Beyond Consumer Capitalism

Beyond Consumer Capitalism

Media and the Limits to Imagination

JUSTIN LEWIS

polity

First published in 2013 by Polity Press

Polity Press
65 Bridge Street
Cambridge CB2 1UR, UK

Polity Press
350 Main Street
Malden, MA 02148, USA

ISBN-13: 978-0-7456-5023-4 (hardback)
ISBN-13: 978-0-7456-5024-1 (paperback)

A catalogue record for this book is available from the British Library.

Typeset in 11 on 13 pt Bembo by
Servis Filmsetting Ltd, Stockport, Cheshire
Printed and bound by T.J. International, Padstow, Cornwall

For further information on Polity, visit our website: www.politybooks.com

Contents

Part IV   Waste and retrieval

Acknowledgements

Many thanks to Kim Humphery and Rick Maxwell for their shrewd and well-informed comments on the manuscript; to Janice Gillian for her wise observations; to Andrea Drugan, Lauren Mulholland, Joe Devanny and Susan Beer at Polity for their professionalism; and to Chloe Lewis for keeping it real.

1

Introduction: The problems of consumer capitalism in the twenty-first century – and why we find it so difficult to appreciate them

People in the developed world are wealthier than at any time in human history. We have access to a vast array of consumer goods clamouring to improve the quality of our lives. A bounty of information and entertainment is available at the flick of a finger tip. Opportunities for communication abound: we can phone and email, text and tweet, post and blog, flickr and facebook, skype and type, all with a global reach and instantaneous response.

Despite this superabundance – and even before the 'credit crunch' arrived to expose the uncertainty of debt-dependent economies – there was little sense that we were living in a golden age. For all their material advantages, children born into the twenty-first century are rarely seen as a lucky generation. The future is rich, instead, with a sense of foreboding.

Doubts hover like storm clouds on the horizon: dwindling economic security, mounting debt, environmental degradation and a creeping sense that a system based on permanent economic growth is unsustainable. There is also a widespread feeling that the way we live now is not quite as good as it could be. The idea that 'things can only get better' has been replaced by the lament 'is that all there is?'[1]

What once drove us forward has become a treadmill, requiring all our effort and energy to simply stay where we are. This sense of stasis is more than simply a reflection of the human condition or, for that matter, our capacity for discontent. The first part of this book begins with the proposition that we have reached a pivotal moment in our social development. Consumer capitalism, for all its abundance and its apparent dynamism, can no longer be relied upon to deliver human progress.

The limits of consumer capitalism

Ever since its emergence as a dominant industrial force, consumer capitalism has had its critics. Despite many attempts to forecast the system's demise,[2] capitalism has proved to be extraordinarily adaptable.[3] Its persistence – alongside the collapse of alternatives – gives the system an air of permanence. Economies may wax and wane, but there is little sign that government-backed consumer capitalism is on the verge of collapse.

What we face in the twenty-first century is less a question of consumer capitalism's viability than its purpose. In an age of abundance, is the system still capable of fostering human development? The question is timely because we can observe a new set of conditions that suggest the system's ability to improve our lot is diminishing. These problems are sometimes difficult to appreciate because they are a product of the system's success.

Consumer capitalism's capacity for proliferation – to turn nature into dazzling aisles of consumable goods – is both its genius and, perhaps, its undoing. Its inexorable rise depends upon its ability to stimulate the production and consumption of objects without paying heed to matters of degree. Our supermarkets, big box stores and Amazonian web-aisles are testimony to the magnitude of the system's productivity. But the benefits of proliferation are finite.

In the 1970s – a decade associated with rising working-class prosperity in developed countries – Jeremy Seabrook documented the attitudes of older working-class people in Britain. He found, even then, both a dependence upon and an underlying disillusionment with consumerism.[4] The optimism of the post-war years had given way to a feeling of limited horizons. As one man told him: 'The only chance of satisfaction we can imagine is getting more of what we've got now',[5] a sentiment that captures the absence of imagination at the heart of consumer capitalism. It is a system that can never envisage a moment when we have enough things.

The rise and fall of orthodoxies litter human history, and yet our collective imagination pins us firmly to the present. We behave and plan only for more of the same. There is no space, in this model, for a post-capitalist society,[6] a place where the superfluity of consumer goods allows us to direct our energies away from the consumption of commodities towards other – potentially more purposeful – activities.

The material limits of a consumer capitalist vision force it into an encounter with the limits of the physical world. The idea of infinite economic growth was always going to fit awkwardly with the finite nature of life on earth. The first part of this book deals with the economic, social and environmental implications of this tension.

The economics of excess in a finite world

The economic recession towards the end of the twenty-first century's first decade was an example of consumer capitalism's tendency to over-reach in an attempt to create prosperity. The constant need for growth pushed us towards a reliance on mounting levels of debt in order to stimulate further the cycle of production and consumption.[7] The system survived because of the largesse of governments who chose to use large amounts of public money to bail it out. This, of course, increased public debt and – ironically enough – increased our dependence on consumer capitalism to fill the gaps left by a more austere public sector.

The 'credit crunch' might have been avoided by a more sceptical attitude towards unfettered financial markets and more prudent government regulation. It is, however, symptomatic of the problems faced by a system that requires constant increases in demand to sustain economic growth. Superfluity becomes a necessity rather than an achievement, a contradiction that becomes ever more burdensome for the increasingly bemused consumer.

In the twentieth century governments were forced to grapple with capitalism's tendency to drift towards monopoly.[8] As companies grew, buying up competitors in waves of horizontal and vertical integration, they were able to make economies of scale and control distribution and publicity channels, driving out smaller competitors. They could then define the realm of choice to their own advantage, using their market power to drive out competition. While this remains a major problem (if we are concerned about the quality as well as the quantity of choice) – most of the world's music, for example, is produced by one of three global companies[9] – it can be dealt with by anti-monopoly legislation.[10] The state has thereby intervened (albeit rather feebly in recent years) to protect consumer choice – without which the system loses its dynamism and purpose.

But the economics of excess have created another paradox, one that pushes the idea of a 'rational consumer' to breaking point. While some might balk at Ben Fine's description of 'rational economic man' as combining 'the basest instincts of a selfish beast with the highest form of commercial calculation',[11] its twenty-first century articulation presents us with a problem. This combination of self-interest (or, in more altruistic societies, ethical concerns) and careful calculation pushes us to buy the best (or most ethically produced) product at the best or fairest price. Rational consumers provide consumer capitalism with its central logic.[12] En masse, or in well-heeled niches, they create a kind of market meritocracy, a place where quality will thrive.

In the developed world rational consumers now find themselves faced with two irreconcilable pressures. The sheer scale of goods available makes choosing what to buy both time-consuming and difficult. There are far more commodities available than there were fifty years ago, but no more leisure time in which to make decisions. We can either devote all our free time to making well-informed purchases, or conclude that this is a poor use of a precious resource (our free time) and give up trying – hoping, instead, that we might be steered by various unreliable prompts.[13] Choice – once a way to assert our independence – becomes an encroachment on the time we have available to act independently.

The unlimited increase in consumer goods (on which the system depends) thus comes crashing up against the finite nature of our time on earth. The rational consumer begins – metaphorically at least – to fall apart. At the same time the value of commodities in an age of superabundance becomes increasingly difficult to maintain, as the empirical impact of each new object on our quality of life lessens with every purchase.

Consumer capitalism and the meaning of life

The social constraints consumer capitalism now faces are no less profound. The system's appeal has always rested on a straightforward deal: capitalism creates wealth, and wealth makes us happier, healthier, more secure and fulfilled. Since the ability of a society to provide healthcare, education and enhance people's quality of life depends upon resources, consumer capitalism's productive flair has been embraced by a broad cross section of political opinion. It could fuel personal wealth *and* public services.

For classical economics, this deal is set in perpetuity. Increasing consumption and the desire for a better quality of life are locked in a permanent embrace. Yet this is also beginning to unravel. A growing body of research suggests that the relationship between a country's gross domestic product and the quality of life of its citizens has a clear and visible end-point. Once a society reaches a certain level of affluence, the evidence suggests, economic growth ceases to have an impact on our physical or mental health.

In the twenty-first century, most developed countries have already passed this point. The push for economic growth is seen as necessary to sustain employment levels, but growth, in itself, no longer delivers clear social benefits. The consumer society's persistent claims to make us happier, healthier and more fulfilled reverberates around the echo-chamber of advertising with an increasingly hollow ring.

Once the relationship between consumer capitalism and quality of life begins to drift apart, the system loses its most compelling rationale. Indeed, for the growing field of quality of life research, consumerism is seen as an increasingly malign influence, a compulsion that pushes us away from those non-material activities that are important sources of pleasure and meaning.

This is not to say that we do not find pleasure and value in objects, or to deny the advantages brought by the growth in affluence of consumer societies.[14] The provision of comfort surrounded by a diversity of goods has all kinds of material and symbolic benefits.[15] But these benefits are finite: our capacity to enjoy consumer goods is limited by time and space. We have now reached a stage where the continual proliferation of consumer goods risks cluttering up rather than adding to the meaning of life.

Consumer capitalism as a threat to our quality of life

The third strike against consumer capitalism today is perhaps the best known. The environmental limitations of our twenty-first-century world – the finite nature of the earth's resources and its delicate ecology – are easy to grasp and well documented. In some ways, these limitations are less immediate than economic and social constraints. The system's genius for transformation makes it possible to imagine doing more with less – recycling and reusing materials with increasing efficiency, for example – to enable economic growth for centuries to come.

The more immediate environmental problems created by consumer capitalism lie in that domain that economists refer to as 'externalities'. The business of transforming raw materials into commodities, of distributing, selling and ditching them, has a myriad of environmental consequences. As the scale of our productive capacity grows, our ability to damage and destroy eco-systems grows with it. While we may be prompted to deal with the more conspicuous and manageable of these 'externalities' (reducing various forms of urban pollution in the developed world, for example) we tend to neglect those with less immediate effects upon affluent societies.

The most alarming of these is the way in which our fossil fuel driven economy is altering the earth's ecology, creating a layer of greenhouse gases that will warm the planet with consequences for life on earth. The Stern Review on the economic consequences of climate change referred to 'the greatest market failure the world has ever seen'.[16] It is possible to imagine consumer capitalism running on clean energy, but the time-lag between cause and effect provides little incentive for either business or democratic governments to do what is required.

When the Intergovernmental Panel on Climate Change (IPCC) published their first comprehensive report in 1990, they described the devastating consequences if we failed to curtail global warming. But these dangers were not immediate: the accumulating impact of greenhouse gases lingers long after their production. The time span of the 1990 report – looking fifty to a hundred years ahead – gave licence for governments to prevaricate.

This, in part, explains our singular failure to address the problem. Since 1990, far from changing course, we have allowed greenhouse emissions to rise significantly, with mounting evidence of risks which draw ever closer. Even when economists described the purely fiscal costs of climate change,[17] the response from business and government was, at best, half-hearted. We are now approaching (or, indeed, may have passed) the point at which we will be able prevent significant climate change or prepare for the subsequent disruption.

In this unhappy scenario, consumer capitalism's drive towards further economic growth pushes the decades of reckoning ever nearer. As a system, it is unresponsive to longer term threats, which might lead it to switch to more expensive but cleaner forms of energy. It is also uniquely intolerant of one of the solutions, which would involve less dependence on the proliferation of consumer goods and economic growth. This is a scorched earth policy in more than a metaphorical sense. Consumer capitalism, in its current form, represents a threat to the collective security and well-being of the developed world.

Why is it so difficult to imagine other forms of progress?

Despite its economic, social and environmental shortcomings, consumer capitalism continues to dominate our field of vision. I write at a time when those on the political right urge public austerity and faith in the market's ability to bounce back, while the left calls for more public spending to stimulate growth in the consumer economy. They share the desire for business as usual, differing only on how best to achieve it.

Neither proposal addresses the model's economic limits, its failure to improve the quality of life or its push towards alarming environmental outcomes. In the developed world, consumer capitalism offers solutions to problems – lack of money for a good life, lack of consumer choice[18] – that are, in affluent societies, increasingly irrelevant.[19] And both sides have, thus far, failed to grasp the profundity of the system's limits.

There is, of course, dissent. Consumer activism[20] now exists side by side with anti-consumerism. Kim Humphery has observed that much of this anti-consumerism is tilted at individuals rather than societies, and is based on moral disapproval rather than more systemic issues,[21] while Jo Littler has shown how 'radical consumerism' and the traditional variety can be two sides of the same coin.[22] There is, nonetheless, an increasing sense of disillusionment with the consumerist project. The Occupy Movement, for example, has expressed both frustration and dissatisfaction with business as usual.[23] It has been criticized for its incoherence and inability to articulate clear alternatives, but this is less a fault of the protesters than the orthodoxy they seek to question. Consumer capitalism appears to have created a cultural system that makes it difficult to conceive other models of human progress. Its economic, social and environmental limitations are sustained by a lack of imagination. The rest of this book looks at some of the reasons why this is so.

Media and the limits of imagination

The Disney corporation, one of the world's largest media companies, has promoted the idea of the 'imagineer' – people who engineer imaginative landscapes.[24] We have created a culture in which our society's principal imagineers – the greatest concentration of creative talent and energy – work in the advertising industry. Part II looks at the ways this industry permeates almost every aspect of our cultural lives and considers the consequences of this relentless intrusion.

The sheer volume of creative time, effort and resources that we devote to advertising has allowed it, as a cultural form, to stretch its own boundaries. Advertising has become much more than just a sales pitch; it can be funny, moving, ingenious and engaging. But for all its wit and skill, it operates under the constraints of the consumerist system that depends upon it. Every story told by advertising rests upon an increasingly untenable proposition: that our quality of life is bound up in the purchase of commodities.

Advertisements may, individually, touch upon many aspects of human experience. Collectively, they repeat the idea that the *only* source of pleasure, popularity, status, security and meaning is in what Sut Jhally calls 'the dead world of things'.[25] They insist that the social world – the source of so much of what we value – is simply an extension of the world of commodities. Even if we ignore or reject most of the advertisements we see or hear (indeed, the ubiquity of advertising means that we must), it is difficult to remain untouched by this volume of repetition.

Advertising, in this sense, pretends to be outside politics, but it is deeply embedded in a series of highly contested ideas. If Part I explores the extent to which consumerism is a partisan, limited and increasingly problematic world view, Part II shows how advertising both sustains and expresses this view – not as some coordinated or conscious effort, but simply in the way it goes about its business.

Part III considers a cultural form that, in some ways, begins from a very different philosophical premise. Journalism is strongly tied to a democratic tradition, to the idea that for democracy to flourish people must be well informed. If advertising circulates conventional wisdom, journalism prides itself on questioning it.

Journalism is thereby well positioned to interrogate consumer capitalism's shortcomings, to report alternative views and make what was once accepted controversial. But it remains constrained by its embrace with commerce. The tawdrier aspects of this embrace – the many ways in which commercialism leads us to redefine public interest as private intrigue rather than civic concern – are well documented. Part III explores a more fundamental constraint: the way in which our understanding of news has been shaped by a business model of news and information.

When journalism became a business, news became a commodity – one that came to be defined by its most profitable form. The democratic value of news is based on the longevity and value of the information it provides. The commercial value of news, by contrast, is based on its impermanence. A newspaper's profitability depends on the idea that news is a flimsy, fragile form of information with a short shelf life, that being informed depends not on the quality of information but on its quantity and regularity.

The rise of a commercial news industry meant that news became defined in part by the notion of built-in obsolescence. The newspaper became the apotheosis of a disposable commodity. Yesterday's news was, by definition, of little value, and news became increasingly bound up with the idea that what mattered above all was the immediate, the current, the here and now. The commercial stress on immediacy pushes journalism away from asking larger, more profound social and economic questions.

This manifests itself in the coverage given to economics and, more specifically, economic growth. The economic, social and environmental problems of our current growth model outlined in Part I are, in theory, grist to the journalistic mill. They pose serious challenges to the purveyors of conventional wisdom. News is precisely the kind of civic space in which these challenges might be aired – instead, we find little questioning of the idea that economic growth is always both desirable and necessary. It is not simply treated as uncontroversial, but as an objective good.

It is hardly surprising, in this context, that most news outlets failed to anticipate the banking crisis. The commodity form of news made investigation of structural economic problems difficult. What needs to be reclaimed and rethought is the democratic purpose of news, a space where our imaginations might flourish, and where we might be able to begin a more profound examination of the limits of consumer capitalism.

Part IV begins by stepping back to look at the communications and creative industries as a whole. While this is an important economic sector in its own right – more than 7% of global GDP – these are industries whose significance surpasses their economic value. They produce commodities that dominate our leisure time and, indeed, our consciousness.

The information and creative industries are dominated by large global conglomerates.[26] Concerns about protecting cultural diversity and the quality of content in its less profitable forms have been played out in the politics of trade agreements (battles over the right to subsidize local production so that it can survive the onslaught of Hollywood, for example) and monopoly legislation. What has received less attention is the way in which increasing dependence on a particular business model shapes our conception of technological progress.

The media and telecommunications industries have always been adept at planned obsolescence: the shift from vinyl to CD, for example, was pushed by integrated conglomerates in order to create new markets for old content and sell new hardware.[27] But the digital age has meant that cultural forms – like music, films, computer software and games – are no longer so obviously bound to physical objects that can be bought and sold.[28] This has pushed the industry towards business models increasingly dependent on upgrading the digital devices that allow us to play with, watch, listen to or use cultural forms.

The industry's pursuit of this new business model has been a spectacular success. And there have, along the way, been genuine innovations in technology and design. It has also been an environmental disaster, shortening the shelf-life of electronic devices – most of which are discarded in full working order – to create mountains of toxic electronic waste amid a frenzy of production, consumption and replacement.

It has also created a culture in which we associate progress with consumption. Progress is bound up less with creating innovative, diverse and well-crafted cultural forms than with the speed at which we dump and replace digital devices. The industry thus not only embraces consumer capitalism, it epitomizes it. Its business model has become a philosophy, a way of life. As long as we are swept along in this constant cycle of replacement it is difficult to imagine other forms of progress, to see how innovation might serve a social and cultural purpose as well as a commercial imperative.

Part IV ends by trying to envisage other ways of moving forward. The final chapter sketches out proposals for opening up the space in which we can conceive new ways of organizing the future. Consumer capitalism may well play a role in that future, but not at the expense of more promising and more sophisticated visions of human development.

Part I

Stretching beyond its limits: The tired machinery of consumer capitalism

2

Consumer capitalism as a cul-de-sac

Consumer capitalism dominates our economic, social and cultural life. Its omnipresence in the developed world has, in part, depended upon the actions of governments to moderate its excesses and harness its profits for public good. In the twenty-first century this understanding appears to have withered, and consumer capitalism frames many of our assumptions.

The notion of a consumer culture now pervades most aspects of private and public life. There is, however, an increasing tension between a consumer culture based on permanent growth in production and the finite nature of our physical, social and psychological landscape.

Consumer capitalism as a way of life

An economic system may simply be a way of organizing the production and distribution of resources, but there is nothing innocent or incidental about these arrangements. Any system of production and consumption imposes its own range of possibilities. Economics can inspire wars and revolutions, it is at the heart of most political struggles, and, perhaps most fundamentally, it can play a central role in our understanding of what constitutes a good life. The way we shape our economy will, in turn, shape us.[1]

We are more than mere cogs in a money-making machine, witlessly obeying its commands. There are many aspects of life whose relationship to our economic system is indirect and diffuse: our relationships with our family and friends may take place in an economic context, but those relationships have a volition that transcends economics. Nonetheless, our goals, values and opportunities are inevitably influenced by consumer capitalism – from the media we consume to the food we eat. Consumer capitalism may not encompass everything we do, but it does, in part, define us as a society.[2]

This point is always easier to grasp when we are looking at systems foreign to our own. Economics is, in this sense, a little like language. Other ways of speaking are distinct and identifiable, whereas the way we speak ourselves seems natural, a point of departure for every other accent or dialect. Consumer capitalism is often discussed as if it evolved as a natural and necessary consequence of human activity in a productive, democratic age. And yet anthropology teaches us that life in contemporary consumer economies is both contrived and distinct.[3]

Accordingly, when we talk about 'capitalism' we are usually implying more than a set of financial arrangements. Consumer capitalism evokes a culture and a lifestyle. We refer, after all, to 'capitalist societies' as often as we refer to 'capitalist economies'[4] – the assumption being that capitalism is a social as well as an economic system.[5]

It is worth pausing here to reflect that, despite its ubiquity, most of us no longer use the word 'capitalism' as often as we might. Since the collapse of Soviet-style communism and the integration of China as a key player in a global capitalist economy (whatever it may call itself), there has been no obvious counterpoint to give meaning to the word. The battle between capitalism and communism defined politics for much of the twentieth century. In the twenty-first, consumer capitalism no longer has a visible alter-ego. Our principal point of comparison has disappeared.

In theory, the collapse of the Soviet model liberated us from a narrow dichotomy, where critical thinking about capitalism would inevitably be reduced to positions somewhere on the continuum between communism and free market liberalism.[6] In practice, it created an intellectual dead-end, whereby capitalism's victory was seen as the final product of an evolutionary process, an idea encapsulated in Francis Fukuyama's well-known tract, *The End of History*.[7] In this vision, capitalist democracies represent an endpoint in human progress, their success a guarantor of the system's superiority. Without a point of comparison, capitalism (or various versions of it) assumed an air of inevitability, stunting our ability to appreciate its flaws and imagine alternatives.

Consumer capitalism's place in our institutions, our social life and our consciousness seems assured, and yet its capacity to enrich our lives appears to be draining away. Thereby lies a central theme of this book: human progress, especially at this moment in our history, relies less on an acceptance and more on our interrogation of consumer capitalism.

The rise, falter and rise of consumer capitalism

It is easy to anthropomorphize consumer capitalism. In 1955, a retail analyst called Victor Liebow wrote – with remarkable prescience and candour – that:

> Our enormously productive economy . . . demands that we make consumption our way of life, that we convert the buying and the selling of goods into rituals, that we seek our spiritual satisfaction, our ego satisfaction in commodities.[8]

This epiphany gives consumer capitalism a commanding voice: we may have created it but, like Doctor Frankenstein's brilliant creation, it refuses to do our bidding. Rather than serving our interests, it is 'our enormously productive economy' that makes demands. It tells us – like a deity or a dictator – how *we* should best serve *its* interests. Its rapacious wants become our needs.

Liebow's gospel is deeply pessimistic, robbing us of our

independence. His use of anthropomorphic metaphors is not unusual (indeed, the observant reader will have noticed that I have already succumbed to this temptation). For its devotees, capitalism is an ingenious and dynamic creature, magical yet rational, one which – like a benign will-o'-the-wisp – will deliver the greatest good to the greatest number.[9] For its critics capitalism can be a merciless despot, a creature red in tooth and claw which, left to its own devices, becomes bloated, corrupt and, *in extremis*, brutal.

The problem with both descriptions is that whether we see capitalism as clever or cruel, it has no ingenuity, no wit, no morality, no feeling and no understanding. It is a collection of financial forces and mechanisms which have, at times, been both efficient and productive. But, while the system has a genius for reinventing itself, its capacity is limited and, like many of its products, it comes fraught with imperfections.

If we ask consumer capitalism to create an information system enabling citizens to understand the world, its best efforts continue to fall well short of our ideals. So, for example, even our wealthiest market system – that in the United States – has been unable to create a news service to rival the breadth and scope of the publicly funded, non-commercial BBC.[10]

For all its adaptability, capitalism fits awkwardly with many contemporary social or political desires. The rise of democracy saw a clamour of politicians, preachers, poets and protest movements speaking out against unfettered capitalism, a system they saw as oblivious to a whole range of human needs. They resolved that we use other means – whether political, legal or cultural – to craft our own destiny, rather than allow history to be guided by the ethereal force of the 'invisible hand'. Their combined will was too insistent to be ignored: some societies tried to bypass capitalism altogether, but most set about restricting and adapting it in the name of the common good.

As a consequence, the twentieth century was characterized as much by the contestation of capitalism as by its promulgation. We saw a raft of regulations to change or modify some of its systemic features (often referred to as 'market failures').[11] Capitalism's flair for wealth creation had a series of unintended consequences – what economists call 'externalities'. It is a technical term that, like the military euphemism 'collateral damage', covers a multitude of ills. It was a Conservative British prime minister in the 1970s who spoke of the 'unacceptable face of capitalism',[12] and whose government was content to preside over the rise of a less avaricious public sector, one more responsive to social goals and created to provide on the basis of need rather than ability to pay.

On the home front, the 'self-correcting' nature of capitalism – the idea that when companies or financial institutions crashed and burned, new business would rise from the ashes – was regarded as unacceptably cruel.[13] The gap between failure and rebirth took little account of the human misery caused by the upheaval. Governments – especially those in the wealthier, developed world – began to intervene in the marketplace to stimulate economic growth and to limit the damage (in their own countries, at least) when things went awry.

The rise of democracy created a demand for careful planning and equality of opportunity – something that, in many realms of life, was delivered more successfully by public rather than private institutions. Despite capitalism's energy, some of the twentieth century's greatest achievements – in healthcare, culture, architecture, education, science and technology – came from public investment rather than private capital. Without public money and political will there would have been no space exploration, no universal healthcare or education systems and no world wide web.

Even in countries like the United States, economic growth was often driven by public investment, regulation and subsidy.[14] Wealthier, developed countries regulated the market to protect various public interests, while creating other economic models for key areas like education, environmental protection, transport, health and law and order. Cruder forms of capitalist development – where ruthless human and environmental exploitation increased levels of profit – were consigned to the poorer part of the world, which, in many cases, did *not* thrive as a consequence.

Some of the most progressive societies to emerge from a century of hard and soft conflict were Scandinavian social democracies – where capitalist forces were muted or displaced by a set of egalitarian principles. These societies, surveys suggest, are some of the world's most equal and content,[15] places where the public good took precedence over private gain.

But capitalism endured. Towards the end of the twentieth century the idealism behind public institutions became tainted by the petty failings of bureaucracy and the cumbersome anonymity of large government institutions. These failures inspired the rise of a neo-liberalist politics – epitomized most famously by Margaret Thatcher and Ronald Reagan – based on a reassertion of the primacy and efficiency of private markets (albeit fuelled and pro-tected, in part, by public spending). Citizens were routinely recast as 'consumers', whose engagement in the world was limited to preferences in the marketplace.[16]

Although consumer activism – boycotting companies or goods – has sometimes managed to persuade consumers to act collec-tively, this cuts against the grain of consumerism, which – unlike citizenship – is based on a philosophy of individual preferences.[17] Hence Margaret Thatcher's famous dismissal of the idea of society and the primacy of 'individuals and families'. As she put it in an interview with *Woman's Own* magazine: 'Who is society? There is no such thing! There are individual men and women and there are families . . . There is no such thing as society.'[18]

One of the ironies of recent history is that as consumerism has expanded the power of consumers has shrunk. As corpora-tions displaying their wares were allowed to grow (enhancing their political clout), the ability of individual consumers to assert their will became, by degrees, ever more feeble. If people decide to boycott their independent local shop, it might – if they make enough noise about it – cause the shopkeeper some concern. If they boycott a national chain of supermarkets because of their poor environmental record, their individual action is far too minuscule to register an impact. Or if they have a preference for a certain product – fruit buns made with wholemeal rather than white flour, to pick a random example – the market, oblivious to individual tastes, will not necessarily provide it.

In mass or even niche markets, preferences are only meaningful if they are widely shared: consumer capitalism has no interest in individuality in its distinct or original sense. The more consumer capitalism pushes towards large units of mass production and consumption, the less sympathetic it is to diversity or idiosyncrasy. For all the rhetoric about individual freedom made by some of its protagonists, consumer capitalism has become a deeply collectivist enterprise. The power of industry lies in its ability to override what distinguishes us as individuals and appeal to – or construct – commonality (otherwise known as 'markets', as in the 'youth market'). While big government is often blamed for creating a disillusioned and alienated electorate, big businesses create a similar feeling of powerlessness.[19]

The role of government, in the new neo-liberal orthodoxy from the 1980s onward, was not to modify capitalism but to manage it. Soviet leader Michael Gorbachev's hope that he might move Russia towards a Scandinavian model of social democracy was dashed by a corrupt capitalist land-grab. China, meanwhile, became a totalitarian capitalist state in all but name. The world's dominant institutions (a mix of governments and global corporations),[20] backed by bodies like the World Trade Organization, worked to ensure that the globalization was organized around the freedom to move money and goods (and to a much lesser extent, people) around the globe.

So it was that, more than five hundred years to the good, capitalism entered the twenty-first century in remarkably rude health. At the heart of this success lie two inextricably linked ideas. The first – one that Victor Liebow anticipated so well – is an image of the good life based on the accumulation of products. Consumerism, almost by definition, sells itself, but its main selling point is its ability to improve our quality of life.

The second is the idea of perpetual economic growth, a notion that has become a central focus of our political life. The economist Tim Jackson stresses how distinct this is to the modern age:

> For the last five decades the pursuit of growth has been the single most important policy goal across the world. The global economy is almost five times the size it was half a century ago. If it continues to grow at the same rate the economy will be 80 times that size by the year 2100. This extraordinary ramping up of global economic activity has no historical precedent.[21]

Both these ideas – consumerism and the importance of growth – involve a celebration of excess, where more is always good and where the role of the market is to supply this superabundance. Today, few governments question these two ideas – even if they were inclined to – and many try hard to exemplify them.

The early period of the global recession towards the end of the first decade of the twenty-first century was an interesting historical moment, one that revealed both the fragility and the strength of the prevailing orthodoxy. A tiny window opened, offering us a glimpse of what it might be like to rethink one of the dominant ideologies of our age. In a metaphorical nanosecond – one that seemed to slip away almost as it appeared – the enormity of the 'credit crunch' seemed as if it might have the potential to bring the whole edifice of an over-reaching capitalist system crashing down.

For the more open-minded members of the commentariat, the air was suddenly thick with contradiction. Big capitalism – from banks to car-makers – insisted on the right to be bailed out by the welfare state. The breezy confidence behind the lend and spend world of twenty-first-century consumer capitalism fell way like the emperor's new clothes. Our system of rewards, so generous to those in the pure business of money making, looked at best misplaced and at worst obscene – especially when ordinary tax-payers were required to give the speculators a lavishly cushioned landing. Even right-leaning newspapers – who tend to be pro-business and anti-regulation – joined the chorus of disapproval.

For some economists, the credit crunch was all too predictable.[22] A heady mix of unregulated financial markets and increasingly debt-dependent growth, they warned, was always likely to end in tears. In an effort to sustain unsustainable levels of growth, the financial sector was encouraged to take risks with credit and devise ingenious forms of speculative investment. The successful financier George Soros describes how governments and financial authorities, in an effort to fuel demand and stimulate continued economic growth, allowed the creation of a 'super-bubble' in the money markets.[23] Governments, for their part, were beguiled by the confidence of the financial sector, which seemed to promise the growth they craved.

Despite the rhetoric of open markets, big business has long

been adept at exploiting various forms of state subsidy, but the rescue packages they sought when the system collapsed were on an unprecedented scale. Risks that had been taken for private gain were paid for by public money. To the political and business consensus – who paid little attention to those outside their own circle who might have warned them – it was a punch in the solar plexus.

Suddenly, it seemed as if we might have the conditions in place for a radical, popular challenge, not just to the neo-liberal orthodoxy but to consumer capitalism as a model for human progress. The idea that Western capitalism was the end point of human history,[24] looked decidedly myopic as the fragility of its internecine and speculative structures were laid bare. This was, perhaps, the beginning of the end of the end of history.

But the broader challenge never materialized. On the contrary, while most of the conditions that precipitated the recession remain, we have lurched back into pre-recessionary ways with remarkable speed. Financial markets remain lightly regulated (a little less lightly in places, but still relatively unrestrained), bankers bonuses are back, the threat of climate change is ignored in the quest for relentless economic growth, and we are urged, once again, to take on debt and carry on consuming (even though, for many, living standards remain stagnant). The price of consumer capitalism's failure led not to the growth of a more stable public sector but to its retrenchment, leaving us even more dependent on private capital and investment.

The entrenchment of a consumer culture

Celia Lury lists the ways in which we now embrace consumer culture.[25] We have seen an extraordinary proliferation of commodities – between the 1970s and 1990s the USA saw a tenfold increase in the number of new goods to hit the market.[26] An array of market reforms have been introduced across the public domain, from welfare to warfare.[27] Shopping is both a leisure pursuit and a focus of material and online public space (in the

USA, only TV viewing takes up more leisure time). We have seen a voluminous growth in the size of retail space (in the USA, a fourfold expansion in the last 30 years).[28] And we have become accustomed to the promotion of consumer debt, the rise of brands and the ubiquity of advertising.

Research from across the humanities and social sciences has tried to take stock of consumer culture, and there is a healthy literature documenting its rise.[29] This work is full of insight about the way we live now, and deserves far more attention than it receives. There is, nonetheless, a tension between some of the more robust critics of consumerism and those who are uncomfortable with dismissing the many ordinary benefits associated with it. Roberta Sassatelli[30] and Daniel Miller[31] both argue against what they see as the disapproving moral tone of some of the anti-consumerist literature. The pleasures and perks of consumer capitalism are so much a part of everyday life, Miller suggests, that few of the system's most eloquent critics are prepared to forgo them. They stress the need to acknowledge that the availability of a wide selection of goods has important symbolic as well as material benefits.

It is not surprising if debates about the nature of consumer capitalism have a moral inflection and often drift towards absolutes, in which the machinery of market economics is portrayed as either benign or malignant. For centuries now these debates have been cast in ethical and political terms, played out across the statistics and spreadsheets of the social sciences and the narratives of the humanities. During the twentieth century our view of the ethics and efficacies of consumer capitalism defined our position on a political continuum.

In this book, I have chosen to sidestep these mighty and enduring arguments to address a new set of problems that beset consumer capitalism in an age of abundance. These are matters of proportion rather than principle, in which the never-ending cycles of production and consumption come up against the increasingly cramped time and space of the human condition. They apply whether we laud consumer capitalism as the most effective form of wealth creation or lament its inequities. They do not add up to an argument for abandoning consumer capitalism, but they do suggest its displacement as our principal modus operandi.

Chapter 3 considers these problems in more detail. What links them is that consumer capitalism is, like many religions, philosophically tied to a notion of infinity. This unbounded world – one with no limits and no horizons – is superficially appealing, manifesting itself in the idea that anything is possible.[32] But in the context of the mathematical constraints of everyday life, it is also implausible. It refuses to appreciate the prevailingly finite aspects of the time and resources available to us.

When the finite world *is* contemplated, it is generally dismissed as a temporary constraint on progress, a set of circumstances that humans will always have the ingenuity to overcome. Even if we were immortal beings living endlessly on an expanding planet, this would be both impractical and philosophically crude. As it is, it creates its own constraints, limiting our ability to appreciate the nature and possibilities of a finite volume of time, space, physical and psychic resources.

How do we reconcile the finite properties of life with a system that depends on the multiplication of choice and perpetual growth? We are, after all, intrinsically finite creatures on a finite planet. Our emotions are finite, our knowledge is finite, our needs are finite, the time we have is finite. Once we begin to understand the character of this finite world, it becomes clear that consumer capitalism's stress on infinite possibility is increasingly out of kilter.

Consumer capitalism's push towards infinity has created a new set of contradictions across a number of environmental, economic and sociological fronts. While these may not bring about its downfall, they oblige us to ask whether there might be a less acquisitive and more fulfilling model of human society. The next chapter highlights various ways in which this is manifest: in terms of the economic and physical world, the social world and our capacities as human beings. In each case, we see the persuasive promises of consumerism and the model of permanent growth flounder in the face of the finite.

3

The environmental, economic and social constraints of consumer capitalism

The problems with consumer capitalism outlined in this chapter bypass many aspects of traditional left/right politics. This is not so much a failure of the old paradigm, but more the consequence of a set of conditions that have become especially pressing in the last few decades. The success of consumer capitalism and economic growth has created a new set of problems about the environmental, social and economic limits of everyday life which most parties across the political spectrum are ill-equipped to address.

Consumer capitalism and the environmental risks of growth

The most rudely material problem facing consumer capitalism is environmental. The producers of commodities are generally not obliged to compensate for the damage caused by the production, distribution or consumption of goods. As a consequence, a system driven by constant growth was, at some point, inevitably going to disrupt the delicate ecology of life on earth.[1] There are many instances when Malthusian doom-mongering proved to be premature, but a perpetual commitment to expansion meant there was always likely to be a time when the finite natural world would struggle to support our increasing demand for resources.[2]

Industrial growth is, of course, not entirely a product of consumer capitalism. During the twentieth century the Soviet Union was as committed to economic expansion as the West – it just wasn't as good at it. But it is in the twenty-first century – with state supported consumer capitalism relatively unchallenged – that the environmental consequences of unconstrained economic growth have reached a critical point. After centuries of growth, we now consume resources at a rate that matches the scale of the earth.[3] Most of this consumption remains concentrated in the developed world, with the wealthiest 20% of the world's population responsible for more than three-quarters of total private consumption.[4]

The list of environmental problems facing us is daunting.[5] Even an optimistic view of some of the most sought-after resources left available – notably oil, gas, agricultural land and water – will not withstand increasing levels of demand for much longer.[6] Those with faith in the ingenuity of the marketplace argue that as the price of some of these commodities rises, we will be spurred on to find more efficient ways of doing things. Such a transition is, however, unlikely to be seamless, and it would be naive to expect the market to manufacture solutions with the alacrity and prescience to avoid serious shortfalls.

Even if we take an optimistic view of our ability to find new ways of meeting the demands of a consumerist economy, many of the environmental consequences of our relentless productive cycles fall outside the normal operation of the marketplace. They are, as economists put it, 'externalities'. And the list of what we might call 'eco-externalities' grows ever more pressing.

In order to maximize the planet's productive capacity we have been obliged to change it to suit the needs of expansion. This has meant wiping out those habitats and species who get in the way in order to make space for increases in our production of goods. The cost of the production, use and disposal of goods, thus far, has been the degradation of 60% of the world's eco-systems.[7]

We produce waste – much of it toxic – at an unprecedented rate, contaminating the soil, the air and the sea.[8] Since waste disposal and environmental protection are not part of consumer capitalism's remit, these duties are either ignored or regulated and funded by public institutions (usually a level of government). The volume of waste produced by OECD countries has more than doubled since 1980.[9] A report by the World Bank in June 2012 suggested that we currently produce 1.3 billion tonnes of municipal waste every year – a figure they predict will rise to 2.2 billion tonnes by 2025, with an annual cost of solid waste management rising from $205 billion to $375 billion.

The report suggests a direct correlation between the per capita level of income in cities and the amount of waste per capita generated. It also highlights the extent to which the public subsidy of waste disposal drains money away from areas like health or education, with poorer municipalities spending between 20% to 50% of their available budgets on often piecemeal urban waste management.[10]

The strains on the public purse means that little of this waste is reused or recycled. Richard Maxwell and Toby Miller write about the mountains of toxic e-waste dumped in the United States:

> It has been estimated that the five hundred million personal computers discarded between 1997 and 2007 contained 6.32 billion pounds of plastics, 1.58 billion pounds of lead, three million pounds of cadmium, 1.9 million pounds of chromium, and 632,000 pounds of mercury. In 2007, the EPA reported that 'of the 2.25 million tons of TVs, cell phones and computer products ready for end-of-life management, 18 percent (414,000 tons) was collected for recycling and 82 percent (1.84 million tons) was disposed of, primarily in landfill.'[11]

Less visible forms of waste – created or dumped elsewhere – accumulate at a dramatic rate. The volume of plastic waste adrift in the North Pacific Ocean has increased a hundredfold in the last forty years[12]. The trade in waste tends to flow from those who consume it to poorer countries for disposal – 90% of exported waste is classified as hazardous.[13] Obsolete pesticides – including poisons banned in most countries – accumulate in stockpiles in Mali, Botswana and other parts of Africa.[14]

These problems may not be insurmountable, but they are increasingly difficult to manage, for two reasons. First, increasing demand in a finite world means that our skill and ingenuity in exploiting resources has less and less room to manoeuvre. Second, consumer capitalism's success comes at an increasingly high price – not only because of the environmental damage it causes but in terms of the increasing costs of managing its waste.

For many people in the developed world, many of consumer capitalism's 'eco-externalities' are blots on the distant landscape. The most daunting environmental issue of the twenty-first century is even less visible. Put simply, one of the key bi-products of our enormously productive economy is a series of gases that, if we continue to produce them, will alter life on earth irrevocably.

Climate scientists have been concerned about the possibility of anthropogenic global warming for many decades. The physics of climate change are relatively simple. A number of gases routinely produced by human activity – notably carbon dioxide, methane and nitrous oxide – have the capacity to form a layer in the atmosphere around the earth and prevent heat escaping. This, in turn, causes the planet's temperature to rise – a fairly straightforward process climate scientists call 'the greenhouse effect'. Evidence suggests that we have passed the planet's ability to absorb 'greenhouse' gases at a sustainable level. Indeed, human activity has reduced the ability of the earth to absorb gases like carbon dioxide – by cutting down forests to make room for increases in the production of commodities – while relentlessly increasing the production of those gases.

As theories go, it is both plausible and – to a large extent – provable. The risks outlined by climate scientists in the 1980s were of such global concern that the United Nations set up the Intergovernmental Panel on Climate Change (IPCC), a body charged with bringing scientists from around the world together and establishing an authoritative consensus. The IPCC produced its first report in 1990, an ambitious project which brought together and reviewed the world's leading research (from Institutions like NASA and Harvard in the USA and Bern in Europe) with data going back tens of thousands of years.

Their 1990 report[15] outlined the nature of the threat. It predicted a consistent and rapid rise (measured in decades rather than millennia) in global temperatures – predictions that have changed little over twenty years later, with volumes of data confirming (and in many cases exceeding) early estimates.[16] The report demonstrated how a small shift in temperature – of a few degrees – has potentially catastrophic consequences for current patterns of life on earth. It recommended taking action – switching to cleaner forms of energy and preserving nature's capacity to absorb greenhouse gases – to prevent the degradation of many of the planet's eco-systems.

Most climate scientists have no particular axe to grind, but in a world where major vested interests depended upon the production of greenhouse gases – notably the oil and car industries, who comprised half of the twelve richest global corporations in 2012[17] – their work had serious political ramifications. Some of consumer capitalism's most powerful players were deeply committed to greenhouse gas production – and in some cases, to the depletion of the forests that absorb carbon dioxide. Climate scientists thus found themselves in the unusual position of facing a well-resourced cabal of consultants and public relations experts busily undermining their work in order to safeguard business as usual.[18] This group – described in vivid detail by Naomi Oreskes and Erik Conway as 'merchants of doubt'[19] – took their lead from earlier campaigns funded by other vested interests, notably the attempt to cast doubt on the toxic effects of tobacco smoke.

Climate science thus became not only inconvenient but deeply controversial. It is hard to think of another group of scientists in recent decades who have been subjected to more scrutiny and criticism. One of the consequences of this was to raise the bar on the level of proof required to legitimate the science. In effect, this meant that climate scientists were obliged not simply to show that climate change might happen, but to wait until there was demonstrable and clear evidence that it *was* happening. For over two decades the IPCC has published and evaluated an increasing body of evidence that has made the case for anthropogenic global warming compelling. Meanwhile, in a collective act of brinkmanship – as if to test the theory to breaking point – we have continued to pump an ever increasing volume of greenhouse gases into the air. Between 1990 (when the IPCC issued its first report) and 2010, global carbon emissions rose by 40%.[20]

The failure of the world's developed countries to stabilize – let alone reduce – their greenhouse gas emissions is one of the striking features of our age. Because of a decline in their manufacturing base, countries like the UK were able to claim movement towards the emissions targets outlined in the Kyoto protocol. In truth, these countries had simply 'outsourced' their emissions to developing countries, who increasingly produced the goods (and thus hosted the pollution) they consumed. So while emissions in the UK appeared to decline by 6% between 1990 and 2004, once activity caused by the UK's consumption of consumer goods is taken into account, we see an increase of 11%.[21]

Inevitably, by the time the IPCC issued their fourth assessment in 2007, the question was no longer one of preventing climate change but ameliorating its worst effects. In practice this means keeping the death toll – from disease, famine, drought, sea level rise, forced mass migration and the increased likelihood of extreme weather events – to millions rather than billions. Politicians and campaigners have identified a 'tipping point' of a global rise of two degrees centigrade – beyond which various 'feedback' processes (such as the melting of polar icecaps, which is likely to trigger further release of methane into the atmosphere) may spiral out of control. Many scientists see this figure as dangerously high,[22] little more than a pact of political convenience, but accept that decades of inaction mean that anything less is now unlikely.

The IPCC's 2007 report indicated that we will need to reduce carbon emissions by between 50% and 85% by 2050 in order to keep climate change within manageable limits.[23] Without a dramatic – and unlikely – breakthrough in geo-engineering, this will not be achieved simply by significant investment in clean technology. Once we factor in economic growth, the targets for reducing greenhouse gas emissions look increasingly unattainable.[24] The world economy has grown fivefold since the mid twentieth century, a rate of expansion which will lead to a global economy eighty times larger by 2100.[25] Even if we fall well short of this expansion, we will need to curtail the perpetual growth of global production and consumption if we are to have a realistic chance of meeting these targets.[26]

According to the 2007 IPCC report, our current planned

trajectory will allow that production to increase to unprecedented levels.[27] And while the IPCC continue to stress that 'many impacts can be avoided, reduced or delayed by mitigation',[28] a key part of the solution is to consume less – notably in the higher consuming economies of the developed world. But this idea is anathema to our current model of consumer capitalism, which devotes considerable resources into persuading us of the benefits of consuming more.

We are, as a consequence, running out of time. As NASA climate scientist James Hansen and colleagues put it:

> Present policies, with continued construction of coal-fired power plants without CO_2 capture, suggest that decision-makers do not appreciate the gravity of the situation. We must begin to move now toward the era beyond fossil fuels. Continued growth of greenhouse gas emissions, for just another decade, practically eliminates the possibility of near-term return of atmospheric composition beneath the tipping level for catastrophic effects.[29]

In November 2011, the International Energy Agency (IEA) released a report that suggested that current plans for industrial growth and energy provision will mean that we will have passed the point of maintaining climate change within manageable levels by 2016. The IEA's chief economist Fatih Birol made the striking assertion that: 'if we don't change direction now on how we use energy, we will end up beyond what scientists tell us is the minimum [for safety]. The door will be closed forever.'[30] The report received little coverage and had little impact on the public or political spheres.

The stakes could scarcely be higher. So why is it that, in the face of one of the greatest challenges to face humankind, we either shrug our shoulders or seem content with a series of half-measures? The collapse of global climate change talks in Copenhagen at the end of 2009 was greeted with little sense of alarm. In inverse proportion to the urgency of the problem, news coverage of climate change has declined significantly in recent years, with economic news pushing the story to the sidelines.[31] For most people outside the world of climate science, one might imagine that the risks of climate change were decreasing.

Accordingly, in the United States, the Pew Research Center for the People and the Press in January, 2010, found that dealing with climate change was at the bottom of a list of 21 priorities for government – with only 28% judging it to be a priority (a fall from 38% in 2007).[32] Similarly, a BBC survey in February 2010 found that only 26% of British people agreed with a statement that reflected the scientific consensus – 'climate change is happening and is now established as largely man-made' (roughly the same proportion who believed that 'climate change is not happening' at all). This was actually a drop from the previous year's figure.[33]

At the heart of this complacency is a paradox: our apparent acceptance of the threat posed by climate change is occurring at a time when we have become increasingly risk-averse. The influential sociologist Ulrich Beck has famously described countries in the developed world as 'risk societies',[34] where fears of everything from terrorism to paedophilia tend to be amplified into a clamour of over-reaction.[35] We live in a time, he suggests, when concerns about health and safety involve systematic attempts to reduce risks to a minimum, and where exaggerated fears of minimal risks – sometimes based on the feeblest of evidence – can induce panic, with very real consequences.[36]

As climate science has become ever more certain, our muted reaction to it remains a vexed question. If Beck's description rings true,[37] why does something as threatening as climate change produce such inertia? If, as the IPCC insist, the worst effects of climate change can still be prevented,[38] why do we continue to dither and stall, inching towards half-measures with little sense of urgency? There are a number of explanations.

While humankind has an undoubted capacity for conflict, we are used to pitting ourselves against clearly defined adversaries rather than well-established aspects of our own lifestyle. A British study, based on a series of focus group discussions published in 2009, demonstrated the difficulty. Put simply, the research found that, for many people, accepting climate change was a much tougher option than adopting a more sceptical attitude.

In the following exchange, for example, a focus group member is recalling a television programme which pitted the idea of anthropogenic global warming against those who suggested temperature changes were the products of natural cycles (and thus beyond our control).

> *Facilitator*: And what made you believe those scientists who said it was natural, if there were two sets of scientists?
> *Respondent*: I suppose because I wanted to. I suppose it sounded better than 'we're ruining the world'.[39]

Which, of course, it does. It is much harder to embrace the idea that the catastrophic potential of global warming to create havoc is not the product of a natural cycle we might unite to overcome, but the result of our own indulgence and disregard.

We are, as a species, ill-equipped to deal with a threat like climate change. For many people, it requires not just one leap of imagination, but three. First, we have to be able to discount our own experiences. When events coincide with climate change predictions – such as floods, or notably warm or hot weather – the weather around us confirms the science. But when they do not – the cold winter of 2010 in Europe and parts of North America for example – we have to override our experience with abstractions. This is, for many, counter-intuitive.

Thus one chilly winter in an influential part of the world gave those inclined to belittle climate science favourable conditions to sow seeds of doubt. As the British newspaper the *Daily Express*'s front page headline blared with incredulity after a cold winter in the UK: 'SNOW CHAOS: AND THEY STILL CLAIM IT'S GLOBAL WARMING'. 'As one of the worst winters in 100 years grips the country,' the paper opined, 'climate experts are still trying to claim the world is growing warmer.'[40] As it happened, those climate experts were soon to be vindicated: figures released by the US National Oceanic and Atmospheric Administration in July 2010 suggested that globally 2010 was on course to be one of the warmest years since records began in 1880,[41] a fact that received far less little attention than stories of freezing temperatures and snowstorms in one small part of the planet.

A second difficulty is the sheer scale of the problem, which requires many people to think globally rather than locally. For those living in cooler parts of the world – such as Northern Europe and parts of North America – the prospect of a warmer climate seems a very benign threat. To appreciate the chaos warming will cause in other parts of the world – through drought, crop failure, flooding and disease – the inhabitants of cooler climes need to attempt the difficult task of imagining other ways of being.

The third conceptual leap is to appreciate the time-lag between cause and effect. What we do now will have consequences that are measured not in days or weeks but decades. One feature of our 'risk society' is our impatience. Our 24-hour news cycle stresses immediacy – both of threats and how we might counter those threats (a point taken up later in this book): your child might be abducted by paedophiles, you might catch a new deadly flu virus, or you might be blown up in a terrorist attack. These risks might be minimal, but it is their potentially imminent nature that makes them both newsworthy and pressing. The gradual nature of climate change, by contrast, invites a more relaxed response.

This combines with the short-term outlook encouraged by our dominant political system. Electoral democracy is, for all its merits, based on mechanisms that are poorly suited to dealing with long-term global problems. Many of the measures needed to tackle climate change involve raising taxes – partly to curtail activities that produce greenhouse gases, partly to raise money to invest in green technology – with no immediate pay off. It also involves significant government intervention to discourage certain activities – from excessive packaging to flying to eating beef – that people find convenient or enjoyable. If the beneficiaries of these actions are governments elected in the future, there is little incentive for governments today to risk unpopularity by acting on their behalf.

Worse, the actions of any single government may involve putting a country at a short-term competitive disadvantage. The lack of powerful global agencies may often be desirable – allowing a degree of freedom and flexibility for nation states – but for a global problem like climate change it makes us dependent on high degrees of international cooperation at the expense of immediate domestic interests. To date, it is more parochial concerns – and the immediate viability of elected governments – that prevail.

All these problems can be overcome. We are capable of putting our faith in abstraction or representations even if they don't concur with our own experience:[42] a range of studies demonstrate the power of media to establish certain assumptions about the world.[43] Benedict Anderson wrote about the way in which nationalism creates 'imagined communities', based on a set of cultural ideas and practices that bind different people in different places together.[44] At the moment these imagined communities tend to work against the appreciation of global problems. But it is possible to imagine a global community bound by the need to deal with a threat on the scale of global climate change.

Governments are, after all, capable of acting collectively for a wider set of interests. Global trade agreements – such as the General Agreement on Tarriffs and Trades (GATT) and the meetings of the World Trade Organization (WTO) – are a case in point. These agreements restrict the ability of governments to protect their own industries from the ebbs, flows and imbalances of global trade in the name of a wider, common interest (free trade). Many have argued that the beneficiaries of this common interest are often the few (those who can move capital around the world and outsource labour to the countries where it is most exploited) rather than the many, but whatever the merits of the WTO, it is a testimony to the possibilities of collective government action.

It would be unfair to blame consumer capitalism for getting us to this point: we can have economic growth and environmental degradation without consumer capitalism, and there is no doubt that the prosperity it has helped create has bought huge advantages. But it would be naive to suppose that the 'invisible hand' is capable of the kind of altruistic planning necessary to avert catastrophic climate change. As it now stands, consumer capitalism, with its stress on stimulating consumption to fuel permanent economic growth, is very much part of the problem. Climate change – a function of living in a finite world – is simply beyond the philosophical imagination of a system premised on infinite growth.

So many choices, so little time

The limited space in which to produce, store, distribute and dispose of commodities is, potentially, less a constraint on consumer culture than the finite nature of time.[45] For astrophysicists time may be a malleable dimension, but for life on earth it is a stubbornly fixed resource. One of the great efforts of public health and medical science has been to maximize human lifespan, to extend the time available to us to enjoy, among other things, the bounty of consumer culture.

For much of the twentieth century, the growth of consumer goods was matched by a growth in leisure time, creating a synchronicity of expansion. The problem we face in the twenty-first century is that the amount of time we have to buy things and to benefit from their possession and use is remarkably flat.

In his book *Time and Money: The Making of Consumer Culture,* Gary Cross suggests that during the 1920s the benefits of economic growth were seen more in terms of increasing leisure time than access to consumer goods. Later, consumer culture would push us in the other direction, and the desire for free time would be eclipsed by a clamour for spending power. Time, as they say, is money, and we find ourselves caught in the tension between the two, creating an 'ironic sense of scarcity in the midst of plenty'.[46]

The demand for gadgetry and goods has become relentless, and the gradual decrease of hours in the working week that defined much of the twentieth century has come to a shuddering halt. No more so than in the United States, where longer working hours and shorter holidays are the prices paid for the ability to consume as much as possible.[47] The model of endless growth, it appears, requires endless effort to keep pace with it.

The average American supermarket stocks five times as many goods as it did in 1975[48] – and yet we have roughly the same amount of time available to do our shopping (arguably less, since the huge growth in media and communication technologies takes up every increasing amounts of our leisure time). The proliferation of consumer goods exceeded our ability to deal rationally with the vastness of choice some time ago.[49] In 1992, for example, US food companies launched a total of 11,500 products.[50] Since most of these were copies or derivatives of things we already had, a deluge of advertising messages were required to sell them.

Many of these products are, themselves, designed to create more demand. Our hair, for example, is kept in good condition by the natural oil (sebum) secreted by our sebaceous glands. Shampoos – essentially a mixture of water and detergent (such as sodium lauryl sulphate) – wash this oil away, creating a demand for another product – conditioner – to compensate for it. The dehydration caused by shampoo means that the more we wash our hair, the more we appear to need to wash and condition it.[51]

Once we accept shampoo as a rather imperfect way of keeping our hair clean – and most of us do – we can then be drawn into a whole variety of other 'hair care' products: 'protection sprays', 'blow dry creams', 'detangle sprays', 'heat protection sprays' and so on. But what is most striking about what is, in essence, a fairly simple chemical product, is the sheer abundance of choices available to us.

Walk along the aisles of a supermarket or through the lanes of a shopping mall and you will find an orgy of repetition. There is difference, certainly, but mainly similarity. We will be confronted by displays of dozens of different brands of breakfast serials, shampoos, pain relievers and pasta sauces, most of which will be small variations on a theme. More means, much of the time, more of the same.

In the summer of 2010, Louise Sutton conducted a survey of one local supermarket to get a measure of the avenues of choice.[52] She found, for example, 188 different types of shampoo and conditioner on display. Despite advertisers' claims, the differences between them was minimal. Apart from detergent and water, most of these shampoos offered similar cocktails of foam producing agents – such as cocamidopropyl – oils, colorants, emulsifiers, emulsion stabilizers and natural or artificial fragrances.

She also found 161 different types of breakfast cereal. While there is undoubtedly a continuum between the highly processed varieties and the more nutritional options, most popular cereals tend to be various incarnations of sugar, highly processed cereals, preservatives, flavourings, colourings, minerals and, in some cases, dried fruit. So, in a typical supermarket, if we want buy something to keep our hair clean and to provide a particular type of morning snack, we have 349 different choices to negotiate.

This tension between the growth of commodities and the stagnation of the leisure time in which to choose and consume them was anticipated by Staffan Linder in his 1970 book *The Harried Leisure Class*. To keep pace with the multiplying demands of a consumer culture, he suggested, we would have to increase our rate of consumption. Whether we end up doing things more quickly or consuming many things simultaneously (the teenager watching TV and social networking on line while they do their homework is an obvious example), leisure time becomes more rushed and, in one of the many contradictions of modern consumer capitalism, less leisurely.[53]

But this squeeze on our leisure time does more than speed up our rate of consumption: it makes consumption itself more difficult. We no longer have enough time to make informed choices based on quality or value for money. Even if we made time to conduct a cursory in-store analysis, in most cases the actual ingredients or component parts of products, where they exist, are hard to read (usually in very small print) and even harder to interpret. Too much choice, psychologists are discovering, is a source of anxiety rather than pleasure.[54]

Barry Schwartz explores how the psychology of choice can rebound on us. The more choice we have, the higher our expectations. Inflated expectations then lead to dissatisfaction – a lingering sense that we could do better. Indeed, his book provides many striking demonstrations of our lack of self-knowledge: we choose choice thinking it will make us happier even if it actually makes us restless and unfulfilled.[55] This is not to suggest that a degree of choice brings no benefits – it clearly does – but that these benefits are finite.

In today's affluent societies we are obliged to adopt coping strategies based on brand loyalties. We either devote time and energy to finding the best product at the best price, or else submit ourselves to be guided by a mixture of whim, fancy, or by yielding to the smooth tones of advertising. The idea that less (choice) might be more (satisfying) is anathema to consumer capitalism, which needs to keep pumping up the volume of goods.

The proliferation of commodities – beyond a certain point – pushes us towards over-consumption, which is the easiest response to an abundance of goods. This may literally be – in the case of convenience food – bad for our health. Thomas Princen calls this kind of activity – where the link with rational self-interest is contradictory at best – 'misconsumption'.[56] This submission to a series of easy decisions involves a loss of self-control.[57] It is not simply that we tend to opt for convenience rather than for challenges: the more choices we are asked to make, the less time and fewer resources we have to make them. Excessive choice becomes a burden rather than an opportunity, diminishing our ability to act creatively or independently.

The proliferation of goods reaches a point where choice becomes, even on capitalism's own terms, dysfunctional. Sheena Iyengar and Mark Lepper's experiment with various food items – jam and chocolate – suggests that while a choice of 24 to 30 different items attracts customers, the bewildering array of possibilities is ultimately off-putting. Customers presented with just six options, they discovered, were more likely to buy something than those with more choice.[58] Iyengar and Lepper's solution to this problem is to suggest that companies decrease the choices they offer. This may be sensible advice, but in macroeconomic terms it represents a real problem for a consumer capitalist project built on the idea of producing more rather than less.

And yet we remain steadfastly bound to the idea that choice is, in itself, a desirable commodity – regardless of degree or circumstance. So, for example, price fixing by cigarette companies was reported on BBC news as being 'bad for consumers'.[59] The well-being of the consumer, in this context, is seen purely in terms of their access to a large choice of goods and services at the lowest price. In truth, what is really bad for the consumer is buying the cigarettes in the first place. Higher prices for tobacco might be good for consumers, because it decreases their ability to pay low prices for something that may later cause pain and suffering. We might say much the same about the enormous range of processed food available to us. What is good for consumers in terms of market logic can be bad for their health and well-being.

The collapse of the Cuban economy following the removal of the Soviet oil subsidy in 1989 is an interesting case in point. While this may have had a number of negative effects on people's quality of life on the island, research suggests that the austerity that followed – in which the choice of food available decreased – had significant health benefits. Obesity levels fell and physical activity increased, creating a healthier, fitter population, with significant declines in deaths attributed to diabetes (51%), coronary heart disease (35%) and strokes (20%).[60]

Even when we are offered something genuinely useful or life-enhancing, too much choice will become a barrier rather than a spur to action. Coping with superabundance eats up our time, requiring a commitment which might otherwise be directed towards doing something that might be more meaningful.

The simultaneous growth in information has created a parallel problem. Most people in the developed world have access to a store of knowledge so sprawling and so vast that it requires both time and expertise to negotiate it. Driven by the desire to spread information and communication, we found ourselves ill-prepared to deal with its superfluity. Email, Twitter, Facebook, texting and the gargantuan intertextuality of the internet all compete for our attention while old media – like television and radio – continue to thrive. Yet ignorance persists in the age of information.[61]

The rational consumer lies at the heart of consumer capitalism: but before the over-burdened 'rational consumer' can begin to research which product most suits them, they need to decide which price-comparison or consumer website is the most reliable. And the rational consumer may well conclude that the time and effort this involves exceeds the rewards of making the right purchase. In short, the rational consumer will make the rational decision to give up being a rational consumer. In the twenty-first century, this is consumer capitalism's Catch 22.

So, for example, the UK government encourages consumers to shop around among energy suppliers to reduce their bills – and there are many price comparison websites offering advice on the best deals. They are, in effect, simply urging us to behave like rational consumers, and thus reward the most efficient suppliers. The problem was that the majority of people did not want to spend their free time researching the intricacies of energy costs. According to the Department of Energy and Climate Change: 'only 15% of households switched gas supplier last year and 17% switched electricity supplier – down from 20% (gas) and 19% (electricity) in 2007, despite the fact that it is possible to save up to £200 from an annual dual fuel bill by shopping around for the lowest online rate'.[62]

This is, if we think about it, a bizarre set of circumstances. We have a public body – in this case a government department – urging consumers to pursue their economic self-interest in order to oblige the market to deliver the best prices. Yet most people take no notice, preferring instead to pay more than they need. To make sense of this we must begin to appreciate how burdensome the unremitting proliferation of choice can be.

Most of us, faced with this kind of excess, are obliged to make compromises based on what is easy and convenient. This means we either stick with what we know or depend on mediators – whether it be advertisers or Google News – to do the thinking for us. In some ways we have become even more dependent on big media than we were when information was less abundant. In order to choose which price-comparison website to use, we are directed by expensive TV advertising campaigns towards one or the other.

One potential benefit of this proliferation has been the growth of movements to promote ethical forms of production. The rapid growth of the Fair Trade movement[63] allows consumers to use ethical concerns to navigate their way through the clutter to make certain choices. While the Fair Trade movement is at a competitive disadvantage (higher wages for producers inevitably means higher prices), it has successfully used branding techniques in a way that turns traditional marketing on its head. Most forms of advertising tend to foreground the moment of consumption – thereby, as Naomi Klein has documented, concealing a multitude of sins.[64] Fair trade products overtly highlight the conditions of production, providing an implicit commentary on the (non-fair trade) products that sit alongside them. This is a remarkable achievement, both accepting and swimming against the tide of a consumerist ethos.

But this success only applies in a world in which fair trade products are an identifiable niche market. Despite the successful promotion of fair trade in certain areas – notably in commodities like sugar, coffee, tea, bananas and cocoa – it represents a tiny proportion of global trade[65] (one estimate puts it at 0.01%).[66] The success of fair trade branding is the consequence of a more general failure to promote ethical standards in the production of commodities. The advocates of ethical production would prefer to see fair trade as a matter of global regulation rather than consumer choice. The development of a market in fair trade goods is, in this sense, only a 'solution' to the problem of product proliferation as long as it remains a niche market.

So when does choice move from being a gift to a burden? In some of the key areas of our lives, we want a degree of choice, and are prepared to devote the time and effort into deciding between the options open to us. But in the twenty-first century the proliferation of choice – particularly in the realm of consumption, where the benefits of choosing one thing over another are usually small at best – has outstripped the finite length of our time on earth.

Can we have consumer capitalism without a model of endless growth? The conventional answer to this is no: assumptions about growth are built into the system. As Tim Jackson puts it, despite the need for a more sustainable economic model, 'there is no clear model for achieving economic stability without consumption growth'.[67] Jackson sees this less as a constraint of economics than a limit of imagination: we simply haven't set our minds to exploring such a possibility.

This is, in part, because an abandonment of growth, on its own, has undoubted negative consequences. If we increase productivity without reducing the number of hours we work, we depend on economic growth to increase the volume of work available. Productivity in the UK more than doubled between 1976 and 2005, but GDP grew at a slightly faster rate over the same period, allowing the creation of jobs to offset efficiency gains and keep employment levels stable.[68] Productivity gains without economic growth will create unemployment – which is, in turn, associated with a significant drop in people's quality of life.

An increasing number of economists – such as Jackson and those associated with the New Economics Foundation in the UK – are challenging the principle of endless economic growth in wealthy countries. They see the current model of economic growth – crudely measured in terms of gross domestic product (GDP) – as both crude and amoral: a place where war is better than peace (if it generates more economic activity) and where waste is a virtue.[69]

The New Economics Foundation propose that we abandon GDP as a measure of social progress, replacing it with a series of indicators that better describe human fulfilment and quality of life.[70] To do so requires a shift in values, so that we begin to exchange money for time. As the economy becomes more efficient, we might begin, once again, to absorb productivity increases by working less. This would have a more profound influence on our quality of life, which is, in wealthy countries, more responsive to chronological than financial gains. Or, to put it another way, in a world replete with consumer goods, we will gain more from increasing our free time than maximizing our ability to accumulate. This, in turn, raises the third problem with consumer capitalism: despite the promises of plenty, it no longer has the capacity to deliver the things that we most value.

Consumer capitalism and the quality of life

In an age of plenty, there is a contradiction between our desires – which are often rooted in the social aspects of life – and consumer capitalism's provision, which is largely material.[71] We have ravaged eco-systems and mortgaged our futures to the hope of infinite growth, yet all we have to show for it is a mountain of things. We may have had fun using them, may even have had fun buying them, but they leave us strangely unfulfilled.[72] Oliver James, a psychologist of consumerism, diagnosed this new malaise as a case of 'affluenza'.[73]

Things are *supposed* to keep getting better – this, after all, is the promise of a consumer society – so we are bound to feel let down if they don't. Consumer capitalism's model of perpetual growth thereby comes up against another constraint: the pleasures of consumerism, it appears, are also finite. The 'retail therapy' of the shopping emporium is a kind of stasis. The satisfaction and meaning it provides may be real enough, and, as Kim Humphery points out, consumerism can be multi-dimensional.[74] But once we reach a certain point it does not improve with volume (either more things to buy or more to spend). This applies whether we get material, emotional or symbolic satisfaction from the things we buy.

A growing body of evidence from across the social sciences suggests that the link between quality of life and our ability to consume has become increasingly tenuous. Ruut Veenhoven's 'World happiness database' has pulled together international data on quality of life,[75] while other studies have explored the relationship between quality of life – including a range of indices such as mental and physical health and risk of crime – with a range of social and economic factors. The results of this research sound a death-knell for consumer capitalism's central promise.

For poorer countries increases in GDP may lead to improvements in quality of life, but this correlation no longer holds true for wealthier nations.[76] While real incomes per head in countries like the USA and the UK have increased significantly since 1950 (tripling in the USA and doubling in the UK), reported satisfaction or happiness levels have either remained flat or declined. Increasing GDP in recent decades also appears to have little impact on overall levels of physical or mental health or a range of social problems.[77]

One of the most dramatic shifts in people's perception of their quality of life occurred in Russia after the collapse of communism, when the supply of consumer goods increased (for some) but reported levels of happiness plummeted.[78] Increases in crime, unemployment, insecurity and instability – all strongly correlated with a drop in quality of life – turned out to be far more significant than the benefits of consumer capitalism.

Richard Layard, summing up the research on quality of life, puts it bluntly:

> People in the West have got no happier in the last 50 years. They have become much richer . . . But they are no happier. This shocking fact should be the starting point for much of our social science.[79]

The 'life-satisfaction paradox'[80] here is that *within* any given society, people with more money tend to enjoy life more than those with less. Research suggests that this is because of the esteem (or lack thereof) that comes with their relative financial position.[81] In a society that links income with status, people like to feel they are doing well rather than doing badly. Those on higher incomes are happier than those on lower incomes in part because of the esteem that accrues from their relative position, *not* because they have more things. Most people, it appears, would rather earn less money if it meant that their position in the pecking order was elevated.[82]

And yet the idea that human progress is directly proportional to our ability to buy remains deeply rooted in our politics and our popular culture. While some governments have begun to acknowledge that quality of life is something that might be measured separately from GDP, every government, regardless of political hue, is committed to economic growth on the assumption that all else – happiness, security and human progress – flows from it. To think more directly about providing the conditions for happiness, fulfilment and security, to divert our energy towards considering what human progress actually means, seems almost a distraction. In essence we are all bound to a system that treats us like spoilt children who just want more stuff and better stuff. And, like spoilt children, we are no happier for it.

On the contrary, if consumerism rests upon an empty promise, it can also make us miserable. This is the theme of Oliver James's 'affluenza' thesis:[83] the constant demands of a consumerist society not only fail to deliver, they distract us from things that are more likely to provide happiness or fulfilment.[84] Studies that focus on those aspects of everyday life that generate meaning, fulfilment and pleasure indicate that our *least* favourite activities on a normal weekday are those involved with earning money: commuting to and from work, followed closely by work itself.[85]

Of course some people, some of the time, will find their work enjoyable or fulfilling, but the data suggest that most people are *more* likely to enjoy their leisure time. A shorter working week, in other words, is more likely to increase our quality of life than the ability to buy more goods.[86] Consumerism pushes us in the opposite direction, towards income maximization at the expense of free time. And, as Staffan Linder predicted, free time itself becomes over-burdened with the volume of consumer goods.[87]

Once we have reached a certain level of comfort, a growing body of empirical evidence suggests that sometimes the best things in life really *are* free. Meaning and pleasure in a consumer culture often come from the social activities associated with consumption (a meal with friends, a night on the town), but it is the social aspects that are integral to these experiences. One of the sweetest paradoxes revealed by research into well-being is that doing things for others – such as voluntary work – increases our own sense of self-worth.[88] Altruism, it turns out, is in our own self-interest. Research even suggests that democratic participation is linked to happiness.[89]

Excessive consumerism, by contrast, is more likely to induce ennui than pleasure. Tim Kasser's review of the literature on the psychology of materialism suggests that far from providing happiness or fulfilment, materialist values are associated with a *drop* in quality of life.[90] Similarly, Juliet Schor's study of children and consumerism suggests that 'less involvement in consumer culture leads to healthier kids and more involvement leads kids' psychological well-being to deteriorate'.[91] An immersion in consumer culture, she suggests, is the key explanatory factor associated with various forms of unhappiness in childhood.

Richard Wilkinson and Kate Pickett's analysis provides a relentless statistical account of the failure of economic growth – past a certain point – to generate positive social outcomes.[92] But they also offer a way forward. Their book, the *Spirit Level*, examined a wide variety of indicators of health and well-being in developed countries and finds many of them linked *not* to the wealth of a society as a whole but to its distribution. More equal societies, their findings suggests, are less violent, physically and psychologically healthier, less prone to social problems and generally more content. This holds true for all levels of society, so that – perhaps counter-intuitively – the wealthy in more equal countries are happier and healthier than their counterparts in less equal societies.

So, for example, countries like the UK, Portugal and the USA, where the gaps between rich and poor are fairly high, are much lower down most of the indices of quality of life than Japan or the more egalitarian Scandinavian countries. Their research reaches the striking conclusion that our current emphasis on the growth of consumer capitalism is entirely misplaced, and that we should focus, instead, on the distribution of income rather than its volume.

Quality of life research is inevitably an inexact science. It depends on a smorgasbord of verifiable measures (like health or crime) and more subjective indicators (like reported well-being) – a mix that is more complex and ambiguous than simple economic indicators like GDP. But it is an attempt to get to grips with what it is that makes life worth living that, in turn, allows us to develop a more sophisticated approach to economic and social policy. The whole premise of consumer capitalism is far cruder, using a GDP as a substitute for quality of life. This would matter little if we set no store by it, but consumer capitalism absorbs our time, our energy and our political imagination. What would a happier, more fulfilling model of human society look like? We're too busy consuming to even ask the question.

Living the contradictions: Media, culture and consumer capitalism

Why do we remain so deeply committed to a system whose benefits are increasingly limited, whose promises are exhausted and whose environmental consequences look increasingly dire? And how might we begin to address these issues and imagine a better world?

These are questions that traditional market economics finds it difficult to address, let alone answer. In theory, as rational consumers, we should drive society towards the fulfilment of our desires. If this were true, of course, things would always get better. In truth, the theory is too simple and too naive to apply to societies where consumerism is no longer a means to an end but a way of life. It depends upon a banal view of human psychology, based on a crude notion of rational self-interest and self-awareness. And it ignores the power of big players within the system – such as transnational corporations and advertisers – to influence outcomes.

But our failure to change course is also rooted in a set of cultural practices, all of which push, nudge and cajole us down a consumerist cul de sac. These practices are so much a part of everyday life that they get in the way of a more deeply felt, sophisticated appreciation of what constitutes human progress. Central to these practices are the commercial giants of media and telecommunications. For all their moments of brilliance and profundity – and, whatever the Jeremiahs may say, there are plenty of them – our information and entertainment media have become increasingly suffused with ideas that sustain consumerism and sideline alternatives. None of these practices are inevitable or irreplaceable, but unless we rethink them it will be difficult for us to imagine alternatives to an increasing jaded system.

The book will focus on three ways in which the media and communications industries keep us conceptually bound to a consumerist credo. First, our most dominant cultural industry – advertising – acts as an unwitting, unplanned propaganda wing of consumer capitalism. Second, the capacity of news journalism to question current orthodoxy is constrained by a focus on 'disposable news', displacing the more democratic function of journalism. Third, the media and communications industries have in recent years come to epitomize the notion of built-in obsolescence based on a perpetual consumerism. Although they have the potential to embrace clean technology, their dismal environmental record leads us in the opposite direction, creating a template for progress based on the endless consumption of objects.

This does not amount to a treatise against consumer capitalism. Its flair for wealth creation has bought all kinds of benefits to humankind. But as the centrepiece for contemporary life, the model has run its course. Our time and space are limited, and even if they were not, increases in consumption levels in the developed world add little to the human condition. For many countries in the twenty-first century we have created sufficient wealth to do almost anything we want. The time has come to stop and think about how best to use it. To do that, we need a different set of stories.

Part II

Selling stories

4

The insatiable age

By the beginning of the twentieth century, capitalism was well established across the developed world. The century ahead would see this transformed into a particular form – consumer capitalism, an economic and cultural system in which the appetite for goods becomes all-consuming and insatiable. The desire for free time would be eclipsed by the desire for more things.

The growth of consumer culture has been made possible by a parallel growth in the advertising industry. The more we have, the harder the industry needs to work to maintain demand. The advertising industry has now colonized our culture, not only as our main form of creative expression, but also as an intrinsic part of nearly all our media, communication and cultural industries.

Selling the insatiable age

At the beginning of the twentieth century, working people in the developed world had tangible dreams of the good life ahead. In the United States, the excesses of the late nineteenth-century 'gilded age' gave way to the progressive era, a more democratic period concerned with equality of opportunity and the common good. Edwardian Britain also saw the consolidation of a new politics based on mass participation, underpinned by significant increases in average income during the second half of the Victorian age. Extraordinary new technologies – planes, cars, transistor radios, movie theatres – were not merely imagined but manufactured.

This was, in many ways, a much more optimistic time than the early years of the century to follow: a time when the growth of democracy alongside an era of unprecedented economic expansion seemed to offer infinite possibilities.[1] And despite the brutal interruptions of two world wars, the twentieth century was a triumph in overcoming many forms of discontent in the developed world. The misery of abject poverty, discomfort and poor public health all diminished, and a new set of freedoms (to travel, to communicate, to play) enlivened cultural life.

But if we got close to a promised era of contentment, it never quite arrived. As the twentieth century matured, it was supplanted by a new culture oozing with gratification yet underpinned by a permanent *dis*content. The desire for a better life became the desire for more things. Our dreams and norms 'were cast more by capital than by church, community or country'.[2] Acquisition went from being about the satisfaction of clearly understood needs to become an end in itself – commodities defined a lifestyle, a pastime, an ambition. Thus began the age of insatiability.

By the twenty-first century the seemingly boundless desire for consumer goods has become one of our society's most defining features. The standard economic account of this (and it is an account rather than an explanation) is to see our current state as a natural development of the human condition. But as Colin Campbell points out, there is nothing natural or inevitable about the unfocused desire of the insatiable age.[3] For while many societies throughout the history of humankind involve conspicuous displays of material lust, these have tended to be specific and defined (such as the desire for gold or land).

Modern consumerism is distinguished by its inexhaustible, flibbertigibbet character, as our desires glide along a ceaseless conveyer belt of things. The 'process is ceaseless and unbroken', writes Campbell; 'rarely can an inhabitant of modern society, no matter how privileged or wealthy, declare that there is nothing new that they want. That this should be so is a matter of wonder.'[4] The condition of wanting has lost its specificity and is, as a consequence, more difficult to resolve.

How did we become like this, creatures flitting from one object to another, always wanting more but unable to predict what 'more' might be? Campbell chastises the mainstream of classical economics for failing even to ask the question, assuming that this is merely a normal, natural state of affairs. For while the consumer society may have been driven, in part, by human desire, the growth of that society has steadily transformed our understanding of what we need and want.

At the beginning of the 1920s our understanding of consumer desire was very different. A US adman of the period lamented that products were so heavily advertised that they were 'scratching gravel from the bottom of consumer demand. The grocer and the chemist look despairingly at their crowded shelves when asked to find places for another breakfast food or a new toothpaste.'[5] A hundred years later, what once seemed an abundance looks like an age of austerity.

A new breed of advertisers – the pioneers of our consumer age – emerged from this apparently saturated market. This was a decade when ads began to create a new set of anxieties and insecurities about winning the approval (or avoiding the disapproval) of others – anxieties which could only be resolved in the marketplace.[6] A 1922 advertisement for Woodbury Soap warned women that:

> a man expects to find daintiness, charm, refinement in the woman he knows . . . and when some unpleasant little detail mars this conception of what a woman should be – nothing quite effaces [*sic*] his involuntary disappointment.[7]

Manufacturers, for their part, could direct their energies towards a new set of products designed to avoid a whole succession of 'involuntary disappointments'. They also realized that the principles of fashion allowed them to persuade people to replace objects purely on the basis of colour or design, rather than their utility. As one advertisement declared delightedly in a 1927 issue of the *Ladies*

Home Journal: 'The plain vanilla . . . of the modern bathroom is turning pistachio and orange!'[8] Taste was not simply subject to change, it was defined by it.

By the end of the 1920s, the gurus of a thrusting advertising industry – men like George Harrison Phelps – charged with selling automobiles – and Robert Updegraff – who sold everything from life insurance to cornflakes – offered glimpses of a future shaped by advertising. Updegraff predicted that:

> By 1950 men [*sic*] will have learned to express their ideas, their motives, their experiences, their hopes and ambitions . . . their desires and aspirations . . . by means of printed or painted advertising, or of messages projected through the air.[9]

It is easy to observe that advertisers like George Phelps and Robert Updegraff were ahead of their time. Much later, at the other end of the twentieth century, George Gerbner would observe the realization of this vision with rather less enthusiasm: 'for the first time in human history', he wrote, 'children are hearing most of the stories, most of the time, not from their parents or school or churches or neighbors, but from a handful of global conglomerates that have something to sell'.[10] This new generation of advertisers, who pictured their industry at the centre of the culture rather than a subsidiary bi-product of retailing, were part of a process that helped shape the consciousness of their age.[11]

Thorsten Veblen coined the phrase 'conspicuous consumption' at the onset of the twentieth century to describe the use of consumer goods as a way of defining one's relationship to others (the idea of 'status symbols').[12] But it was during the middle of the twentieth century – the boom years from World War Two to the early 1970s – that the transformation to a consumer society was most flagrant. During this period, high levels of economic growth – fuelled by state investment, technological innovation and consumer capitalism – became an expectation. In the 1950s, social scientists and other observers could still remember a time when expectations were different, before the rampaging accumulation of goods became so central to everyday life. This prompted them to raise questions it rarely occurs to us to ask today.

Philosophers, economists and commentators sought to account for the lurch towards a consumer culture, as well as question the value and sustainability of a society based on the manufacture of plenty. The economist John Kenneth Galbraith observed that the growth of consumerism was not an inevitable development but the emergence of something quite new. Supply and demand, he suggested, was no longer a simple equation for the satisfaction of human needs. As markets became saturated again in the 1960s (or so people imagined),[13] definable needs were being replaced by less defined wants – an idea developed by Herbert Marcuse in his 1964 book *One Dimensional Man*.[14] In an age of affluence, Galbraith argued, 'the urgency of the wants can no longer be used to defend the urgency of the production'.[15]

Galbraith advanced this idea in *The Affluent Society*, first published in 1958, where he challenged the traditional economic assumption that increasing production was simply a natural response to increasing demand. Sociologists like John Goldthorpe pondered the emergence of 'the affluent worker',[16] while the journalist Vance Packard published a series of books – notably *The Hidden Persuaders* (1957) and *The Wastemakers* (1960) – attempting to document the logic of the new consumer society, where accumulation becomes an end in itself, and when, Packard observed, it was 'just assumed that any growth is good'.[17]

Leaving aside, for the moment, the diagnoses offered by mid century thinkers like Galbraith, Packard or Marcuse, their work signals the recognition of what we might now call a 'paradigm shift' – the move from one set of assumptions and beliefs to another. They saw the emergence of a different kind of society – one which conflated human desire with the endless accumulation of commodities. This had not happened overnight, of course, but it was possible for them to see that as consumerism became central to our social arrangements, we needed new ways to understand the world. This was both a cultural and an economic change – our culture and our economy locked in a new symbiosis defined by consumerism.

It is useful, at such historical moments, to think about the road not taken, to imagine how economic and social forces might have led in other directions. History, as Susan Strasser suggests, becomes a way of imagining a different future; it 'provides us with a viewpoint from which we may observe some other way to be human, and where we might ask heretical but important questions'. One of the most notable of these, when we look back over the last hundred years, is to 'interrogate the costs of commercial values framing all facets of life'.[18] So, how might we imagine a different history, one with a different set of imperatives? What would have driven a less insatiable, post-war age of plenty?

We might, for example, have seen substantial increases in our free time. To have the freedom to choose what we do, unconfined by any financial imperatives, is one of the great possibilities of the technological age. The first few decades of the twentieth century were full of a well-versed desire for cashing in productivity gains for time rather than money.[19] In the United States, for example, both the Republican and Democratic parties included shorter working hours in their platforms up until 1932. But as the century wore on, historian Benjamin Kline Hunnicutt describes how 'shorter hours have ceased to be an important part of public discourse':

> The dreams of the utopian writers of the four hour day and the hopes of those who believed that progress involved leisure as much as it involved economic growth have evaporated, and labor's old demand for 'the progressive shortening of the hours of labor' has been forgotten.[20]

Our abandonment of the pursuit of free time – the once cherished promise of innovation and efficiency – suggests an acceptance that is characteristic of our contemporary lack of imagination. We may wish to revisit these 'utopian dreams'.

We might also have redirected our energy towards supplying those people who might have most benefited from consumer goods, using our dynamic productive capacity to spread new found prosperity to poorer parts of the world. While this idea did gain some currency – notably with the publication of the Brandt Report in 1980[21] – its recommendations were cast adrift in the 1980s. Free market conservative governments (symbolized by Margaret Thatcher and Ronald Reagan) exploited a disenchantment with 'big government' and declared a new faith in market economics aided and abetted by sympathetic governments (an ideological movement often referred to as 'neo-liberalism').

The Brandt Report was written at the end of a period when the redistributive philosophy behind the growth of welfare states still had political momentum. At that time, the idea of extending this largesse to push the production of goods towards the poorer people in the world who would benefit most from them was, in many ways, an obvious development. Once a redistributive philosophy became unfashionable, the machinery of consumer capitalism – which is not built for altruistic purposes – was set to push its productive energy towards the 'haves' rather than the 'have nots'. Its mechanisms were directed towards those with most money, *not* towards those most in need. There was, it was felt, generally more to be made in selling superfluity to the rich than necessities to the poor. If the spirit of the Brandt Report survives,[22] one of its main selling points is a form of enlightened self-interest, which sees economic growth in the developing world as a way of sustaining global growth by increasing demand.

Which leaves us with what Colin Campbell calls the 'puzzle' of modern consumerism. The conditions outlined in Chapter 3 – consumer capitalism's failure in an age of plenty, to deliver quality of life, its dependence on a series of economic contradictions and its hostility to the environment – make this even more of an enigma.

If consumer capitalism does not make us happy or fulfilled, if it is economically and environmentally unsustainable, and if it caters more for those who already have a wealth of consumer goods than for those who don't, why do we still associate it with progress? If we are to imagine another form of human development – to rekindle the spirit of freeing our time from the workplace, for example – we need to understand what drives and sustains consumerism. We need to see why it is that we find it so difficult to imagine 'some other way to be human'.

Writers like Galbraith, Packard and Marcuse offered various explanations for the new age of insatiability. While their understanding of advertising was not always subtle, they all recognized its centrality in a consumer economy. At the beginning of the

twentieth century, advertising was a young industry whose rel-
evance was less apparent in a world where people's needs were
more tangible. To put it bluntly, people had a fairly clear idea
of what they wanted. But over the next few decades, over-
production required a system that could identify new – and rapidly
expendable – forms of desire. At this point, writes Sean Brierley,
'Advertising emerges as a tool to try and stimulate markets to
pay for over-produced goods.'[23] By the start of the twenty-first
century advertising would – without any clear democratic mandate
– become the most ubiquitous form of creative expression in our
culture.

Selling a culture: The growth of advertising

At the end of the nineteenth century, most buying and selling
was done face to face. Shopkeepers and buyers were, between
them, able to negotiate directly the landscape of consumers goods
in response to the customer's needs. As the mass production and
proliferation of goods increased the choices available, businesses
and manufacturers wanted the chance to bypass this cosy interaction and appeal to customers directly. Mass communication
and mass production gave birth to the use of advertising on an
industrial scale, and between 1880 and 1910 corporate advertising
expenditure grew from $30 million to $600 million per year.[24]

By the 1920s the US advertising industry established itself as a
necessary partner in the development of markets for mass production. The new consumer society needed not just an infrastructure
but a culture – one that, as US President Calvin Coolidge put
it, 'ministers to the spiritual side of trade'.[25] But by the 1950s it
seemed that the success of this enterprise – flooding the USA with
consumer goods – would be its undoing. Amid this new clutter of
commodities, a headline in *Advertising Age* declared plaintively and
with a notable lack of pizzazz, that in the new era of abundance:
'Creating Desire for Goods Gets Harder'.[26]

If the aim of advertising hitherto was to channel needs and
desires, it was now faced with the more difficult task of inventing

them. As economists like Galbraith pointed out, the advertising industry's primary function, in the drive to create consumer desire, was to meet the need of producers rather than consumers. Their role was to make it possible, as Galbraith put it, for production to fill 'the void that it has itself created'.[27]

Vance Packard's account of the growth of consumerism pushed the advertising industry to centre stage. The purpose of the industry, he suggested with more than a whiff of disapproval, was to invent 'strategies that would make Americans in large numbers into voracious, wasteful, compulsive consumers – and strategies that would provide products assuring such wastefulness'.[28] His book, *The Hidden Persuaders*,[29] was a rollicking ride through the many motivational strategies used by advertisers to create a consumer culture. Although Packard's analysis is often slipshod and ad hoc, his vantage point – as an observer of the rapid emergence of consumerism – allows him a certain licence.

His work also exposed a fault line in classical economic theory, which tends to collapse 'needs' and 'wants' and see both as arising spontaneously in humankind.[30] Because the level of affluence enjoyed by many white Americans in the 1950s was sufficiently new and distinctive, social critics like Packard were able, at certain moments, to identify another possibility – of a society happy with its lot, where most people had what they needed to live a good and fulfilling life. A few years later in 1963 the British sociologist John Goldthorpe would ask similar – if rather narrower – questions about the culture of a more affluent working class.[31]

While economists were captivated by what Packard called 'growthmanship', the question that motivated critics like Packard was *why* the possibility of a genuinely contented society – one where people had enough money to expand their free time to dwell further on the less overtly material aspects of life – had so palpably failed to materialize. Being happy with one's level of possessions can be seen be as an eminently desirable possibility, but writers like Packard, Galbraith and Marcuse saw such contentment as a problem for an economic system that insisted upon permanent growth. In short, consumer capitalism had a clear interest in fostering discontent, and thereby persuading wealthier sections of society to carry on consuming.

The advertising industry found itself at the heart of this endeavour – their importance grew as the need for consumer goods dwindled. Tom Crompton, Guy Shrubsole and Jon Alexander make the point that despite its centrality, there is remarkably little research on the role advertising plays in our economy or our culture.[32] Advertisers themselves – perhaps reluctant to be portrayed as a malign influence – are often coy about their impact, modestly asserting that all they do is spread preferences around, nudging us from one product to another. Unless, of course, they are talking to their clients, when they tend to make bolder claims. As Arthur Asa Berger puts it, 'advertising agencies are forced to talk out of both sides of their mouth at the same time'.[33]

And yet much of the evidence – such as it is – tells a clearer story. In a study published in 1995, Chulho Jung and Barry Seldon indicated that 'consumption not only affects advertising, as previous research has shown, but that the converse is also true: aggregate advertising affects aggregate consumption'.[34] More recent work by Benedetto Molinari and Francesco Turino comes to a similar conclusion.[35] Indeed, as the choices available to consumers expand, advertising grows proportionately to defend market share in some areas and increase it in others. In this great game of accumulation there have been more winners than losers. Every time we seem to have reached a saturation point in consumption, advertising steps up a gear and pushes us beyond it.

From a global perspective, advertising has conspicuously failed to spread its messages equitably. It has, for some time, celebrated the paradox that those in greatest need of its services were those with the greatest resources, thriving on the principle that the more things people have, the more advertising they need. And the extraordinary proliferation of manufactured objects since the 1950s obliged consumers to become increasingly dependent upon advertising to differentiate between one product and another. Advertising helped create over-consumption, and then brought order to the chaotic superabundance.

The consumer society as we now know it blossomed amid the greatest uncoordinated, unwitting propaganda effort in the history of humankind. Global advertising spending grew from 7.5 billion dollars in 1950 to 72 billion dollars by the end of the 1970s. In the

1990s, researchers in the USA estimated that by the age of 18 the average American has seen around 350,000 commercials.[36] By the end of 2011 – when the superfluity of the 1950s looked positively meagre – we were spending half a trillion dollars a year – most of it in the wealthy, developed world – trying to persuade people to buy more things.[37] This is a mammoth cultural effort – more than 15 times the value of the total global box office receipts for all films released in 2011.[38] For developing nations like China, advertising spending has increased at a blistering pace – thirteenfold in the decade from 1997 to 2006.[39]

Advertising is now our dominant cultural industry – what Stuart Ewen calls 'the prevailing vernacular of public address'.[40] It sucks up our talent for art, design, creativity and story-telling and sets it to work on the manufacture of that most precious of commodities, human desire.

It is worth remembering that many of our information and entertainment media began as ventures that were far less dependent on advertising than they are today. The first thirty years of British broadcasting, for example, required no advertising – a public service model that saw broadcasting as a public good and which was widely adopted throughout Europe. The film industry has always been a profit-making business, but films themselves were generally commercial free for most of the twentieth century. And while the rapid growth of pop music industry from the mid 1950s to the early 1980s was also a largely commercial enterprise,[41] it maintained a clear distance from the world of advertising, which was obliged to make up its own tunes. The credibility of pop music as a creative form relied, in part, upon this distance. Using music to sell things was seen as a debasement of the ability to convey mood and meaning through music. Jingles might be catchy and fun, but no one took them seriously as an art form.

The rapid growth of newspapers in Britain during the nine-teenth century was fuelled less by the lure of advertising revenue (which was taxed until the second half of the century) than by a rampant radical press promoting the democratic rights and welfare of working people.[42] The internet began, in the early 1990s, as a publicly funded, largely non-commercial space for the exchange of information, the development of civic networks and as an educational resource.[43] The early years of online were greeted by many as the dawn of a new democratic age.[44] I recall my colleague Michael Morgan (at the University of Massachusetts in the early 1990s) enthusing about this remarkable development, one with the potential to expand and deepen the public sphere, allowing citizens to inform one another and to create their own information and communication networks.

All these media have, since then, been transformed into increasingly commercial domains dominated by advertising. Although each media form has its own characteristics, what unites them is a purpose. In most cases their existence – economically speaking – is defined not by the ability to inform, inspire, move or entertain, but their ability to deliver audiences to advertisers. This is not to say that films, TV programmes or websites are incapable of speaking beyond the needs of commerce – they clearly are – but each medium now depends upon an increasing volume of advertising for its economic survival.

On television, the proliferation of channels has been driven largely by private companies, so that the proportion of publicly funded spaces has shrunk with alarming speed.[45] The UK, for example, has moved from a carefully constructed ecology based on public service – with a mix of well-funded commercial, semi-commercial and publicly funded channels producing a wide range of high quality programming – to a predominantly commercial system with a politically fragile public service component.[46] Not only does British television have a greater proportion of purely commercial channels, it also allows more commercials on those channels, a preponderance that was hitherto considered detrimental to the integrity of broadcasting. Pressured by demands from an expanding commercial sector, UK regulators have gradually relaxed limits of the volume of advertising on British television so that the average viewer is now exposed to 48 TV commercials a day.[47]

Countries like the United States of America – who have always had predominantly commercial systems – show more advertisements now than at any time in their history. An analysis of US primetime TV in June 2009 found that commercial messages took up 41% of viewing time, and nearly half of viewing time during reality and late night TV shows.[48] A survey of primetime television in Australia found that limits on commercial time (13 minutes per hour) were consistently flouted – with some hours registering 19 minutes of advertising per hour (or 32% of viewing time).[49] These proportions are well beyond the reach of any other television genre.

While advertisements can be lavishly produced, witty or entertaining, their presence – unlike almost every other form of programming – has nothing to do with viewer demand. On the contrary, when asked, most viewers would prefer less advertising, and find themselves increasingly annoyed by the constant interruption of all our other cultural forms.[50] In other words, the expansion of the time devoted to encouraging consumer demand has occurred *in spite of* consumer demand.

The drift towards the growth of advertising time on television is possible, in part, because advertising displaces audiences from their position as consumers. Although we are accustomed to talking about media audiences as if they were customers for the programmes on offer, when programmes are funded by commercials, their economic relationship to them is tenuous. The customers – the people who pay – are the advertisers. Audiences are the commodity being bought and sold. It is not surprising if it is advertisers rather than audiences whose wishes hold sway.[51]

This becomes apparent when we introduce other economic models allowing audiences to express a preference for less advertising. In the USA, commercial free channels like HBO can charge a premium for allowing viewers the privilege of watching programmes that are not continually interrupted by (or written around) advertisements. HBO promises a different kind of television, in part, simply because advertising does not dominate its content. Channels like HBO could hardly claim to be entirely commercial free – the programmes themselves have become ads for various spin-offs[52] (part of what Andrew Wernick calls a 'promotional culture').[53] But their emergence and success is based on the value audiences give to an environment with less commercial clutter.

In the UK, when the BBC and a commercial channel broadcast the same event simultaneously, the BBC will invariably get a *significantly* larger audience than its commercial rival – between three to five times the size – simply because people would rather watch programmes broadcast for their own sake than ones that are regularly interrupted.[54]

Given this distinct lack of public enthusiasm, it is perhaps unsurprising that the growth of TV advertising occurred with little public deliberation. In the USA, the 1996 Telecommunication Act, which pushed US media further down the road to a purely commercial ethos, received almost no serious media attention (and when it did, more as a fait accompli than as a matter of debate).[55] In the UK, an Ipsos-Mori survey in 2006 suggested that the majority of people had either never heard of or knew little about the main regulatory authorities for broadcasting or the press.[56]

This matters, because despite the new media revolution, television continues to dominate our leisure time. Despite predictions that new media would replace the old, the average person actually watches more TV now than ten years ago.[57] Television remains the big beast of contemporary culture and the information age. Yet, with little public consultation or discussion, governments have created or changed broadcast regulations so that the genre that dominates most multi-format commercial television networks is not drama, sport, film, comedy, reality competitions, quiz shows or soap opera, but advertising itself.

Media – like film – that were traditionally ad-free spaces are now funded by product placement deals and commercial tie-ins.[58] So, for example, the Bond film *Die Another Day* raised $120 in revenue by promoting Samsonite luggage, Omega watches, a Phillips heart rate monitor, Bollinger champagne, Heineken beer, Sony security systems, laptops and British Airways.[59] Even more lucrative, however, are product spin-offs, in which the movie becomes an advertisement, writ large, for a range of merchandise. So, for example, the Disney film *The Lion King* made a fraction of its profit at the box office. The film's revenues were around $300,000, but it made a billion dollars from nearly 200 items of *Lion King*-related products.[60]

The same is true of the pop music industry. The word 'jingle' – the tunes written to sell things by – seems almost a quaint throwback to a time before the popular music and the advertising industries merged in a money-making symbiosis. From the industry's point of view, the use of popular music in advertising is both a source of income and an opportunity to provide an artist with exposure. The advertisers, meanwhile, are able to cash in on pop music's emotional resonance, capturing the musical mood and associating it with the consumption of commodities.

There are many milestones in pop music's gradual embrace of advertising. For some, the use of the Beatles song *Revolution* in a 1987 Nike commercial was the moment when pop music sold its soul to Madison Avenue. Music journalist Dave Marsh captures the sense of outrage well: 'The artistic community, people who thought rock was art, were up in arms when Nike bought the Beatle's *Revolution* . . . to defile . . . the whole idea of revolution, if it comes down to what sneaker you choose to wear . . . what sweatshop you choose to abuse.'[61]

Another key moment, identified by Bethany Klein in her account of the increasing commercialism of the pop music indus-try,[62] was the release of Moby's album *Play* in 1999. For the first time, every one of the 18 songs on the album was licensed for use in commercials, movies or television. Once, non-conformist punk rockers like Johnny Rotten (butter) and Iggy Pop (car insurance) fronting up commercials would have been unimaginable. Now they follow a tradition in which the music and advertising indus-tries have become inseparable, where the *idea* of non-conformity is used to sell things. It would be foolish to suppose there was ever a time when the artistry and authenticity of popular music were untainted by commerce. What has changed is the depth of the relationship, in which both are subsumed within the broad discourse of advertising.

The increasing role of advertising in the cultural industries is, in part, a consequence of the growth of the online world. The world wide web went from being a public information tool to an ad-dominated medium with a speed that, in a less commercial age, might have raised concern. Some of those who celebrated its potential now lament the shallow, addictive and commercial beast it has become.[63]

Much of the enthusiasm around the information age has imag-ined that information had its own agency and volition, seeping its way into the daylight of its own accord. But the creation of information does not happen by itself. R. L. Rutsky points out that consumer capitalists have 'an obvious interest on seeing information as a kind of capital on which they can earn a return'. [64] The great strength of the internet – its capacity to receive or display a huge corpus of content at little cost – is also, in financial terms, its weakness. For most 'content providers'– whether they are journalists, artists or musicians – the *only* way to raise revenue online is through advertising.[65]

The internet has thus evolved into a cultural form that promotes the idea that information and entertainment are only viable if advertisers are willing to pay for them.[66] The amount we are prepared to pay for our news or our music is declining, even while expectations about its quality remain the same. What we have lost here – apart from a grasp of the basic mathematics of cultural production – is an appreciation that such things have value beyond their ability to connect audiences with commodities.

Advertising has, in these various ways, colonized our culture. It wallpapers our public spaces – on billboards, buses and buildings – and brands the clothes we wear. All our communications media – the mail, the internet, social networking sites, even the phone – are increasingly channels for pitching products. As each medium becomes saturated, advertisers look for new spaces – from sports pitches to concert halls – in which to make their appeals.

George Monbiot, writing in the *Guardian*, chastises the dominance of the advertising industry and its negative social and environmental impact, but bears witness to its ubiquity:

> I detest this poison, but I also recognize that I am becoming more dependent on it. As sales of print editions decline, newspapers lean even more heavily on advertising. Nor is the problem confined to the commercial media. Even those who write only for their own websites rely on search engines, platforms and programmes ultimately funded by advertising.[67]

For the emerging generation of online community news sites, the paucity of funding means that the debate is not where to raise income, but merely about who to accept advertising from (between those who favour local companies and those who adopt a less discriminating approach).[68]

At one time we associated the idea of 'selling out' with artists – writers, actors, musicians and so on – who compromised their craft for commercial ends. The triumph of consumerism is such that the phrase is rarely used anymore. As George Gerbner observed, our culture is manifestly *about* selling, if not selling out. The next chapter describes how this is not merely a social development but also a political one.

5

Tales of sales: The politics of advertising

The advertising industry shapes our culture in three profound ways: first, by the sheer volume of its presence as our most conspicuous cultural genre; second, by the way in which other cultural forms – like commercial television – are constrained to accommodate it; and third, by the content of advertisements themselves. Because we tend to treat advertising as a source of income rather than content, as innocent rather than ideological, these points are generally overlooked.

The promotion of consumer capitalism is not a value-free, apolitical endeavour. Part I brings together a series of pragmatic concerns about its ability to drive human progress in the twenty-first century and stresses the need for us to imagine a world in which consumer capitalism plays a less dominant role. The advertising industry is, in this context, a subtle but relentlessly partial voice, pushing us towards consumerist goals, ideals and solutions and blotting out alternatives.

The strategy adopted by much contemporary advertising is revealingly self-contradictory. It promotes the idea that all good things in life and the solution to every problem are matters of material consumption. And yet it has so little confidence in this proposition that it makes every effort to link products with the non-material world of human relationships. On one level, this works very well: it pushes advertising outside the realm of regulatory scrutiny and guides us through a world in which product proliferation – a plethora of similarity – has made traditional forms of rational consumption impossible. But it also obscures the political nature of the central pitch.

It is a politics that has encouraged us to abandon the push to exchange the productivity gains that come with technological innovation for increases in our free time. Despite evidence to the contrary, it encourages us to believe that we must, for our own well-being, sacrifice time in order to maximize our spending power.

Policy makers, by allowing advertising to dominate our culture, have allowed it to shape our priorities. Most of our cultural and information industries now depend on it, and it has become a ubiquitous part of our cultural environment. The decisions that have encouraged this development may have been pragmatic but their consequences are deeply political. If we are to imagine other forms of human progress, we need to restrain the influence of the advertising industry.

Commercial confines

At times when it looked as if there was no more room in our lives for more things, the growth of advertising has encouraged wealthy societies towards insatiability, moving past points of saturation to continue along an upward spiral of accumulation. More advertising means more goods, which, in turn, requires more advertising to help guide us through the clutter. The advertising industry has swept us along a very particular path: our society's central vision of the future – more of the same – reflects its single-minded focus.

Most of the stories created by our information and creative industries are not there because they are helpful, compelling, moving or significant, but because of their ability to connect us to commercial messages. The ingenuity of cultural producers working within these commercial constraints may be dazzling or banal, but a series of economic imperatives[1] inevitably limit our cultural and creative horizons.[2]

Those cultural forms that fail to fit the marketing format are, regardless of their profundity or importance, less likely to see the light of day – and certainly not in television's primetime. A compelling television drama written to hold our attention for an hour – or even half an hour – is simply unsuitable for a commercial television format based on providing increasingly regular interruptions. A primer on TV writing in the USA reminds the aspiring writer that 'television shows (are) structured around commercial breaks'. This means, for example:

> For hour-long dramas or action-adventures, the stories are built in four acts, often with a teaser and tag. Each act needs to go out on a strong hook, especially at the half-hour mark, when viewers are most likely to change the channel. Most hour-long shows weave together three plotlines: the A story, which drives the bulk of the episode; a B story, featuring supporting characters; and a C story or 'runner', usually lighter in tone, that serves as comic relief.[3]

Advertising thereby defines the grammar of commercial television as a cultural form, shaping its narrative conventions and structuring its content.[4]

The United States is, perhaps, the most conspicuous example of a commercial culture. The USA spends more on advertising – over 2% of GDP – than most other countries – around double the rate of countries like Sweden or France.[5] Its dependence on advertising has a longer history – especially in key areas like broadcasting – so that its citizens have become accustomed to cultural events that are defined by the promotional needs of the corporate world. Their biggest annual TV event – the Super Bowl – has long been a showcase for Madison Avenue's latest ad campaigns. The advertisements have become part of the spectacle, with an increasing number of people tuning in to watch the commercials rather than the game.[6]

Why has football (soccer) – the world's biggest sport – failed to capture the imagination of the United States? Principally because football – where the ball is in play for most of the two 45-minute halves – does not fit the commercial format that has dominated US broadcasting since the 1930s. The sports that dominate US culture – American football, baseball, basketball and ice hockey – have all evolved around this constraint. The 'time-out' – a stoppage featured liberally in all of them – may slow a game down, but it allows the networks regular opportunities to insert commercial breaks.

Advertising has thus become a part of the customary order of sporting life. Instead of 'rain stopped play' we have the altogether more contrived 'advertising stopped play'.

For viewers who have grown up in countries where television is – or was – less remorselessly commercial, some of these built-in stoppages seem strange. So, for example, the sole purpose of the 'two-minute warning' in American football – a sport specifically redesigned to fit the needs of TV advertisers[7] – is to enable TV networks to show commercials towards the end of the second and fourth quarters. The American version of football has thereby contrived a stop–start structure ideally suited to the needs of commercial television. Open play occupies only 6% of a three-hour television broadcast.[8] This contrasts with the world game, where two 45-minute halves provide fewer opportunities for commercial interruption, and any attempt to slow the game down would be bitterly opposed. It is the centrality of advertising in US broadcasting that, above all, explains the mystery of football's failure to capture the North American imagination.[9]

But advertising is more than a series of constraints and interruptions of other forms of creative expression, it is a cultural form in its own right. There is a literature describing how its many stories help sustain and promote a range of ideas about the world.[10] But when media regulators debate the role of advertising in broadcasting, discussion is usually predicated on the idea that advertising is, first and foremost, a matter of economics rather than part of the culture.

If we are asked what we watched on television last night, we will list the programmes but forget to mention that we may also have watched dozens of commercials.[11] Advertising is, in this sense, so ubiquitous, so much a part of our cultural life that its presence seems, most of the time, unworthy of comment. Our dominant cultural industry thus remains remarkably untroubled by critical scrutiny.

This is not to belittle the growing politics of anti-consumerism, which has an array of antecedents in forms of religious morality and a long-standing environmentalist movement.[12] It is also fair to say many people are, at certain moments, aware that advertising can promote unhealthy forms of consumerism. The advertising

industry is almost certainly our least beloved cultural industry –
like a parasite, it clings to other cultural forms, and unlike them,
its presence is rarely sought. One of the reasons my own students
feel so comfortable applying a critical distance to advertisements
(as opposed, say, to the Disney films they grew up with) is because
they have so little emotional attachment to them. But neither anti-
consumerism nor a general lack of enthusiasm has inspired a serious
challenge to advertising's cultural predominance.

When the content of advertising *is* debated – such as the selling
of junk food during children's programmes – the advertisements
themselves are usually taken at face value and treated on their own
merit (buy this soft drink, buy that brand). Advertising *en masse* is
seen as no more than the sum of its parts. The problem, by implication, can be reduced to a particular set of product ranges, thereby
avoiding larger questions about the broader politics of advertising.

This reflects the view of advertising regulators, who insist that
advertisements be considered individually rather than collectively.
Commercial messages are treated on a case by case basis as no
more than 'facts about products'. The Federal Trade Commission
(FTC), responsible for the regulation of advertising in the USA,
adopts a sympathetic stance towards the genre, regarding it as a
generally benign source of information:

> Most of the time, advertising enhances market performance by provid-
> ing useful information to consumers and by enabling firms to promote
> the attributes of their products and services and, thereby, to compete
> better with each other.[13]

This is a highly questionable claim, but the FTC is above such
considerations, confining itself to policing a line that advertisements may cross if they become offensive or overtly unhelpful to
consumers:

> On the other hand, advertising may adversely affect market perfor-
> mance when businesses use it to transmit deceptive or fraudulent
> messages on which reasonable consumers are induced to rely to their
> detriment. When this happens, we tend to refer to the result as 'market
> failure'.[14]

Regulators busy themselves with preventing such 'market failures', while ensuring that advertising does not mislead, harm or offend. The remit of most regulatory bodies, such as the FTC or the UK's Advertising Standards Authority, is limited further by their own definition of what might be fraudulent or misleading:

> Although, in principle, the FTC may challenge any deceptive advertising claim, it is the Commission's long established practice not to challenge claims that are purely subjective (e.g., 'best', 'brightest', 'great taste', 'feels and looks great'). This type of claim generally is considered 'puffery.' Instead, the FTC concentrates on challenging false or misleading claims about objective facts (e.g., 'fat-free,' 'proven effective by scientific tests').[15]

Advertisers, aware of these regulations – as well as the power of a symbolic rather than a utilitarian pitch – tend to steer clear of the difficult terrain of 'objective facts'. In a world cluttered with similar commodities it is easier to appeal to a symbolic rather than a more practical domain. Advertisers draw heavily upon this form of poetic licence, and the great bulk of advertising content – seen by the regulators as mere 'puffery' – is left free from scrutiny.

There are a small number of exceptions to this generally benign overview – notably for *some* of the products that are demonstrably bad for public health. Despite their public modesty (unless they are pitching to clients), research confirms that advertising generally increases demand.[16] To limit this demand, a number of countries (including the USA) impose limits on advertising alcohol or tobacco. Few have extended this to other areas of public health (notably the wide range of high-fat, high-sugar, processed foodstuffs that tends to dominate the world of food and drink commercials),[17] and none are prepared to consider the role of advertising in general or stand in the way of its increasing ubiquity.

The broad implication of these regulatory structures – and of the general acceptance of advertising they represent – is that the stories told by advertisements are essentially trivial, entirely peripheral to larger political questions. If we take most advertisements on their individual merits, this seems both apt and reasonable. In *The Hidden Persuaders*, Vance Packard's famous critique of the advertising industry, there is a tendency to portray advertising as if it were a *coordinated* campaign, the self-conscious propaganda wing of a voracious economic system.[18] This reflects an assumption we often make about cultural forms, where judgement is made in quasi-legal rather than sociological terms, and where influence only 'counts' if it is a matter of deliberate intent. If we make this assumption, then broader questions of influence are easy to rebut: advertisers do not conspire or act in consort: they produce messages with the limited ambition of selling a particular product.

And yet Packard was right to see advertising as more than the sum of its parts. Our experience of advertising – and its meaning – is cumulative. Each advertisement may take up only a tiny part of our attention, but the *discourse* of advertising is far more pervasive. Collectively, advertisements reverberate to a tune that is both political and relentless. The moral of the thousands of different stories advertising tells is always the same: regardless of how much we already have, the only way to secure pleasure, popularity, security, happiness or fulfilment is through consumption.

The idea that advertising promotes a consumerist world view is so self-evident that it scarcely merits discussion: it thus remains largely unspoken. So too is the idea that consumerism is an ideology with political ramifications. Both points have been left, thus far, to a few critical voices without entering the mainstream of public debate.[19] So, for example, Arthur Asa Berger suggests, reasonably enough, that 'advertising often distracts us from paying attention to the need for social investments ... and thus, by its very nature, tends to be politically conservative'.[20] Rather than act collectively to reduce the smog, we are encouraged to buy eye-drops. But these observations are generally bypassed, so while Michael Schudson suggests that the industry 'may shape our sense of values' he spends little time interrogating the seriousness of this claim.[21]

Others, like Mica Nava, have suggested that advertising is so ubiquitous that it cannot be reduced to regimes of production and consumption.[22] Advertising, she points out, is about more than simply selling things: they tell stories which may have little to do with commerce. But while advertising offers some diversity – a useful strategy, after all, to get our attention – it is far more ideologically constrained than most other cultural forms. It has a functional purpose in a way that most other cultural forms do not. While advertisements may be fragments across a rich firmament of meaning, they are defined by their requirement to sell as well as tell. To ignore this point, while dwelling on all the *other* ideas advertisements may communicate, is to miss the wood for the trees.

Nava's argument is, in part, a counterpoint to absolutist ideas about media. Neil Postman, for example, has tried to advance Marshall McCluhan's notion that 'the medium is the message' in relation to television.[23] The difficulty with this argument is that while television may have certain characteristics and properties that are particular to it,[24] as a technology it is comparatively value-free. Television can, in theory, be consumerist or environmentalist, capitalist or socialist, racist or multi-cultural, feminist or patriarchal. So, for example, the idea that television shortens our attention span is more a consequence of its commercial development (and the need for regular interruption) than a feature of the technology itself.

In the same way, the feminist critique of advertising allows us plausibly to imagine an advertising industry that does *not* depend on gender stereotypes. But if advertising has, in theory at least, the freedom to tell stories across a number of ideological divides, consumerism is inevitably an issue on which it can never be anything other than deeply committed.

This does not make us witless consumers of this consumerist message: we may respond to advertisements in many different ways. A TV commercial may be witty, stylish or visually appealing without inspiring any desire for – or even interest in – the product being sold. Young people may 'play' with the meaning of commercials in ways that disregard their central pitch.[25] The sheer scale of advertising, after all, stretches many thousand times farther than our ability to absorb or act on their individual parts. Most of them will, on an individual level, inevitably fail. The need for advertisers to entertain us makes it possible for us to focus on something other than the desirability of the product, but it would be foolish to ignore the sheer ideological weight that underpins the vast landscape of advertising.

Sonia Livingstone makes a similar point when reviewing the evidence about the link between television advertising and childhood obesity. The causes of childhood obesity and children's relationship with television are both complex areas of inquiry. In both fields, it is difficult to gather evidence that shows a dramatic and instantaneous cause and effect. We are, after all, active agents engaging with cultural forms rather than passive creatures simply doing what we are told. But we are influenced by this engagement, and we depend upon those cultural forms to provide us with narratives for understanding who we are and the world around us.[26] There is, accordingly, a volume of data to suggest a link between advertising and obesity, a link that has very real consequences for children's health.[27]

This has led the World Health Organization to ask governments and businesses to reduce the volume of advertising promoting unhealthy food. Subsequent campaigns to restrict advertising on children's television have further stimulated academic work in this area, including research suggesting that one of the most cost-effective tools available to government to tackle childhood obesity would be to impose restrictions on advertising.[28]

The response from most governments, under pressure from the powerful food and beverage industry, has been minimal, relying on 'self-regulation' in spite of the volume of evidence in favour of more binding intervention.[29] A few countries – such as Sweden – have gone further, seeing children under the age of 12 as a special group in need of protection from advertising. The Swedish position takes us well beyond the jurisdiction of most advertising regulation, directly challenging the premise that most advertising is benign or useful. It is, nonetheless, a very limited challenge. Even in Sweden, regulation is limited to broadcast media, creating opportunities for other cultural forms – notably those online – to exploit this gap in the market.

The Swedish approach also presumes that after 12 years of age we are beyond advertising's purview. This judgement is based on assumptions about the capacity of older children (and, of course, adults) to make discriminating judgements – even when the information available is one-sided and unhelpful. But in their review of research in this area, Sonia Livingstone and Ellen Helsper suggest that advertisements *do* influence what children choose to eat, regardless of age. Although we tend to think of older children as more savvy and media literate (and thus less in need of protection), the evidence suggests that teenagers are just as likely to be influenced by advertisements as younger children.[30] We may become older and wiser, but our immersion in consumer culture does not foster an ability to think critically.

Even the campaign for media literacy, founded to foster a critical awareness of media content and institutions, has increasingly been appropriated by the discourse of consumerism. Media literacy, in this user-friendly format, is reduced to a consumer's ability to make the most of media technology.[31] So, for example, the UK media regulator Ofcom publishes a 'Media Literacy e-bulletin' to encourage consumers to use digital media safely and to best exploit all the services on offer.[32]

The evidence linking television advertising with obesity casts a shadow over government policy across the globe. In most countries, governments have allowed media to become increasingly dependent on advertising, as well as presiding over a cultural landscape which has become littered with commercial messages. But it also raises a larger question. If advertising promotes consumerism, then surely it plays an overtly *political* role in our culture – one which makes it harder to appreciate the environmental, economic and social problems of contemporary consumer capitalism.

This question is well beyond the jurisdiction of most regulatory authorities, which tend to assume that advertising is at best informative and at worst harmless. These authorities do, however, have their antennae attuned to *certain* kinds of political discourse. Advertisements designed to promote human rights, for example, are seen to pose a problem. So, for example, between 1994 and 1997 the UK Radio Authority prevented Amnesty International from using advertising to publicize the genocide in Rwanda. Amnesty, they argued, constituted a body with a political agenda,[33] and their use of advertising thus breached a commitment to political impartiality. Amnesty successfully challenged this ruling in the European Court of Human Rights, and the decision was overturned in 2002, proving that, at the very least, the notion of what we mean by a 'political' message is a slippery one.

When Amnesty took on consumerism more directly, their use of advertising created even more discomfort. In 2010, they produced an advertisement designed to draw attention to the human rights record of the Shell oil company in Nigeria (to coincide with Shell's London AGM). The advertisement compared Shell's $9.8bn profits with the plight of the people of the Niger Delta. Shell's oil spills, Amnesty claimed, have polluted drinking water, contaminated fishing waters, farmland and the air. On this occasion, Amnesty did not attempt to place the message on radio or television, preferring the more relaxed regulatory arena of print. Nonetheless, the *Financial Times* – who were free of any constraints on political advertising – refused to print it.

The newspaper's decision may have been informed, in part, by fear of litigation from a wealthy corporate client, but it is emblematic of a striking double standard. Consumerism is now so embedded in our culture that the promotion of it – through the proliferation of advertising – is regarded as innocent and apolitical. An oil company painting a rosy pictures of its environmental record – employing a kind of smoke-free puffery – slips into the ether unchecked. Questioning consumerism, on the other hand, is seen as a rude and unwelcome interruption.

The logic behind this double standard is difficult to sustain, relying as it does on the questionable assumption that consumerism is either an unimpeachable force for good, or that it is apolitical while anti-consumerism is not. It is an acceptance that allows advertising to spread across the cultural horizon, promoting a consumerist approach across an increasing array of social institutions. Citizens are understood as consumers, communities as markets, taxpayers as customers.[34]

Judith Williamson pointed out some time ago that the political discourse of advertising is also, in part, a matter of what is hidden from view.[35] In the ad-world, the production and distribution of commodities is either romanticized – the traditional Italian family making pasta sauce, for example – or invisible.[36] Equally absent are the growing problems of post-consumption – the disposal of our increasingly toxic array of consumer goods. The problem is not just that, as Tim Edwards put it, 'Consumer society remains socially divisive – inclusive and inviting to the affluent, mobile and able; exclusive of the poor, the isolated and the impaired',[37] but in the ad-world the many inequities of global production and the environmental consequences of distribution and disposal are somebody else's problem. This is a manifestly political proposition.

Advertising and the good life

Chapter 3 suggested that there is little empirical evidence behind advertising's central, unifying theme that all good things come from the accumulation of commodities. On the contrary, what is remarkable about quality of life research is the failure of the growth of consumer goods in affluent societies to make us happier or more fulfilled. Research suggests that a walk in the park or an evening spent in the company of friends will do more for our well-being than any amount of 'retail therapy'.[38] This is not to say we do not derive pleasure from commodities or the process of acquiring them, or, indeed, that in a consumer society we can easily separate consumption from other pleasures (an evening with friends may well involve consuming food or drink, and even a walk in the park might be enhanced by the purchase of comfortable footwear). But the pleasures of consumer goods are limited and finite.

Advertisers themselves are well aware that fulfilment often comes from outside what Sut Jhally calls 'the dead world of things'. They understand that we care more about the social and physiological world, about good relationships, status, good health, relaxation and human interaction than the attributes of objects.[39] The content of advertising reflects this, skipping lightly into the social world to capture our attention and stir our emotions.

Television advertising, in particular, rarely bases its appeal on the properties of the commodity being sold. In an age of product proliferation it has become increasingly difficult to distinguish between the properties of things, obliging advertisers to look elsewhere to make their appeal. Many 1950s TV commercials look old-fashioned because they sometimes list, in as much detail as time allows, the positive features of the car or the toothpaste they are selling.

These commercials look faintly comic now, partly because a pitch that provides us with relevant information is seen as a less subtle form of persuasion than one that nonchalantly ignores the product's features. As John Berger put it, 'publicity is about social relations, not objects'.[40] We thus find ourselves entering into a strange pact: on television we enjoy stories more than descriptions, and are happy to be persuaded as long as both we – and the advertiser – can pretend we are simply being entertained.

The craft of most contemporary advertising is to bypass informed judgements about quality and price and to juxtapose the object with an emotion or idea. The aim is to create a symbolic association between a product or a brand and something more ephemeral – images of popularity, attractiveness, family harmony, sophistication, good health or any other of the social values we hold dear.[41] A mobile phone is usually sold on its image (used by fashionable people) rather than its functionality (good sound reproduction). Research even suggests that democratic participation is linked to happiness,[42] a notion anticipated by the Pepsi commercials in the late 1980s linking their cola with the collapse of the Berlin wall.[43]

These coy come-ons are one of the contradictions of the consumer age – so much so that we have become accustomed to advertising that contains no information about the product at all. An advertisement for a Flake chocolate bar features an attractive woman in a long, luxurious 'flake-like' dress dancing in slow motion against a black background to the sound of a gentle classical piano[44] (the Flake bar itself is shown briefly at the end, without comment). An advertisement for Doritos depicts a giant Dorito chip hovering over London, then cuts to scientists examining pieces of it – ending as one scientist takes a sheepish bite.[45] A lavishly produced Chanel ad stars Keira Knightley in glamorous settings adopting various poses (and seen briefly holding a bottle of Chanel).[46] A TV commercial for RAC's breakdown service shows a montage of cars broken down in various locations to a version of the Carpenters' song 'Close To You'.[47] None of them tell us anything at all about the commodities they are selling. They all engage us by associating the product with images that have an appeal *outside* the 'dead world of things' (with sexuality, humour, glamour or sophistication).

Others make only brief evaluative statements. An advertisement for Wall's sausage rolls is narrated by a man from 'middle England' offering a humorous description of his family's weekend spent enacting medieval battles. It ends with him eating a sausage roll as he lays 'dying' with the tag line 'Wall's – proper food, bring it on'.[48] The statement (along with the narrative) *suggests* that Wall's uses wholesome ingredients without making any explicit (and therefore questionable) claims. This is puffery dressed up in a succession of comforting clothes.

The symbolic work of advertising – with its focus on the social rather than the material world – is not new. At the beginning of the twentieth century, the development of the department store represented an important shift away from the utility of goods. Some of the first campaigns for department stores neglected to mention what you might find inside them, promoting them instead as lush emporiums, places of culture rather than exchange.[49] But as the proliferation of goods increases and relative utility of objects diminishes, advertising is forced away from telling us why something is worth having and towards appealing, instead, to symbolic associations somewhere on the continuum between vaguely plausible and arbitrary.

It is worth pondering on the widespread acceptance of the shift from a descriptive to a symbolic sales pitch. We flatter ourselves that it reflects our own sophistication as consumers. An attempt to persuade us about the merits of a product's intrinsic qualities looks too obvious for us now. And yet we accept the far stranger proposition that we buy something on the basis of being told little or nothing about it. So, for example, we might dismiss a car commercial that lists its positive features as boring or trite, but we allow an appeal based on the idea that that the people driving it are 'cool' to wash over us. This might be seen as a decadent form of sophistication, but it could hardly be described as savvy.

There are, from the advertisers' perspective, significant advantages of symbolic forms of persuasion. Free from the constraints of the product itself, they are free to paint any picture they want. They can move effortlessly – with wit, style, narrative or aesthetics – beyond the realm of truth and verification. By associating a soft drink with young, popular, attractive people, they are simply offering us a link (one they hope will register in our minds) rather than making any specific claims.

These strategies make the various regulations and codes on advertising standards largely irrelevant. As an article on alcohol advertising in the *British Medical Journal* pointed out with some frustration:

> The documents we analysed show that attempts to control the content of alcohol advertising have two systemic failings. Firstly, the sophisticated communications and subtle emotional concepts such as sociability and masculinity that comprise modern advertising (and sponsorship) often defy intelligent analysis by the regulator . . . Secondly, producers and agencies can exploit the ambiguities in the codes and push the boundaries of both acceptability and adjudication.[50]

A more rational consumer response to advertising – in the classical economic language of informed consumer choice – would be very different. Savvy consumers would understand, first of all, that we have been given very little useful information about the value of the product/brand. They might then make the plausible assumption that if the product had any particularly noteworthy features we would have been told about them. They would also understand that the high cost of the campaign would have to be recouped in the price of the product, and that as a consequence they are paying more than they might do otherwise. Unless the advertised product generates sufficient sales enabling economies of scale to compensate for the spend on advertising, the more lavish the campaign, the higher the price. A smart response to the more costly forms of advertising would thus be to *avoid* the promoted products and seek alternatives.

It could be argued that this kind of rationality fails to acknowledge that the symbolic work of advertising adds value to a product.[51] So, for example, if we accept the symbolic association between the product and the social world – and thus imagine that owning the product makes us *feel* sophisticated, popular or attractive – we are making a kind of rational choice. The problem with this argument is that the concept of rational choice in market economics relies on a more conscious calculation. There may be instances when we are aware that we are buying an image – we may want the kudos that comes with brand names but accept that this comes from the advertising rather than the product itself – but this is hardly typical consumer behaviour. We are more likely to endow the object with the symbolic properties conjured up by the advertiser. This may feel real, but given the arbitrary nature of the association it would be hard to describe it as rational.

The 'seductive but misleading' tales woven by advertising create what Avner Offer calls a 'spurious differentiation of identical goods'.[52] The consumer – without the time to conduct a more evaluative analysis of what is on offer – is obliged to resort to an arbitrary world of symbolic associations.[53]

Advertising operates, in this sense, like a form of drug addiction. It helps to create a world directed towards the acquisition of consumer goods. The volume of goods available gradually becomes overwhelming. We then depend on advertising to enable us to function when the level of choice exceeds our capacity to make rational decisions. While the system 'works' on its own terms – and in the stark, limited language of GDP growth, with some success – it is hard to see it as a leap forward in the human condition.

For Jerry Mander, 'the goal of all advertising is discontent'.[54] Advertising, after all, is about happiness postponed, or what Andrew Wernick calls the 'perpetual deferral of the promoted object'.[55] Its relentless logic declares that satisfaction is always another product away. And yet, for advertising's main audience (those with disposable income), the evidence suggests that advertising is more a source of misery, insecurity and anxiety than it is of joy, pleasure and comfort.

Advertising is, in this sense, deeply contradictory. Its purpose is to link fulfilment with consumption, and yet its strategy for doing so tacitly acknowledges the emptiness of the promise. It is not just that, as Bill Leiss, Stephen Kline and Sut Jhally put it, 'goods simply cannot deliver the promised happiness shown in advertisements';[56] the hyper-consumerism advertising promotes can actually make us unhappy.[57] Sut Jhally argues that this is because it distracts us from the things that *do* bring satisfaction – we engage with objects rather than with people, and we sacrifice our free time so that we might earn more money and consume more. In other words, the concentration of effort on consumption means a diminishment of the other pleasures that come with affluence. Most notable of these is the freedom and opportunity that comes with an increase in our free time.

Diminishing the value of time

In one sense, of course, an increase in leisure time provides further opportunities for producing a new range of goods to amuse us.[58] But once people were free from want, we also had the tantalizing prospect that many people would use their wealth to be free from work (in the form of shorter working hours) – even if it meant sacrificing their ability to maximize their earning potential.

During the first half of the twentieth century, we used increases in wealth to exchange work for leisure. The average working week fell significantly from around 55 to 60 hours a week (depending on the sector) in 1900 to around 40 hours a week by the 1950s.[59] The shortening of the working week continued in the second half of the century, but at a much slower pace (especially in the United States). Between 1880 and 1995 leisure time for the average American worker more than tripled (from 1.8 to 5.8 hours a working day).[60] But by the end of the twentieth century, the move towards a shorter working week in developed countries – particularly the United States – had ground to a halt.[61]

We see the same slow down or reversal of the shortening of the working week in Europe. France introduced the 35-hour week in 2000, but the legislation was subsequently weakened. The UK, meanwhile, battled hard to opt out of the European Working Time Directive, which limited the working week to 48 hours, a higher level than the average working week in the late 1940s.[62] This is a long way from John Maynard Keynes' prediction of a 15-hour working week by 2001 – a plausible dream in the 1950s, a time when expectations of working less had become the norm.

A more recent report published by the New Economics Foundation – calling for a 21-hour week – detailed the range of benefits such a reduction might bring for our quality of life.[63] The evidence suggests that once we reach a certain level of prosperity (around $25,000 per capita per year)[64] the quality of life in wealthier societies will benefit more from increasing our free time than increasing our spending power.

For while many people undoubtedly find satisfaction in paid employment, studies based on 'experience sampling' – where people are asked to record their feelings throughout the day – suggest that most people place more value on their time *away* from their workplace. Derek Bok sums up the research in this area thus:

> The most striking result from experience sampling is that almost all the pleasurable activities of the day take place outside of work . . . The less pleasant aspects of the day involve activities associated with one's job, including commuting.[65]

One study, for example, divided the day up into a list of 18 different activities (dinner, watching TV, cooking etc.). The three activities at the bottom of the list (those that people least enjoyed) were the morning commute, working and the evening commute (the evening commute being slightly preferable, presumably because people are leaving work).[66]

In the decades when our leisure hours were decreasing we appeared to value our time at work more. Conversely, our economic system's failure to reduce our working hours in recent decades has increased the value we put on leisure time. In 1955, the percentage of Americans who enjoyed non-working activities (more than work) was 49%, with 38% preferring work. By 1991 the ratio had shifted from 68% to 18%. Research suggests that levels of job satisfaction have further declined in the years since.[67]

Despite these palpable trends, the prospect of reducing the average working week is more distant than at any time over the last hundred years. The possibility of a 15- or 21-hour week now seems almost outlandish, in part because we have created a culture that constantly stresses the need to maximize our spending power. The repetitive dance of advertising encourages us to assume that any increase in income should be spent buying objects rather than hours. Indeed, Keith Cowling and Rattanasuda Poolsombat's research suggests that the volume of advertising messages in the

United States, in particular, has pushed the American workforce away from the pursuit of free time, so that they work far longer hours – and enjoy much shorter holidays – than most Europeans.[68] Juliet Schor pursues this theme in her book, *The Overworked American*, documenting its negative impacts on quality of life.[69]

Stuart Fraser and David Paton's research finds the same relationship in Britain, with advertising pushing us towards the maximization of income at the expense of free time. After several decades of reductions in the UK working week, average working hours stabilized in the early 1970s at around 42-3 hours per week. Their modelling suggests that this stagnation was not inevitable, but a choice promoted by increasing advertising expenditure, which stressed the importance of money (to buy goods) rather than time: 'an increase in advertising is associated with an increase in hours worked . . . causality runs unidirectionally from advertising to hours'.[70]

It is hard to underestimate the effect of this on our economics. Tim Jackson explores this point in his report, *Prosperity Without Growth*. As the production of goods and services become more efficient, we have a choice: we can cash in those efficiency gains in the form of time or money. But if we always choose money rather than time, we need perpetual economic growth to prevent efficiency gains from creating unemployment:

> As long as the economy expands fast enough to offset labour productivity there isn't a problem. But if the economy doesn't grow, there is a downward pressure on employment. People lose their jobs . . . Growth is necessary within this system just to prevent collapse.[71]

This keeps us tied to a model in which economic growth is necessary to prevent significant increases in unemployment (with all the associated increases in social problems and adverse impact on quality of life).

And yet we have reached a stage where earning more money is only beneficial if it increases our income relative to others. Working shorter hours, by contrast, has an absolute correlation with increases in our quality of life.[72] There may come a point when this is not longer true – when the working week is so short that further reductions are no longer beneficial – but we are some way from reaching this happy work/life equilibrium.

Freedom from advertising

In the 1960s, Raymond Williams described advertising as 'the official art of modern capitalist society'.[73] The breadth and scope of the industry's voluminous presence, since then, has also made it our most conspicuous art-form. But despite its endlessly repeated promises, the success of advertising in promoting the constant accumulation of consumer goods has brought neither happiness nor meaning.

This stark failure is almost entirely ignored in government and policy circles, where consumer choice continues to be an abiding principle, while the reach and scope of advertising is allowed to increase with every passing decade. Reviewing the evidence on consumerism and quality of life, Richard Layard argues that legislation *banning* advertising is a far more plausible policy for increasing quality of life than extending consumer choice.[74] Such a drastic step may be both impractical and, in some ways, undesirable, but policy makers have moved in the opposite direction – testimony, perhaps, to the persuasive power of consumer culture.

If a world without advertising is politically untenable, it does provide food for thought. At the very least, our policy makers should acknowledge the waning benefits of extending consumer choice. They might also consider the credible and popular proposition that we might all be better off with less advertising, and thereby pursue other ways to pay for our cultural forms.

For advertising has become a lead weight on our culture. It limits our creative ambitions and our conceptual horizons. It binds our understanding of human progress to the tether of relentless consumption. It makes it difficult for us to appreciate some of the problems – notably climate change – it has helped create, and discourages us from seeking pleasure and meaning outside consumption. As long as advertising constitutes our dominant form of cultural expression, it will be difficult to muster the political will to move to a more sustainable economy, or to imagine forms of social progress that do not depend upon consumer capitalism and perpetual growth.

Since advertising carries no right of reply, its voluminous presence has created a lop-sided political landscape. Imagine, instead, what the world might be like if all that creative energy were spent encouraging us to think beyond consumer capitalism. It would represent nothing less than a seismic shift in our cultural environment.

Part III

Reporting consumer capitalism

6

Disposable news and democracy: Rethinking the way we report the world

Journalism is linked – both historically and philosophically – with democratic progress and the questioning of orthodoxies. These instincts, combined with their centrality to the public sphere, give the news media a special place in our culture. Even in a commercial system, journalism has a licence to interrogate the increasingly fragile assumptions that equate consumer capitalism with social progress.

News media often fall short of these deliberative ideals, and much has been written about the way in which commercial imperatives corrupt and degrade their loftier mission. For many, journalism is at its boldest when free from commercial constraints. The problem with this view is that it overlooks how deeply embedded consumerism is within the culture of journalism.

Once news became a commodity it was obliged to adopt its most profitable form. This involved stressing the 'newness' of news, a form of planned obsolescence that encouraged us to discard yesterday's news and replace it on a regular basis. The disposable nature of news quickly became one of journalism's core values, epitomized by the breathless rush of today's 24-hour news cycle.

As a consequence, journalism contains within it two very different notions of 'the new'. One, informed by a democratic tradition, stresses new ideas; the other, informed by a commercial tradition, depends upon a more banal, temporal notion of 'the new' which prizes currency over substance. The first form of journalism is well placed to question conventional wisdom about consumer capitalism; the second is more inclined to embrace it.

Journalism, democracy and consumer capitalism

Democracy relies upon a well-informed citizenry fuelled by an independent information system. This, in turn, depends on many features of an open, civil society – people employed to do independent research, the production and publication of statistics, access to public and private institutions and so on. But even in the information age, any discussion of the way we understand the world is obliged to consider the quality and nature of the news industry.

Journalism's mode of address is, in some ways, a counter-point to advertising. At its best, it does not seek to persuade or beguile, but speaks to us as citizens rather than consumers.[1] It assumes that we think about, discuss, react to and even shape the world around us. In so doing it fulfils a deeply egalitarian purpose – that of informing people about the world and enabling them to make considered democratic choices – or, indeed, to take history into their own hands. Even in thoroughly commercial news operations this civic role is well understood, enshrined in legal frameworks (such as rules about the impartiality of broadcast news) and cultural traditions (ideas such as 'balance' and 'accuracy').

If journalism's instincts are democratic, it is, like other cultural forms, dependent on advertising – and all the more so in the online age. Several studies have examined the way in which advertisers directly or indirectly influence news content,[2] while the role of public relations in promoting news stories and shaping news agendas is a cause of increasing concern.[3] Media conglomerates are not above incorporating their news divisions into cross-promotion strategies, using 'soft' news stories to promote their other media.[4]

The research literature is also replete with the flaws of trusting our key information system to a small group of privately run concerns.[5] This has inspired a neologism to describe news borne of commercial interests: 'churnalism' – mass produced news produced by a cash-strapped fourth estate, where efficiency savings limit time for scrutiny or investigation, forcing reporters to churn out redrafted press releases and agency copy and to surf the ever-growing tide of public relations.[6]

Robert McChesney and John Nichols have written a book lamenting the current condition of the US news media – compromised by years of cost-cutting and the needs of commerce. What we need, they suggest, is more rather than less journalism. They insist that its social value goes beyond commercial considerations and that our democratic dependence on journalism, for all its many compromises and transgressions, obliges us to see it as a public good.[7] News, in its ideal form, is seen to occupy a *space outside* consumerism.

If the literature on journalism sometimes reads like a catalogue of failures, it is because it adopts a civic idealism as its point of departure. The quality of journalism is measured by the extent to which it advances public debate or furthers public understanding. And, despite all the pressures and distractions of commerce, the utopian model of journalism remains palpably intact. It is an ideal immediately understood by both journalists and critics, not only among public service broadcasters, but also in the practices of commercial newsrooms. As a consequence, ideals of a deliberative public sphere remain a touchstone for the way we understand the role of news.[8]

It is easy to be cynical about journalism in a commercial age. A series of Ipsos/Mori surveys between 1983 and 2011 asked people to rate the trustworthiness of various professions. Journalists consistently come at or near the bottom of the list – fighting it out with politicians for last place. For more than a quarter of a century the proportion of those surveyed who trusted news reporters to 'tell the truth' did not rise above 22%.[9] Surveys in the USA suggest only marginally higher levels of public esteem.[10] The unsavoury revelations that emerged from the Leveson Inquiry into the British press confirmed what many already feared, revealing the depths to which some newspapers were prepared to sink in pursuit of gossip, scandal and tawdry titillation.[11]

To many journalists (and, indeed, politicians) this seems unfair, the many being tainted by the excesses of the few. More than this, the notion that news is central to democracy remains something to cling to, a self-defined civic space to protect and nurture the very idea of citizenship. Without it, the whole democratic endeavour will wither on the vine. News is, in theory, a place where the short-comings of consumer capitalism – its failure to deliver an improved quality of life, its environmental consequences and consumerism's diminishing returns – might be highlighted and debated. News has the potential to take us beyond current orthodoxy, to be the place where other possibilities may emerge.

In Chapter 2, I described how the seismic failure of financial markets in 2008 created the conditions for a more sceptical attitude towards business as usual. This was, after all, a systemic failure. For the economist Tim Jackson, an economy dependent on permanent consumer-led growth shaped its own downfall:

> Allegiance to growth was the single most dominant feature of an eco-nomic and political system that led the world to the brink of disaster. The growth imperative has shaped the architecture of the modern economy. It motivated the freedoms granted to the financial sector. It stood at least partly responsible for the loosening of regulations, the over-extension of credit and the proliferation of unmanageable (and unstable) financial derivatives.[12]

If this analysis was, perhaps, more uncompromising in its assessment of dominant economic assumptions than many were prepared to countenance – especially for those bound up with the comfortable litany of financial experts who dominate economic news – we saw a momentary shift towards a more questioning form of journalism. In some quarters, this involved a healthy dose of self-criticism: journalists wondered whether they had become so deeply embed-ded in the financial sector (and its political boosters) that they lost their critical distance.

How might we rekindle the spirit of interrogation we glimpsed (however faintly) in 2008? What might inspire our news media to use the information available – from the new economics, the growing body of quality of life research and the rich vein of environmental science – to ask big questions about the way we live now? What is that prevents news from becoming a truly open, civic space – a place where conventional wisdom is questioned rather than recycled?

What's new

There are many practical reasons why it is easier for journalists to replicate rather than question dominant ways of thinking.[13] News, whether run commercially or as a public service, is often served up in the context of consumer culture. Questioning consumerism may not be off limits, but the importance of advertising to commercial news revenues could hardly be said to encourage it.

The presence of advertising softens those moments when consumerism *is* interrogated. So, for example, on those occasions when commercial television shows a documentary that explores or debates the downside of consumer capitalism, it is interrupted by a series of vignettes that soften and ease these concerns, presenting a commercial world in tune with all we hold dear. I recall watching *The New Rulers of the World*, a documentary made by the campaigning journalist John Pilger and shown on the UK's main commercial channel, ITV. The documentary offered a critical view of global capitalism and the rising power of transnational corporations, a view interrupted every 15 minutes or so by advertisements. One of these commercials – for just the kind of large, global corporation under scrutiny in Pilger's documentary – was for the Peugeot 307.

The Peugeot commercial featured a series of uplifting images of people struggling against adversity to the backdrop of Labbi Siffre's anti-apartheid song, 'Something Inside So Strong'.[14] It was, in a symbolic sense, perfectly in tune with Pilger's message – so much so that Pilger used the same Labbi Siffre song (rather more appropriately, perhaps) during a subsequent documentary.[15] A programme critical of global capitalism thus passed seamlessly to a commercial *for* a global corporation. The commercial break was, in its soft, implicit way, a symbolic refutation of the points made by the film.

But the commercialization of journalism goes well beyond the role of advertising or a capricious proprietor's control. Among journalists there is a vague, general appreciation that news needs to sell as well as tell, and that these two motivations – one commercial, one democratic, may conflict. The best-known complaint is that increasing commercialism has led to a 'dumbing down' of news content,[16] with coverage of celebrity or human interest stories eclipsing news with a wider public significance.

So, for example, John McManus describes how a good story is sometimes more a matter of drama than substance. A woman's scurrilous attempt to sue a fast-food chain – after putting a co-worker's fingertip (severed in a work accident) in their chile con carne – made the front page of the *San Jose Mercury News* eleven times in one month. It was, in many ways, an irresistible story, but it was of little consequence in the wider world. In the same month, he reports, they ran only one story about the US war in Iraq. 'Some would argue,' he suggests, that a war 'killing hundreds of thousands of Iraqis . . . costing thousands of American lives and more than a billion dollars a week merited the front page more than the saga of a small-bore grafter.'[17]

These complaints – like the commercialization of news itself – have a long history. In 1947, the Hutchins Commission in the USA spelled out what it saw as a conflict between public and commercial interests. The press, the commission suggested, were 'caught between its desire to please . . . its audience and its desire to give a picture of events and people as they really are'.[18] Critics see commercial interests as a form of interference, interrupting or detracting from public interest journalism. John McManus for example, defines the commercialization of news as 'any action intended to boost profit that interferes with a journalist's or news organization's best effort to maximize public understanding of those issues and events that shape the community they claim to serve'.[19]

But the contradictions within the contemporary practice of journalism go much deeper than this. If human interest stories – with little connection to the public understanding of issues and events – are sold as news, it is because they are sanctioned by long-standing custom and practice.[20] This tradition is now so deeply embedded in the culture of journalism that its origins are largely unquestioned.

For over a hundred years, the style, content and expectations of what defines 'news' has been shaped – in part – by the needs of a mass-produced consumer culture. As a result, news as commerce and news as civic knowledge have become so entangled that we have become confused about the purpose of news in an open society.

McManus's idea of commercial interests *interfering* with a 'news organization's best effort to maximize public understanding' suggests that news itself – uncontaminated – has a certain purity of purpose. While we can begin to imagine what this kind of news might look like – as the public journalism movement in the USA has tried to do[21] – we not only need to understand how business interests constrain democratic endeavour,[22] but how certain forms of commercialism have informed the definition of journalism. The critical idea in this process – one generally overlooked – is the idea that news should be 'new'.

The link between what is new and what is news seems so obvious – the two words have a common derivation, after all – that it scarcely seems worth pondering. Terhi Rantanen has written a compelling analysis of the way in which news has, through the ages, reinvented itself as 'new'.[23] But the very idea of 'new' is not as straightforward as it seems. In Rantanen's narrative, we can see how news degenerates into a kind of crude chronology. The 'new' is, in this sense, about moving forward, a constant reiteration of the present. News may be the first draft of history, but unlike the discipline of history it has less interest in the past. History dissolves as the stress on 'newness' pushes us towards 'nowness'.

This chronological sense of the new is fairly banal – little more, in the end, than a way of marking time. But if we think of news as an information system, the notion of 'new' has a more profound inflection. New information can do more than simply register the present; it can enhance our understanding of the world. Information may be new in the sense that it adds something to our stock of knowledge. This can be practical – something our local council is doing on a matter we care about, for example – or it may be epistemological, allowing us to see the world anew. The 'newness' of news is thus more than simply a matter of being up-to-date: it encapsulate new ideas, new forms of understanding.

The first meaning of newness encourages routine; the second enables change. Although our current notion of news retains both meanings, there is no doubt that the first has eclipsed the second, as news punctuates the present with a kind of ersatz urgency. News has, in this sense, often lost sight of what makes information useful or significant. An obsession with being up-to-date has meant a neglect of new ideas, making journalism a more conservative endeavour that it might be.

The focus on the new in its more limited, chronological sense has reached its apotheosis in the repetitive rush of the 24-hour news cycle.[24] News has thereby become the ultimate disposable commodity, one whose very dispensability, almost by definition, devalues it as an information system. It is a view encapsulated by one of the twentieth century's champions of modern mass production: while the gist of Henry Ford's sentiment – 'History is (more or less) bunk' – is well known, it is worth recalling his remark in full: 'We don't want tradition. We want to live in the present, and the only history that is worth a tinker's damn is the history that we make today.'[25] This captures the narrow sense of the newness of news, as well the way in which a stress on the new fits with a commodity form of news in the age of mass production.

We can trace this dichotomy – a chronological versus an epistemological version of the new – through the history of journalism. The first emerges most clearly as one befitting a consumerist model; the second remains present throughout – under pressure from the first but remarkably resilient nonetheless.

Useful versus disposable news

The rise of journalism is inevitably intertwined with moments when new ideas worked their way into the public sphere. Journalism is, after all, deeply implicated in the rise of democracy.[26] In early nineteenth-century Britain, for example, radical newspapers like the *Penny Politician*, *Black Dwarf* and the *Poor Man's*

Guardian were forceful agents for democratic change, promoting the ideal of a universal franchise at a time when only a certain class of property-owning men could vote.[27]

For radical reporters like Henry Hetherington (editor of the *Poor Man's Guardian*), news was, in part, about educating citizens and encouraging them to take history into their own hands. The British governments of the day were, for their part, so rattled by the spread of these ideas that they imposed a series of 'taxes on knowledge' in an unsubtle attempt to price popular titles out of business. Newspapers like the *Poor Man's Guardian* refused to pay the most direct of these taxes – stamp duty – printing instead the phrase 'Knowledge is Power' in place of the conspicuously absent red stamp of official approval.

Hetherington's use of such a phrase may seem a little portentous now, but it encapsulates a form of journalism committed to the spread of new information and ideas, a necessary prerequisite for understanding society and imagining something better. So, for example, the *Poor Man's Guardian* account of the meeting of the Operative Builders Union in London concerned itself less with details of events than their import:

> a grand national organization, which promises to embody the physical power of the country is silently, but rapidly, progressing . . . Their report shows that an entire change in society[,] a change amounting to a complete subversion of the existing order of the world[,] is contemplated by the working classes. They aspire to be at the top instead of at the bottom of society – or rather that there should be no bottom or top at all.[28]

The 'newness' of news, in this account, is bound up with possibilities of social change.

This was not to say that radical forerunners of mass circulation news were simply high-minded purveyors of information about public affairs. This was no pristine era of reporting unsullied by the more salacious arts of popular story-telling.[29] The radical press may have championed democracy, but they were also bound by the need to make ends meet and attract an audience. Henry Hetherington was a hero for many radicals – someone who went to jail for his journalism – but he could muckrake with the best of them. He once vowed that his newspaper would deliver 'Murders, Rapes, Suicides, Burnings, Maimings, Theatricals, Races, Pugilism and . . . every sort of devilment that will make it sell'.[30]

Henry Hetherington's populist sensationalism used the more banal notion of the new – new stories rather than new ideas – in a way that exploited the ambiguity of newness. But it was used less as a pitch for profit than an appeal to a wider public sphere. The British radical press may have been pragmatic in spicing up their fare, but they were defined by a self-proclaimed civic role – the idea that the need for democratic change had to be understood before it could be enacted. This was news for the sake of something more than itself. The use of 'every sort of devilment that will make it sell' might now be seen to define the modus operandi of sections of the modern tabloid press, but for papers like the *Poor Man's Guardian* it was the beginning of a process rather than an end, a mechanism to communicate new ideas to an increasingly literate working class.

By mid century, the British government realized that heavy-handed attempts to suppress the radical press had failed. The 'taxes on knowledge' – stamp duty, as well as taxes on paper and advertising – effectively penalized all forms of popular journalism, stunting the growth of a newspaper industry that might be more in tune with men of property and the governing class. Of all these taxes, the duty on advertising most clearly constrained newspapers as a profit-making enterprise, and it was no coincidence that this was the first to be repealed (in 1853).[31]

The adoption of a more reformist, less punitive tax regime allowed the growth of commercial mass circulation newspapers, requiring a level of capital investment and advertising support that favoured more establishment forms of ownership. According to Thomas Milner-Gibson, President of the Association for the Promotion of the Repeal of Taxes on Knowledge, a more open market would create 'a cheap press in the hands of men of good moral character, of respectability, and of capital'.[32] This declaration proved to be prescient, and newspapers gradually moved out of the hands of radical reformers and became big business.

What followed, in the second half of the nineteenth century, was a shift away from the communication of new ideas towards a more effective business model for newspapers.[33] Encouraged by the government's adoption of a more liberal approach to the press, news become more skilfully crafted as a commodity, and the nature of news would be redefined by this transformation. In their seminal account of the history of British journalism, James Curran and Jean Seaton describe this as a moment when 'market forces succeeded where legal repression had failed in conscripting the press to the social order'.[34]

But journalism's democratic zeal did not disappear. On the contrary, it developed *alongside* the desire to titillate, entertain and recycle the present in the pursuit of profit. The civic spirit of news was bolstered by the rise of broadcasting across Europe. Unlike the press, where the principle of private ownership was well established by the 1930s, broadcasting required public intervention. The limits of the broadcast spectrum meant that an open market was a recipe for chaos: government was thus obliged to set up agencies to license the airwaves and prevent broadcasters transmitting on overlapping frequencies. The airwaves were, after all, public property,[35] and governments were obliged to establish a principle that the airwaves should be used in the public interest.

The birth of the BBC in the 1920s consolidated these ideas to create public service broadcasting – a medium that would be independent of both government and business, free to serve the public interest. The development of broadcast news (constrained, in the early years, by the lobbying power of a newspaper industry fearful of competition) was thereby tilted towards the civic role of journalism, encapsulated by the principles of impartiality and accuracy.

Even in the United States, where the principle of public service broadcasting was much weaker, and where governments have generally been deeply committed to keeping journalism in the hands of private enterprise, broadcast news developed a strong *cultural* commitment to notions of fairness and objectivity.[36] This, in turn, influenced journalism more widely, and many newspapers felt an obligation to adopt similar ideals (in theory, at least). This remained true in spite of the relaxation of the Fairness Doctrine for broadcast news in the 1980s (inspired by a Reagan administration keen to roll back public service regulation) until the emergence of Rupert Murdoch's partisan Fox news channel in 1996.[37]

Nonetheless, the growth of news as a business – its industrialization and absorption into capitalist form of production from the late nineteenth century onwards – had already created a distinct set of impulses. The style, content and expectations of what we think of as 'news' was quickly shaped by the needs of an emerging consumer culture. This meant a gradual shift away from news about public affairs towards the reporting of crime, sport and other forms of 'human interest'.[38] But it also created a working definition of news based on the need to sell it as a *disposable commodity*. Once news became a manufactured object, its commercial success relied upon the creation of a transitory world – one where information can be quickly discarded and replaced – rather than a space designed to build common knowledge.

The history of journalism – like the history of media generally – is often understood as an inexorable process prompted by a series of demographic and technological developments. But if the growth of the daily newspaper was made possible by urbanization, the growth of transport networks and efficient printing presses, its viability as a business *depended on making news a constant celebration of the new*. Whether this was more a matter of appearance than substance,[39] it became a necessary ritual for journalism to be seen as constantly up-to-date. The more people could be persuaded that what mattered was the here and now, the more regularly they would buy newspapers. The newspaper thereby evolved into an object that represents a consumerist dream and an environmental nightmare – something that, *by definition*, needs replacing on a daily basis.

The idea of newness is thereby intrinsic to a consumer capitalist business model, which requires 'things consumed, burned up, worn out, replaced, and discarded at an ever increasing rate'.[40] Journalism was thus partly defined, at a key stage in its development, by the notion of built-in obsolescence. The phrase 'yesterday's news' captures this consumerist credo perfectly. News is seen as losing its value not because it is no longer relevant or useful, but because it is past its sell-by date. Its value, as a commodity, is less to do with its ability to inform than with its sense of immediacy. Indeed, we might say that consumer capitalism succeeded in making news the ultimate dispensable item, one that needed replacing on a time scale even the fashion industry would regard as premature.

Thus began a cultural economy based on the thirst to be first – a point famously satirized by Evelyn Waugh's novel *Scoop* in the 1930s. In this disposable world, newness is all. But what passes for new, in this context, is rarely novel or original. The 'shock of the new' remained an important idea in the culture of journalism, and in developed democracies this – in principle, at least – involved ideas that change the way we view the world. But all too often news became new only in the banal, temporal sense that it was recent (and often not even then).

So while journalism – bolstered by a tradition of public service broadcasting – retains a laudable sense of democratic purpose, it is constrained by its form. News became a commodity almost as soon as it was defined as news. Those in the newspaper business quickly understood that to become profitable, news had to become disposable. The more rapidly news could be made to appear out of date, the more regularly it could be sold. Its currency is, in part, its currency.

The business model of news became a philosophy. The idea that consumer goods should be built to last – rather than used up and replaced – has become almost passé, while we have contrived to create a world in which it is usually both cheaper and easier to replace something than to fix it. If journalism still has the capacity to go beyond this model, it is restrained by the degree to which it encapsulates it.

This is most clearly manifested today by rolling news channels, who have allowed themselves to be defined by a desperation to be up-to-date. Indeed, the development of 24-hour news channels rests on a strange paradox. Hitherto, commentators complained that broadcast news stories were sometimes too rushed and too superficial to allow viewers or listeners to really understand an issue.[41] This criticism could be rebuffed by pointing to practicalities: news bulletins typically had only half an hour or so available to them, and were thus obliged to cover a great deal of ground in a short space of time. History, context and explanation were all luxuries to be carefully rationed.

Freed from such constraints, 24-hour news stations had an opportunity to offer something different. With a whole channel to fill all day, everyday, with nothing but news and current affairs, there was ample time to provide context and analysis and, most importantly, explain the significance of a story in the wider scheme of things. And yet bizarrely, bulletins on 24-hour news channels have become *more* rushed and *less* analytical than conventional news bulletins. A comparison of the BBC's half-hour evening news programme on their main channel with a typical half hour of news on the BBC 24-hour news channel found that, despite the lack of time constraints, stories on the news channel contained less historical background, less supporting evidence, less contextual information, less detail and less explanation of the story's wider meaning.[42]

There are, of course, moments when news channels can stay with a story and devote more time on it. But research suggests that these moments are the exception rather than the rule, and the stock-in-trade of 24-hour news has become a rolling cycle of breathless bulletins.[43]

There are practical reasons for this. Once viewers began treating 24-hour news as 'news on tap' – a place to get quick, up-to-date bulletins at any time of day – news channels felt obliged to deliver precisely that – mindful that the viewer's stay was likely to be fairly short. But the adoption of a rushed, fast-paced format was not simply a response to audience expectations. Schooled in a culture that places such a value on 'newness', news channels simply assumed that audiences shared this obsession.[44]

This demonstrates a striking truth. For most 24-hour news channels, their most precious commodity – time – is seen as less valuable than their ability to endlessly inhabit the here and now. The ability to inform is sacrificed by the desire to be immediate. This is news in its most disposable form.

The stress on being instantaneous is exemplified by the news channels' obsession with 'breaking news'. In a review of the BBC's news channel for the UK government in 2002, Richard Lambert insisted that 'an absolute determination to break news first must be at the heart of everything the channel does'.[45] The report did not explain *why* this should be the case – it is not at all clear, for example, that this determination is shared by audiences, or that this idea serves *any* civic purpose – but the zest for being first struck a chord with an industry devoted to the celebration of the new.

During the 2000s, news channels began to devote increasing amounts of time to 'breaking news', and the ability to be 'first with breaking news' became a key objective for both public service and commercial channels. Breaking news quickly established itself as a regular part of 24-hour news, while the threshold of what constitutes a 'breaking' story has lowered to include almost anything that might be described as 'new'. Breaking news stories have thus become increasingly predictable and routine:[46] the latest development in a crime story, a (well-rehearsed) ministerial statement, a footballer's injury. It would be an understatement to say that this is more time-shift than paradigm-shift. Meet the new news, same as the old news.

The same research also shows that breaking news stories offer less diverse content and are more likely to be delivered by a studio presenter than a reporter on location. They are rarely the result of the news organization's investigative efforts, and when competing channels both report on the same breaking story, the time difference between broadcasters is often less than a minute.[47] What the boast 'first with breaking news' generally means, in effect, is that a news channel has taken information received from another news agency and put it on air with less fact checking, less appreciation of its significance and less consideration of how best to communicate it. This is 'churnalism' at its worst: being first with breaking news is more likely to be an indicator of *poor* journalism than a badge of honour.

The fact that this point is so poorly understood – even by public service broadcasters like the BBC[48] – is indicative of how intrinsic rapidity has become to our understanding of news. Being first with a story trumps all other considerations. It is hardly surprising, in this context, that the democratic purpose of news gets lost.

The celebration of the new is also manifested by the increasing prominence of 'live' news, broadcast in real time. First associated with rolling news channels, the strive to be live has become a common feature of most forms of broadcast journalism. The reporter on location talking live to camera – often in conversation with a presenter (the 'two-way') – has become a routine part of most news bulletins. This rarely involves delivering important up-to-date information (information that was unknown before the broadcast began): its purpose is to signify a sense of being 'right here, right now'.

This is not to belittle those moments when the ability to provide live coverage is a useful service, and or to suggest that there is no value in those rare occasions when news channels allow us to watch a major event unfolding before our eyes. Elections, for example, are events in which new information regularly trickles in and where many people will value the ability to watch this happen in real time. But most live news coverage is low on explanation and high on routine. The preference for covering stories live has become a contemporary fetish.[49]

At its worst, this involves a reporter on location who has little to add to a story, but is required to spend their time speculating on camera rather than finding out what might be going on – what former war correspondent Martin Bell has derisively called 'rooftop journalism'. Their presence at the scene – whether in a war zone or in front of the White House – gives the coverage a sense of authenticity, but generally adds little substance.

Most events do not simply unravel before our very eyes – they require context and explanation to become meaningful. Unless we are already well versed, we need informed journalism – and a sense of distance – to appreciate a story's significance. Live coverage is more about manufacturing the new than revealing it. Dispatching reporters on location generally requires planning, meaning that 'live' coverage will tend to favour what Daniel Boorstin calls 'pseudo-events', which are 'planned, planted or incited' ('we go live to the minister's press conference').[50] This allows those with sufficient clout or resources to create events to set the news agenda. So, for example, a study of CNN by Livingston and Bennett found that 'live news' is more likely to be informed by the usual suspects from institutions and officialdom than 'non-live' news.[51] And while many journalists do an admirable job of thinking on their feet to provide live commentary, this is one of the more superficial journalistic arts, more concerned with presentation than with news gathering and analysis.

If we privilege information that can be transmitted live rather than information that can be gathered from various sources, we make journalism a cruder, less resourceful profession. We lose its ability to gather information, analyse its significance, and recount it in a way that engages us and speaks to our interests and concerns. And we tilt the balance of agenda-setting further towards well-resourced institutions. Like breaking news, live news represents a victory of form over content. The origins of both forms lie in the notion of news as a disposable commodity, permanently transient and constantly in need of replacement.

This is as much the case with 'hard news' stories as it is with human interest vignettes. A study of the use of interviews on UK news channels suggested that their main focus was to create heat rather than light, to manufacture news rather than inform it.[52] An interview with a politician becomes a way of generating statements that can then be used in subsequent news bulletins. If we view news simply as a commodity, this is extremely efficient: the reporting of one story becomes a way of creating another. We then move through a series of claims and counter claims, assertions and attacks, jostling busily from one new story to the next.

The interview with an expert whose purpose is simply to evaluate or explain may be more informative, but it adds little value to news as a commodity form. It spreads out rather than pushing forward, adding nothing to the 'newness' of news as a disposable commodity. So, while this style of interview certainly forms part of the fabric of contemporary news, it is often seen to have less value than a confrontation that generates another ('new') story. Politicians are, for this reason, more likely to be interviewed than people who have knowledge or expertise to impart. A study of those interviewed on broadcast news stories found that around half came from just four professions: the worlds of politics, business, law and order and the news media itself. By comparison, the five main knowledge-based professions (from the academy, medicine, science and technology, thinks tanks and government/public agencies) made up, between them, only 9% of all sources.[53]

In the next chapter I look at the way in which an emphasis on disposable news impedes a more critical examination of consumer capitalism, pushing a growing body of new and challenging information aside. New iterations of tired old formulae are often preferred to genuinely new and original thinking. The problem here is that once news becomes useful – information that enables us to better understand the world – it is no longer disposable. It becomes something we want to retain, something to build on, changing our stock of knowledge. To recapture this sense of the new, to rediscover the purpose of news in a democratic society, means challenging the time-honoured traditions of its dominant business model.

7

Disposable news, consumerism and growth

The idea that news has to be current, up-to-date and disposable has enhanced the profitability of news, but a form based on the planned obsolescence of information has done little to advance our understanding of the world. On the contrary, the insistent demands of the news cycle to replace 'new' stories clashes with journalism's more democratic ideals, making it more difficult to understand the world or to question conventional wisdom.

Part I described how the idea of permanent economic growth based on endless consumer demand is becoming increasingly untenable as a driver of human progress, and yet it remains one of the dominant orthodoxies of our age. Its flaws have emerged in recent decades, as the sheer volume of productivity and consumption finally begins to jar with finite fixities of human life. This has given us a new body of evidence which encourages us to embrace new ideas about our politics, our economics and our culture.

Journalism's democratic instincts may encourage it to debate these new ideas, but the consumerist model of disposable news ties it to the prevailing orthodoxy. While the idea that 'growth is good' is increasingly contested, news coverage continues to reflect a political consensus in which the virtues of consumer-led growth are seen as an objective truth.

If journalism is to respond to the need to imagine other, more functional models of human development, it must come to terms with the contradiction between its democratic, questioning impulses and the development of news as a disposable commodity. We need a slow news movement, one that prizes the sustainability of information and the ability to think the world anew.

Throwaway news

The preceding chapter outlined the shortcomings of the business model that has created 'disposable news'. The journalism it delivers may be pertinent, dramatic or voyeuristic, but the business model obliges it to embrace the 'new' in the most superficial sense. Shanto Iyengar's research has shown how the episodic form of much of our news – a place where events just happen, one after the other, with little sense of broader social context or responsibility – works against public understanding. The form of these 'episodic' stories, he found, makes it hard for viewers to place these events in a social, political or economic context and, therefore, to hold anyone to account. News with a more thematic focus, by contrast, tends to root issues more clearly in a context which enables a discussion of causes and solutions.[1]

Crime news is, perhaps, the most prominent example of this form of episodic, disposable news, and has long been a part of the journalist's stock-in-trade.[2] Kevin Williams's history of British journalism, mindful of the confluence between commercialism and crime in the history of the press, chose (the early twentieth-century British press baron) Lord Northcliffe's clarion call *Get Me a Murder a Day* as its title.[3] Lord Northcliffe, a key figure in the creation of a mass-circulation popular press in Britain, was a well-known adherent of the idea that 'if it bleeds it leads'.[4]

The appeal of crime stories was undoubtedly appreciated by early nineteenth-century journalists in a less commercial age. But there was also a sense that this was a form of enticement that had little to do with the provision of useful information. Henry Hetherington, the editor of the *Poor Man's Guardian*, may have used 'Murders, Rapes, Suicides, Burnings, Maimings . . . and every sort of devilment'[5] to enliven his radical newspaper purpose, but his paper's principle was to promote new thinking about democratic reform.

As newspapers became more profit-oriented businesses – committed to the manufacture of built-in obsolescence – the genre of crime news flourished.[6] Crime news proved a highly disposable form of entertainment – one that added little to a reader's understanding of the world, but required regular updating. Crime became regarded as news in the same way that a new government policy or an earthquake was news. If some news outlets are less inclined towards the salacious end of the genre, they still assume that crime – regardless of its typicality or wider impact – is a normal, everyday part of what constitutes journalism. Crime stories are now deeply entrenched within a popular understanding of news – a prominent part of the fare offered by both public service and commercial news operations.[7]

There are, of course, circumstances in which crime reporting may provide us with useful information about crime trends, relative risks or – in the case of local news – events in the close vicinity that may touch our everyday lives. But these are the exceptions. Most of the time, the origins of crime reporting are a set of dramatic conventions.[8] A crime tends to be reported not because it is typical or widespread, but because it is egregious, shocking or unusual. Crime news is, in this sense, closer to crime fiction than it is to day-to-day experience. Neither news nor fiction has much interest in shoplifting, traffic offences or petty theft.[9]

These dramatic conventions mean that crimes are reported in an almost inverse relationship to the level of risk they pose. So, for example, the chance of a parent having a child abducted and murdered by a stranger while on holiday is so tiny as to be almost negligible. For this reason – along with its dramatic possibilities – such a crime is likely to receive a great deal of news coverage, especially if the parents and/or the child are seen as attractive and sympathetic. The abduction of three-year-old Madeleine McCann from a British couple on holiday in Portugal in May 2007 ticked all these boxes.

The deluge of news coverage that followed was entirely

speculative. Deborah Orr, writing in the *Independent* five days into the story, observed that a succession of stories about the McCanns' plight 'add nothing to anyone's understanding . . . They do not educate, inform or entertain . . . They exploit the interest of readers in a way that can only chime with their own worst fears and insecurities, and augment their own distress and panic.'[10] Her lament went unheard, and despite the lack of any new information, the case continued to dominate front pages in the UK and became a major international story. In September, when coverage was at its peak (following news that the parents were being investigated as suspects) the *Express* carried a Madeleine McCann story on its front page every day for the entire month, making it the front page lead 23 times. And yet, as John Jewell points out, 'to this day, the fact that Madeleine has disappeared is the *only* fact of this terrible affair'.[11]

Even if the story had contained more of substance, it told us nothing about the risks we or other people face. Worse, these kinds of stories can foster a misleading impression about the world of crime, encouraging us to guard against unlikely risks and over-estimate crime levels. It is now well known among criminologists that perceptions of crime bear little relation to crime trends or any sober risk assessment.[12]

Even when crime statistics suggest a long-term decline in crime levels, public perceptions, encouraged by an unrelent-ing crime wave in news coverage – may indicate the opposite. In the first decade of the twenty-first century the British Crime Survey[13] repeatedly found falling crime levels – including violent crime – *alongside* a perception that crime was increasing. This was particularly dramatic in the case of more frequently reported crimes – notably knife crime and gun crime, which 93% and 86% (respectively) of those surveyed reported as increasing, even while figures suggested the opposite. What is particularly striking about these perceptions is the distinction between people's view of crime levels at the national and local level: people are much more likely to imagine that crime is rising nationally than locally. Their local experience, in other words, turns out to be much more accurate than their media-informed picture of national crime trends.[14]

If we judge crime news by its ability to inform our understanding of the world, we would have to conclude that it is spectacularly unsuccessful. The survey data suggest that we would probably have a more informed view of crime if there were *less* reporting of it. Seen in Henry Hetherington's terms, this failure is unsurprising. As public information, crime news has little or even negative value. As a commodity – a form of disposable news – it is admirably fit for purpose. The narratives of crime stories often follow a sequence of crime, investigation, arrest, trial and verdict, all with well-rehearsed rituals and conventions (testimony from witnesses, family and friends of victims and suspects, police and judicial responses and so on). Each stage can be billed as 'new' – one of the reasons why crime stories make up the biggest category of breaking news stories.[15] Crime news is perfect disposable news: while those involved will bear the scars, the rest of us move on the next story – generally none the wiser – for the same cycle to be repeated.

And yet the longevity of crime news in journalistic culture has given it legitimacy as a form of news. Even Nick Davies, an investigative journalist whose book *Flat Earth News* offers a trenchant critique of the decline in the standards and independence of British journalism, bemoans the demise of beat journalists doing the rounds of police stations and courts.[16] This kind of crime reporting is, he suggests, proper journalism. Which, in a sense, it is – but in terms of the properties that define it as a genre, it is neither useful nor informative journalism (the kind of journalism, indeed, that *Flat Earth News* seeks to promote).

For the remainder of this chapter I return to the main theme of this book, and consider in more detail how an emphasis on disposable news makes it more difficult to question the limits of consumer capitalism and entertain alternatives. The 'newness' of news, it seems, makes it difficult to depart from the same old stories.

The growth orthodoxy

For 'the first time in history', wrote Vance Packard at the beginning of the 1960s, politicians, economic thinkers of all stripes, business leaders and unions were united in their 'clamour for growth':

> Marketers talk of the need to increase sales of consumer goods and services . . . Labor spokesmen have called for 'rapid expansion' . . . In 1960, both party platforms called for more growth and differed only on how it should be achieved.[17]

Packard proceeded to question why, in the richest country the world had ever seen, the central question in public life was not how to use or enjoy this abundance, but how to become richer still. Decades on, developed countries have grown significantly wealthier (the 'affluent society' of the 1950s and 1960s[18] now looks, to people in the developed world, almost stoic) and the clamour for growth has become an integral part of public discourse.

In the opening chapters of this book I described various ways in which growth has become a problem for wealthy, developed countries creaking under the weight of commodities. Growth economics has failed to deal with fundamental features of a finite world; it insists on more choice even when the proliferation of goods makes this burdensome; it ignores the failure of growth in the developed world to enhance our quality of life; and it neglects the dire environmental consequences of growth without sustainability. In short, the link between human progress and economic growth is becoming increasingly tenuous.

There are undoubtedly negative consequences if people in the richer parts of the world spend less money. But this is, in part, because we have designed an economic system that depends upon debt-led consumerism, where production is tied to the demands of a consumer economy rather than human need or desire. Developing nations are encouraged to export commodities rather than become self-sufficient, tying them to the vicissitudes of global capitalism. A drop in global demand is bad for these economies because they are there to serve global consumers rather than local interests.

Because we are no longer prepared to reduce the length of the working week, we rely on growth to maintain levels of employment as new technologies produce rises in productivity. Since unemployment generally lowers people's quality of life, growth is the easiest way of making efficiency gains while avoiding unemployment. Devising alternatives to the 'growth model' – what Tim Jackson calls 'prosperity without growth' – will necessarily be difficult and slow to enact – too rapid an unravelling of existing structures will create as many problems as it solves.

Relying on growth to avoid short-term negative outcomes is, in part, a function of the way we manage our economy. Yet the evidence of consumer capitalism's failings is becoming too significant to be ignored: it is no longer possible to assert the idea that 'growth is good' as a simple objective truth. Any virtue attributed to growth depends on how it is measured, managed or achieved. It follows that some forms of economic growth may *not* be good, while many of the conditions for positive human progress lie elsewhere.

These points may be given an airing in news programmes, but they are usually confined to the spaces reserved for quirky, counter-intuitive ideas. So, for example, British Prime Minister David Cameron departed briefly from the traditional script to quote Robert Kennedy's observation that GDP measured everything 'except that which makes life worthwhile'. This observation ran so counter to conventional wisdom that it might have invited a flurry of interest in larger questions about the relation between growth and quality of life. Instead, his proposal to add a new 'quality of life index' to the canon of official statistics was greeted with either amusement or scepticism. The BBC's political correspondent offered a typical response:

> The risk is it is seen as a woolly-headed distraction. A self-indulgent fad at a time of spending cuts, job losses and benefit changes. So while Mr Cameron may be keen on the idea I suspect many of the more hard-headed individuals around him are a good deal less happy.[19]

Part of the problem, of course, is that Cameron's government maintained a commitment to GDP growth and showed no appetite for following those countries with the best record on most quality of life indicators (notably the social democratic Scandinavian countries).[20] So, while the growing body of research on quality of life is occasionally discussed, it is generally treated as a 'lifestyle' issue rather than hard economics, and often with suspicion. Economic growth is seen as a more plausible indicator of social progress, even while the data to support such a view are collapsing.

Constrained by bipartisan political assumptions, the news media follow a political culture that finds it hard to countenance an alternative to an economic system of borrow and spend, or, by inference, an environmental model of consume and trash. Indeed, the 'growth is good' framework is so central to story-telling about the economy that it pushes all conflicting concerns aside. Witness the way in which the problem of climate change was side-lined during the recessionary years after 2008.[21] An environmental problem caused by rapid economic growth was put aside to focus on the need to return to economic growth.

The assumption that consumer-led growth is good remains so pervasive in our culture that the news media can be excused for replicating it. There is, nonetheless, an opportunity for journalists to call upon one of the most prized journalistic values – the questioning of political orthodoxy – and chip away at the conventional wisdom that props up the consensus about the inexorable virtue of GDP growth. The adoption of a questioning attitude towards something that politicians and business leaders tell us is good for us, is, after all, one of journalism's core values. But first we must recognize what stands in the way of this particular form of public interest journalism.

The rise of business news

There is an abundant literature on the establishment and maintenance of journalistic orthodoxies. The tendency of mainstream news services to reflect the range of opinion among political, economic and military elites is well documented. So, for example, towards the end of the 1990s, despite the lack of a significant military threat (following the collapse of the Soviet Union) and lukewarm public support in both the USA and the UK, military and political elites in those countries were keen to return military spending back to Cold War levels. As the *Washington Post* put it in a 1999 headline, 'Consensus builds for increased defense spending'.[22]

And increase it did, both the UK and the USA boosting military expenditure from the late 1990s onwards. This was a case in which public and elite opinion diverged (the former being far less enthusiastic than the latter) – but the reliance of most news media on senior political and military figures meant that the news media tended to reflect their concerns rather than public surveys which suggested other priorities.[23] In the UK, for example, between 1999 and 2009 64% of articles in the British broadsheet press were weighted towards arguments advocating an increase in military spending, far more than the combined number weighted towards maintaining, reducing or debating expenditure.[24]

The USA spends far more on its military than any other country, while the UK is (with France) by far the biggest spender in the EU and near the top of most global lists.[25] Yet because there is a consensus among political and military leaders for these priorities, the rationale for choosing to spend more than other comparable countries is rarely questioned or discussed. It is, in this context, unsurprising if the political and business consensus around economic growth were to receive similarly uncritical treatment.

In the 1970s and 1980s, a corpus of research by the Glasgow Media Group suggested that the views of business leaders tended to receive more favourable news coverage than the unions representing the people that worked for them. Their series of books – *Bad News*, *More Bad News* and *Really Bad News* – reported a systematic bias towards a pro-business view.[26] And yet, more than thirty years on, the world they describe – in which there was at least *some* attempt at balancing a union and management perspective – seems a far more robust public sphere than the one we are offered today. The genre of 'business news' has grown to become a significant part of everyday news reporting, while unions – or others representing working people – have almost disappeared from view,[27] displaced, almost entirely, by the voice of the 'consumer'.

The growth of business news began most conspicuously in the USA, with the emergence of business news channels – such as Bloomberg, CNBC and CNNfn – and a threefold increase in the number of business journalists in the USA between 1988 and

2000.[28] The increased prominence of business news subsequently spread to most parts of the developed world,[29] with, for example, more than 10% of BBC news devoted specifically to business.[30]

This is, in theory, something to be welcomed. If much of the twentieth century was about the growth of big government, the last few decades have been characterized by the increasing power of big business. A report by the Institute for Policy Studies in 2000 found that the world's top 200 companies had grown significantly faster than global GDP. The growth of big business was accelerated by a political shift – from the 1980s onwards – towards a neo-liberal politics, with an embrace of a business-friendly form of globalization (notably the lowering of taxes and tariffs and a relaxation of restrictions on the growth of monopolies). By the end of the twentieth century, the Institute calculated that 51 of the world's 100 largest economies were businesses rather than countries, with the world's top 200 firms generating 27.5% of the world's economic activity – while, interestingly, only employing 0.78% of the world's workforce.[31] The report's authors concluded that power was increasingly in the hands of global corporations rather than nation states. It makes sense, in this context, for journalism to be increasingly mindful of the need to scrutinize business in much the same way as it scrutinizes government.

And yet most business news is narrowly focused, divided between the interests of businesses (with news of stocks, shares, markets, profits and losses, regulation, takeovers and mergers, appointments and announcements) and consumers (new products, consumer protection etc.).[32] The bigger picture – examining the role of business in society – is obscured by details of who's up and who's down. The rise of business news may reflect the growing power of the corporate world, but it does little to challenge it.

A comprehensive review of UK business reporting for the BBC Trust in 2007 deliberately avoided some of the ideological questions raised by the growth of business news, generally hailing it as a positive development. They sidestepped the broader question of whether a focus on business creates a slant toward a particular view of the world and focused on the narrower question of whether business was viewed from a consumer or a company perspective:

We note that many of the BBC's business stories are framed through the perspective of the consumer. We believe the BBC's intention in adopting the consumer's viewpoint is to try to engage its audiences by approaching issues in a way that it thinks affects them and about which they care . . . However, such an approach can create a prism through which much business coverage is seen as a battle between 'unscrupulous' company bosses and their 'exploited' customers.[33]

The report appeared to desire a more consensual approach. And yet business, by its very nature, pits different interests against one another. While consumers may have an interest in businesses remaining profitable, they have little interest in making business owners (and/or shareholders) rich. Consumers want the best product at the cheapest possible price, while businesses want to spend as little on the product and sell it for as much they can. One wants margins low, the other wants them high. Do we favour the interests of the many (consumers) over the few (business owners), or do we overcompensate in favour of business – on the basis of wider involvement in pension schemes and other shareholding activity – and strike a balance between them?

The weight given to these different interests in news coverage is an interesting but limited question. Whether we see things from a business or a consumer perspective, most business news tends to assume that, almost regardless of the nature of the enterprise, we want more rather than less of it. The citizen – who takes a broader view of the role of business in society – has no place in this framework. Although the BBC Trust's review did not explore this point, they did point out that:

Around 29 million people work for a living in the UK and spend a large proportion of their waking hours in the workplace. However, little of this important part of UK life is reflected in the BBC's business coverage . . . the audiences are served in their identity as consumers. But they are not that well served in their role as workers.[34]

In our working lives, we have interests that are distinct – we want well-paid, secure jobs with profits shared among the workforce rather than passed to owners, shareholders or consumers. For many workers in the developed world, outsourcing jobs to low-wage economies – in what Jeremy Brecher and Tim Costello described as a race to the bottom (as countries compete to offer businesses cheap labour)[35] – lowers prices and depresses wages. In short, for both businesses and consumers cheap labour is a good thing; for employees it is not.

This is much debated territory, encapsulating different visions of the world. For the BBC Trust reviewers to ignore the ideological ramifications of these conflicting interests was understandable – if unduly meek. While there is clearly a case for devoting more attention to labour as well as business/consumer interests, there is a much broader issue about the whole nature of the genre, and its ability to address larger questions about our economy and society.

The wave of anti-globalization protests in the late 1990s was a missed opportunity to explore the politics of the push towards global free trade – one of the key political issues of our time. Gary Merrill conducted an analysis of the UK news coverage of the controversial WTO talks in Seattle in 1999. The talks became a focal point for protests against a form of globalization that was seen to favour business over worker or environmental interests. Merrill discovered that most coverage of the WTO talks did not tackle the globalization debate, favouring elite business and political sources from the developed world and tending 'to reproduce the dominant neo-liberal discourse' and portray 'a liberalized trading regime as the logical end-game'.[36]

In the same vein, Mike Berry's study of the BBC's coverage of the 2008 banking crisis (on their flagship *Today* programme) found that some reporters did raise important questions about regulation and the banking industry. Overall, however, their coverage relied on the same well-heeled sources that created or failed to anticipate the crisis in the first place. More prescient economists who had issued warnings about the fragility of the system were generally ignored.[37]

While there are examples of reporting that considers the wider social or environmental role of businesses – so, for example, around 6% of broadcast business news in the UK touches on environmental issues[38] – there is a broader pattern here. Most business and economic news reporting tends to assume that what is good for business is, generally speaking, good for society. A growth in the volume of commodities – whatever they are – is portrayed as something that is assumed to enhance our quality of life.

Studies of economic/business journalism by Gillian Doyle[39] and Damien Tambini[40] explore some of the constraints of business and economics reporting and the ways in which it encourages the recycling of conventional widom. As one economics editor put it: 'In terms of economic development, we write about, say, whether countries have been successful in reducing their debt level but we don't ask why we have a system whereby countries have debts in the first place. We don't challenge – but I'm afraid that's the deal.'[41]

Recycling the growth orthodoxy

If we look at how economic growth is reported in the UK and the USA, we find the same uncritical climate. In a study of press coverage, Richard Thomas and myself examined 591 newspaper articles which explicitly referred to economic growth in developed countries in the British and US press[42] in a ten-month period during 2010 and 2011.[43] The newspapers chosen were those generally acknowledged to be at the 'top end' of journalism, where we might be most likely to find a degree of critical reflection.[44] The sample was evenly divided between articles in the business sections and those in the main news sections (including opinion, editorial and review articles, where there is ample space to interrogate prevailing attitudes).

This was a period in which there were clear opportunities to question the assumptions behind the growth model. Some of the research described in Chapters 2 and 3 was trickling its way into public discussion. So, for example, the British government launched its plan to use surveys about well-being to measure quality of life in November 2010, and in February 2011, Prince Charles made a speech in which he tackled the growth model head on, urging us to move away from the model of economic growth based on increasing consumption.

While some of the newspapers in the sample had clear editorial slants, they would all claim to separate fact from opinion. Yet only a very small proportion of articles adopted a neutral position on the subject of economic growth. Just 2% referred to both positive and negative aspects of growth, and only 3% avoided using any value-laden language. The great majority (94.5%) represented economic growth – either by their use of language or by overt statements – as positive.

We found the growth orthodoxy so deeply ingrained in the routines of reporting that most articles – four out of every five – felt able to use positive language about growth without even specifying *what* the advantages of economic growth might be. This example from the *Guardian* is typical – a no-growth economy is pictured as a bleak, stagnant place:

> The Office for National Statistics confirmed the economy grew by 0.5% in the first three months of the year after contracting 0.5% in the last three months of 2010. Analysis showing the economy stagnated for much of last summer reveals an even bleaker picture of zero growth for eight months.[45]

The dominant metaphor, we found, is one of movement (as in 'we need to get the economy moving again') where growth is associating with moving forward and progressing. These articles from the *New York Times* and the *Daily Telegraph* are typical examples of this conflation:

> The reports suggested growth was being hampered by a combination of bad weather at home and supply disruptions caused by the March earthquake in Japan, and analysts said the economy should regain momentum by the second half of the year.[46]
>
> Still, slow growth is better than none. With growth of less than 1% this year, Britain is increasing exports, particularly in manufacturing. A total of 286,000 new jobs have been created. Helped by the weak pound, we are staggering back to our feet. Progress is likely to remain painfully slow.[47]

Those that did offer details on the benefits of growth (15% of the total) gave various reasons, some of which were more tangible than others. The most common explanations were that growth creates employment and that it provides revenues which makes it easier to reduce levels of national debt. These examples from the *Washington Post* and *The London Times* were particularly explicit:

> The US economy needs to grow about 2.5 percent annually to keep unemployment steady given continual growth in the labor force and in worker efficiency; even stronger GDP growth is needed to bring unemployment down.[48]
>
> The deterioration in the Government's finances is partly the result of much weaker growth, which will drag down tax revenues.[49]

While these arguments are widely accepted – by both supporters and critics of the growth model – they offer only a partial view. So, for example, we might sustain employment by reducing people's working hours rather than relying on growth. Or, since both the USA and the UK devote a significant proportion of government spending to defence, a reduction to more moderate military spending levels could make major inroads into deficit reduction without damaging public services.[50] None of the 591 articles we looked at raised either possibility.

Other positive reasons for economic growth were more speculative. This leader article from *The Times*, for example, opened with the premise that we needed growth to cheer us up:

> First job is to restore the nation's spirit of optimism. Growth is good, whatever some environmentalists might say. Increasing the rate of economic growth, even by a little over a long period, makes a big difference to a country's prosperity.[51]

This assertion is firmly tied to conventional wisdom about the link between GDP and a nation's well-being, but is offered with no supporting evidence (unsurprising, perhaps, since supporting evidence – discussed in Chapter 3 – suggests that the link between economic growth and well-being – or indeed, most other positive social indicators – has evaporated).

Barely a handful of articles – three out of 591 – focused on the negative aspects of economic growth. If we add to these the 2%

that gave a more balanced view of the merits of growth, we can begin to see some tiny cracks in the growth consensus. Of the 591 articles, seven referred to the environmental consequences of growth, five referred to the idea that quality of life could be measured in other ways, and four referred to some of the positive economic consequences of low growth.

These references are clearly very much on the margins. Indeed, of the few references to the environment most fell short of questioning the wisdom of growth itself, advocating instead the idea of 'green growth', with major investment in clean technologies. Typical was an article in *The Times* about the growth of car usage. The article briefly pits economic growth against the environment, before suggesting that technology will provide the answer for the maintenance of both:

> In the long run the improvement of our roads will increase road usage, and while this advances the economy it is potentially bad news for the environment. But the answer is to reduce the pollution and noise caused by cars, not to constrain the traffic.[52]

This imperative – that we can protect the environment without limiting the increase of traffic – is a metaphor for the coverage overall. We can tinker with the flaws in the growth model as long as we do not challenge growth itself. Research on the news coverage of climate change suggests that this focus on 'techno-solutions' to environmental problems is fairly typical.[53] Unfortunately the scale of investment in clean energy required to offset the worst effects of climate change are daunting enough at current levels of economic activity. Tim Jackson has explored the grim mathematics involved: put simply, if we insist on using economic growth as a way to sustain high levels of employment, the targets for reducing greenhouse gas emissions suggested by the Intergovernmental Panel on Climate Change are made considerably more difficult to achieve.[54]

Similarly, the few references to quality of life tended to portray these measures as existing *alongside* GDP growth as an indicator of human progress. Only two articles dealt with the failure of growth to improve quality of life in developed countries: a book review (in which the reviewer adopted a faintly mocking, sceptical attitude) and a report of a speech by Prince Charles (in *The Times*)[55] in which he offered a more thorough-going critique of growth than anything else in the sample (his speech referred to evidence that growth fails to promote well-being while damaging the environment). We did find two other reports of the speech, both of which focused on his comments on the environment rather than the broader questioning of economic growth.

Amid an overwhelming consensus of sources from the political, financial and business sectors, the one critical voice in the sample was a member of the British royal family. This is, in many ways, bizarre, but it highlights the notable absence of others – notably critical economists, environmental scientists, and social scientists – who might have offered a very different view of the merits of growth. So, for example, the New Economics Foundation – whose research offers a trenchant critique of the growth model – were entirely absent.[56]

Instead, we have the familiar recourse to a tired set of solutions. It is suggested, over and over again, that it is our duty as citizens to keep consuming in order to put momentum back into a sluggish economy. Our failure to do so is a problem, as this article from the *New York Times* puts it:

> For now, it is clear that the traditional drivers of recovery – consumer spending and residential real estate – have failed to rebound, with the latest report showing consumers extremely cautious about spending on anything and the housing market stuck at its post-bubble lows.

The crisis, here, is not the late consumerist sense of malaise or the environmental problems ahead, but a *lack* of consumerism:

> Weak demand leads to slow growth, and slow growth leads to high and rising unemployment, which then reinforces weak demand and slow growth, and so on, in a vicious cycle from which the economy, obviously, has found no escape.[57]

It is a view of the world that is as widely held as it is narrow. Another perspective might suggest instead that the 'vicious cycle' is built into the consumer capitalist model itself, with the constant need to accumulate goods to sustain a never-ending quest for economic growth. As long we cling to the assumption that prosperity depends upon growth, there will be no escape from a cycle that is less of a merry-go-round and more of a treadmill, with all our effort focused on staying where we are.

News that endures

The supremacy of the growth model in news coverage reflects the dominance of the model in political and economic spheres. It also reflects the philosophy of 'disposable news', a commodity requiring constant replacement: news must 'move on' just as the economy must 'move on'. In both cases, this movement is thinly defined. It is not a profound leap forward to a new place populated by new ideas. It is a momentum defined by the spirit of consumer capitalism, where more is always good and where the main requirement is to keep up.

The problem, in other words, is one of both content and form. The practice of disposable news – with its reliance on well established sources, its preference for quick solutions and its lack of interest in reflection – will always favour rather than question conventional wisdom about consumer capitalism. There is plenty of evidence with which to interrogate the idea that economic growth is the foundation of our security and well-being, but the unrelenting speed of the disposable news cycle makes this difficult.

The current crisis in the business model of news in many developed countries[58] – a commodity that, in the superfluity of the online age, people seem increasingly reluctant to pay for – may be an opportunity to go back to first principles. If news as a commodity is failing, then perhaps we should redefine it in more sustainable terms. If we free ourselves from an obsession with the here and now, we can begin to develop an idea that has always been there, but that is often bypassed in the rush to be fast and first. The notion that news is about enriching the quality of democracy remains part of newsroom culture. Perhaps it is time to give it room to breath.

Ronald Wright, in his historical review of progress across the ages, argues that we have become trapped in various dead-ends in which we substitute more profound forms of social progress for a series of various technological advances. This, in turn, leads to a failure to address more deep-seated problems – like climate change – and embrace wider visions of progress.

> The reform that is needed is not anti-capitalist, anti-American, or even deep environmentalist; it is simply the transition from short-term to long-term thinking.[59]

This might involve borrowing an idea from the politics of the 'slow food' movement, a rebellion against fast, processed food towards more nutritional and carefully prepared fare. Perhaps we need a 'slow news' movement, with a similar emphasis on well-prepared and (metaphorically) nutritional information and ideas, a place where news can be more profoundly new.

Once we foreground the more enduring, democratic value of news, we can begin to focus on information that adds to our knowledge of the world rather than simply confirming what we already know. Most journalists would see challenging conventional wisdom as part of their job description. If we are to rethink the tired, increasingly flawed model of human progress based on perpetual increases in the demand for goods, we need give them the time to do it.

Part IV

Waste and retrieval

8

Obsessed with obsolescence: Confusing hyper-consumption with progress

This digital world of media and communication has an ephemeral quality. Behind this virtual lightness of touch is an industry that uses resources and produces toxic waste at an alarming rate. Media and communications are now at the cutting edge of consumer capitalism's central strategy for sustaining rates of production and consumption – the idea of planned obsolescence. This has transformed the clean genius of the digital age into an industry that values quantity rather than quality and epitomizes profligacy and waste.

The media and communication industries are an increasingly significant sector of the global economy, but their importance goes well beyond their share of GDP. Their dominant role in our culture gives us a definition of progress based on the principle that the shorter the lifespan of objects, the faster we are moving forward. Progress and planned obsolescence are thereby seen as intertwined. This blots out space – not only for exploring how we might use digital technology to broaden our horizons, but for imagining other forms of human development.

The vanguard of consumerism

My focus, thus far, has been on two of our most strategically significant creative industries. Advertising, our modern cultural behemoth, has become intrinsic to most forms of contemporary culture, ever-present at every point in the vast panoply between fact and fiction. News, while more limited in reach, is our most widely consumed source of information about public life. Advertising amplifies and reinforces the routines of consumer capitalism, pushing the space for alternative ideas to the margins of public contemplation. News retains a more democratic spirit of debate, but is hampered by (among other things) its disposable commodity form, tying it to the prevailing orthodoxy. In this chapter I look across the media and communications industries more generally to consider how their embrace of a consumerist business model informs our attitude to freedom, progress and technological advance.

By conventional measures, the media and communication industries have been one of the economic success stories of recent decades. They now represent around 7% of global GDP, with annual growth rates that have generally outperformed other sectors. Across the OECD countries, growth in the sector has been between 5% and 20%.[1] In the United States, for example, media and communications achieved compound annual growth rates of 8.1% – outperforming GDP growth between 1975 and 2009.[2] The US Consumer Electronics Association suggested that global spending on consumer technology devices surpassed $1 trillion in 2012.[3]

The growth in media and communications has pushed us towards unprecedented levels of media consumption, squeezing out the finite amount of time we have for doing other things. In the USA, hours devoted to using or consuming media and communications devices rose from an average of 2,843 hours per person in 1975 to 3,532 hours per person – or 68 hours a week – in 2009.[4] More time is now spent consuming or using media technologies than any other activity – including sleeping or working (the two other activities that dominate our time).

There are, of course, all kinds of ways in which other

sectors of the economy – from finance to agriculture, energy to transportation – shape our experience of the world. But none of them captures our attention as the media and communications industries do: it is this industrial sector that occupies our time and provides the cultural landscape of contemporary life. This may be a cause for celebration for those in the media and communications business, but it raises much larger questions about the shrinking space it leaves for other aspects of life.

This domination of our waking hours gives the media and telecommunications industries a special place in our consciousness. In this chapter I argue that this is not just because of *what* they produce, but *how* they produce it. The production practices pursued by the creative industries have made them especially important in defining a particular ethos of consumer capitalism. This involves reinforcing the idea that progress is linked less to the quality of our lives than to quantity of things we consume.

The aviation industry is often criticized for its production of greenhouse gases. Environmental groups routinely oppose airport expansion and the tax subsidies aviation receives,[5] while the concept of 'air miles' – once associated with passenger bonuses – has become part of the environmentally aware lingua franca. Many of those who have calculated their 'carbon footprint' will know that the easiest way to reduce their own emissions is to fly less.

Meanwhile, with far less fuss or scrutiny, the media and communications industries produce the same volume of greenhouse gases as aviation.[6] This may seem counter-intuitive: the airline industry's core business, after all, involves burning large quantities of fossil fuel. They leave trails of smoke across the sky as a visible reminder of their environmental impact. By contrast, the sounds and images of the media and communications industry seem to pass quietly and unseen through the air. This is a sector whose industry is invisible, but whose voracity is as all-consuming as heavy manufacturing.

Take, for example, the energy required to power computer servers. Richard Maxwell and Toby Miller point out that:

> In 2010, US server warehouses consumed between 1.7 and 2.2 percent of the total supply. In 2006, Google's server warehouse in Oregon was

using the same amount of power as a city of 200,000 people, even though Google is considered more efficient than the bulk of the data center industry . . . [These companies'] electricity consumption in the United States and the European Union could double every five years. Yet their existence and impact are largely immaterial to consumers.[7]

Despite the efforts of various pressure groups trying to be heard above the quiet hum of technology on standby, the extent of the pollution and clutter produced by media and telecommunications is one of the untold stories of our age. Until we find a way of flying planes without burning fossil fuels, the growth of aviation is always going to be environmentally damaging. But the growth of media and telecommunications might have used sophisticated post-industrial technology to embrace a cleaner model of development. They have chosen not to. Or, more precisely, their skilful application of consumer capitalism has pushed them away from this green embrace.

The media and telecommunications industries have, instead, bundled clean and dirty technologies together in a manic orgy of production. The fashion industry, observed Gilles Lipovetsky, is emblematic of new, fast-paced consumerism. Fashion's 'abbreviated time span and its systematic obsolescence have become characteristics inherent in mass production and consumption' as a whole.[8] Fashion, by definition, determines that regardless of their physical durability, the symbolic value of each new creation withers quickly away.[9] From this ethos we derive the central tenet of consumer capitalism in an age of plenty: the notion of planned obsolescence, where things are designed not to endure but to become outdated as soon as possible.

The concept of 'progressive obsolescence' was developed, appropriately enough, in the advertising literature of the late 1920s.[10] It helped to define a strategy of using marketing campaigns to shorten the lifespan of objects and make way for new waves of production. As objects proliferated, the advertising industry became adept at infusing them with symbolic value – things, that, by creative association, would make us feel popular, pampered, healthy, distinctive, cool or secure. This has created what Juliet Schor calls 'the materiality paradox': goods are increasingly sold by associating them with non-material values, encouraging us to increase our consumption and, thereby, our material impact on the world.[11]

The media and communications industries are, in this sense, at the sharp end of consumer capitalism. They have perfected a world where objects are designed to become passé, where inadequacy is inscribed into their fibre. Michael Taussig described this kind of obsolescence as a place 'where the future meets the past in the dying body of the commodity'.[12] It is a vivid metaphor, except that while human lifespans have gradually increased, the lifespan of objects has shortened dramatically, littering the planet with the dying bodies of objects at an ever-increasing rate.

With every passing decade, the various bits of hardware that bring us information, entertainment and the ability to communicate become increasingly throwaway. Computers, mobile phones and electronic entertainment devices are designed to become antiquated at a ruthless and unrelenting pace.[13] Technologies for relatively simple pleasures – like playing music or making a phone call – now have the brief shelf-life of fashion accessories. Traditional telephones once epitomized particular decades of design; like theatrical props, they can evoke the 1950s or the 1960s. This lingering sense of purpose and style is long gone. Americans now replace their cell phones once every year, trashing 130 million as they do so.[14] They are driven by business models in which new objects are introduced to replace their predecessors every 12-18 months – a level of planned obsolescence that once would have been unthinkable.

The relationship between computer hardware and software sweeps us along in a highly profitable cycle of replacement. As software is 'upgraded' it requires greater computer memory and speed. This, in turn, obliges us to replace our computer technology continually – PCs, laptops, iPads and so on – to keep pace. What was fit for purpose is always temporary because the business model continually alters that purpose. These software upgrades were, at first, significant improvements. They have since become institutionalized, while the benefits of each new upgrade become increasingly marginal. Most users of office software programmes, for example, use only a fraction of their capability even before they are upgraded to offer still more. It is the profit margins of the industry – rather than the demands of users – that urges us to adopt them.

This is hyper-consumerism – a system that tells us not only that we need to surround ourselves with new things, but also that we need constantly to replace what we already have *before* it is broken or worn out. It is a way of life that insists that our ability to communicate, receive information or amuse ourselves must be reconfigured to a new set of devices with remorseless regularity. In the space of ten years, televisions moved from analogue to digital, changed shape to a wider screen, changed shape again to a flat screen, only to be reinvented once more to a higher definition of image (which, in turn, requires a larger screen to appreciate it).

The great Ukrainian pole-vaulter, Sergey Bubka, broke the world record an extraordinary 35 times. We might imagine that this was because, unlike most athletes, his ability to pole-vault improved at a slight, gradual and consistently incremental rate. But the number of Bubka's records was rather more contrived. The substantial rewards offered by event promoters for breaking a world record gave Bubka an incentive to reign in his obvious prowess (he would often clear a world record height with some distance to spare), and to break each new record one centimetre at a time.

Developments in media and communications observe the Bubka principle, but with less perfection and more guile. This is a sector, observes Jonathan Sterne, where 'obsolescence is not only planned but also forced and engineered'.[15] Workplaces have become so accustomed to expect constant innovation that they build it into their forward planning, assuming that even though we may not think there is anything wrong with a piece of hardware or software, we will need to replace it regularly simply 'to keep up'. This is not to say that these changes do not bring about improvements; they often do. But each step forward is faltering and limited, simultaneously introducing a new set of problems to be overcome.

The move from analogue to digital sound – records or tapes to CDs – was sold, initially, as a move towards audio perfection. There were undoubtedly advantages to the new format, which is easier to store and use. Nonetheless CDs, it turned out, jumped, skimped and deteriorated just as vinyl did, as well as using a process that, according to many audiophiles, lost the fidelity and richness of analogue reproduction.[16] The industry pushed CD technology hard – issuing new releases only on CD to force people to adopt the new format – in part because, in an industry dominated by a few large global players, switching formats boosted sales. The new technology allowed integrated companies like Sony to sell new appliances (CD players) and then resell music as people switched to CD.[17]

Vinyl's obsolescence was propelled more by the economics of replacement than its inferiority. Nearly two decades after the move from vinyl to CDs, sales of vinyl records began to increase once again,[18] suggesting that what matters about technological change – for the industry – is less the technology than the change. When, in 2011, the head of recorded music at Warner Music Group suggested that 'Vinyl will definitely outlast CDs because of the resonance, the sound',[19] it was a prediction that laid bare motives behind attempts to engineer its demise.

The next move – towards direct downloads – was actually a step back in sound quality – with digital data being compressed for convenience. So while the MP3 player or the iPod may be able to carry more music, in many cases they offer sound quality no better than the Sony Walkmans of the 1980s. This has nothing to do with technological possibility; it is a necessary part of the business model which thrives on imperfection. Perfection, after all, can only be sold once.

While replacing vinyl with CDs was highly profitable for the industry, the second of these technological shifts – from CDs to downloads – was quite different in character. It pitched one set of industry players (the manufacturers of those devices that store and play downloaded material) against another (the producers of content) – for whom the manufacture of physical (and imperfect) objects (such as records, tapes, CDs and DVDs) meant high profit margins. While companies like Apple seized the opportunity to produce an array of devices for downloaded material, the content producers – whether music, film or television – were reluctant to lose control over their copyrighted material to a virtual world that was more difficult to control. Although the new technology

slashed distribution costs, lucrative business models have traditionally been based on the sale of physical objects which deteriorate or
become obsolete when new formats are introduced.[20]

The move to digital downloads was, as a consequence, less
clearly industry driven than the introduction of CDs. On the contrary, since digital formats will be difficult to dislodge, the ability
to design obsolescence into something as intangible as a download
is limited.[21] The industry, pushed onto the defensive in an era
when digital technology transcended physical objects, has become
increasingly focused on policing its intellectual property.[22] Industry
leaders (like Apple) have shifted the focus from selling content
onto the increasingly rapid replacement of the devices that play
that content. But both technological shifts have more to do with
convenience than quality – providing access to as much as possible
with as little hassle as possible. Their focus is on acquiring volume
and extending choice rather than the quality of the experience.[23]
Quality, indeed, implies durability, which represents a problem for
this kind of consumerism.

For film and television, the move to digital involved technological advantages that were more closely associated with quality of
image reproduction. But this was a faltering step forward, providing potentially sharper images but introducing new flaws such as
the break-up of pictures (pixelation), picture freezing and other
digital glitches. Other benefits – such as interactivity, once sold
as the dawn of a new age of audience empowerment – have been
greatly overplayed.[24] At almost every stage these televisual devices
have tended to become *less* energy efficient, each new gadget or
appliance eating up more power than the thing it replaced. In
the UK, sales of flat-screen TVs have been estimated to increase
carbon emissions by 70% between 2006 and 2010.[25]

In the USA, the Consumer Electronics Association calculated
that in 2008 the average US household spent over $1400 per year
on a total of half a billion consumer electronic devices.[26] By 2011,
the International Energy Agency suggested that the significant
growth in the demand for residential electricity was fuelled by
the proliferation of power-hungry digital equipment, with over
ten billion devices powered by external power supplies (including
two billion TV sets and a billion personal computers).[27] In a vivid

example of the rapacious demands of a single device, Richard Maxwell and Toby Miller tell the story of video-gaming consoles, whose use by 40% of homes in the USA in 2009 meant that they 'collectively consumed electricity at the same annual rate as San Diego, the ninth-largest city in the country'.[28]

Michael Thompson observes that this takes place alongside an increasingly stark disparity between the economic and physical longevity of objects. The consumerist economy relies upon a rapid decline in the economic value of objects which, in a physical sense, take centuries to degrade. Ideally, he writes, 'an object would reach zero value and zero expected lifespan at the same instant, and then disappear into dust. But, in reality, it usually does not do this; it just continues to exist in a timeless and valueless limbo.'[29]

This limbo – the vast accumulation of e-waste that is the most conspicuous outcome of hyper-consumption – is hidden from the view of most Western consumers.[30] Susan Strasser's *Social History of Trash* describes how, before the 1890s, Americans produced very little consumer waste. By the twentieth century, the production, consumption and use of objects began to be seen as separate from the matter of their disposal.[31] One hundred years later this disposal has reached epic proportions. In 1998 the USA discarded 20 million computers. By 2005 the figure was up to 47 million,[32] and for every new computer manufactured in the USA that year, one became obsolete.[33] The UK, for its part, throws 1.5 million PCs into landfills every year.[34]

Elizabeth Grossman calculates that Americans now own about 3 billion electronic products, with a turnover rate of about 400 million units annually: 'in the USA alone, the Environmental Protection Agency estimates that over 372 million electronic units weighing 3.16 million tons entered the waste stream in 2007 and 2008. Less than 14 percent was recycled, while the rest went into dumps and incinerators.'[35] The waste from televisions, monitors, laptops, portable DVD players with LCD screens – and many other playthings of the information age – is highly toxic, so even when it is recycled, disposal or reuse of the more valuable minerals a hazardous business.

Richard Maxwell and Toby Miller's book on *Greening the Media* reminds us of the human misery involved in this toxic production cycle. Since e-waste is one of the most complex, bulky and non-biodegradable forms of trash ever created,[36] both the manufacture and the disposal of these devices has, in large part, been exported (via subcontractors) to the world's poorer countries. An estimated 50% to 80% of the e-waste sent for recycling in the USA is exported to Asia, Africa, and other developing economies,[37] where labour is cheap and environmental laws are lax – with dismal consequences for the health of those involved.[38] At the beginning of the twenty-first century the electronics industry was, according to the Basel Action Network, 'the world's largest and fastest growing manufacturing industry, and as a consequence of this growth, combined with rapid product obsolescence, discarded electronics or e-waste, is now the fastest growing waste stream in the industrialized world'.[39]

Workers in Mexico's TV component factories see their productivity go up and their wages go down, making the devices they produce far beyond their means. Meanwhile, half a million second-hand computers are dumped every month in Nigeria, where local populations run the gauntlet of a smorgasbord of health risks from the array of toxic chemicals spilling out of the innards of once clever machines.[40] A huge volume of e-waste has been exported to southern China, to small backyard workshops where workers with no safety equipment burn plastics over open flames. In one such community, Guiyu, in Guandong province, electronics recycling has rendered the local water completely undrinkable.[41]

Toxicity and waste is bound up with production as well as disposal. Despite the sleek designs of many telecommunications devices, they are resource intensive to produce. Four times as much energy is spent on making devices like computers or flat-screen TVs than on using them.[42] So however energy efficient we try to be (and frankly, most of us are not), it is the frequency with which we replace our digital gadgetry that is most responsible for draining resources. So, for example, a desk-top computer and monitor require 530 pounds of fossil fuels, 50 pounds of chemicals and 3,300 pounds of water to produce – roughly the same volume of resources used in the manufacture of a large automobile.[43]

The manufacture of computers, phones, digital cameras and

other devices is a dirty business, and the more we produce, the dirtier it gets. 'If you dig down beneath the thin surface crust of Silicon Valley,' writes Jennifer Gabrys:

> you will find there are deep strata of earth and water percolating with errant chemicals. Xylene, trichloroethylene, Freon 113, and sulfuric acid saturate these subterranean landscapes undergirding Silicon Valley. Since the 1980s, 29 of these sites have registered sufficient levels of contamination to be marked by the United States Environmental Protection Agency as Superfund priority locations, placing them among the worst hazardous waste sites in the country . . . Of the 29 Superfund sites, 20 are related to the microchip industry.[44]

The information age is thereby built on submerged mountains of toxic waste, an unsustainable use of resources and dependence on fossil fuels. While some might see this as the inevitable cost of progress, this is not a sufficient rationale. The breakthroughs in information, communication and entertainment technology *might* have created a cleaner, smarter, more democratic world. Instead, the industries that have profited from these technologies have contrived a level of planned obsolescence few other industries can match. Media and telecommunications have thereby placed themselves in the vanguard of a consumerist ecology. They have succeeded in making the idea that things should be 'consumed, burned up, worn out, replaced, and discarded at an ever increasing rate'[45] seem a natural part of modern life.

There is, of course, a market for some of the cast-offs of this consumer culture, with a small, informal network of flea markets, car boot sales, garage sales, charity shops and the like recycling cultural objects – such as books, comics or vinyl records – to collectors, enthusiasts and bargain hunters. In some ways this activity – like the early days of the 'punk aesthetic' – subverts the logic of consumer capitalism, extending the life of objects, reducing the need for more production and decreasing the cost of consumption. As Will Straw points out, it also extends the range of cultural possibilities and encourages the fusion of old and new styles.[46] But even this subversion operates within a cultural imperative based on the continual acquisition of objects.

Quality, quantity and cultural meaning

There is no doubt that amid this toxic flurry of production and disposal there have been some beguiling leaps forward in media and communications. But to what end? James Carey, casting an historian's eye over the much-trumpeted promise of new media technologies, recalls 'the vast outpouring of trade books ... extolling not just the potential, but the reality of the internet as an agent of an unprecedented social transformation'. The 'enduring peace, an unprecedented rise in prosperity, an era of comfort, convenience and ease' all failed to materialize, and instead the 'new man and woman of the new age strike one as the same mixture of greed, pride, arrogance and hostility that we encounter in both history and experience'.[47]

Various people at various times have undoubtedly made remarkable use of new technologies, but this is usually at the margins of consumer capitalism's production cycle. Despite the constant reinvention of audio and visual devices, it would be hard to argue that the quality of the programmes we watch or the music we listen to has improved a great deal over the last two decades. The proliferation of television channels is sustained by a commercial model that depends upon the large-scale recycling of old programmes – no bad thing, in itself, but hardly in keeping with the relentless updating of audio-visual hardware.

This divergence between hardware and content suggests that, in most cases, the medium is *not* the message. One of my teenage daughter's favourite shows – the US sitcom *Friends* – began before she was born and aired its final episode before she knew it existed. The show itself lasted a decade, outliving most of the TV screens on which it appeared. Indeed, those intent on keeping up could have replaced their TV sets four times during the show's duration, and few households even possess a TV screen that dates back to the early episodes that are still regularly recycled on 'new' channels.

Many other US sitcoms (such as *Married With Children*, *The Jeffersons*, *Cheers*, *Frasier*, *Mash* and *South Park*) have endured even longer. Indeed, while the screens themselves have a diminishing shelf life, the longevity of television programmes remains a constant feature of our culture. So while the quintessential 1950s sitcom *The Adventures of Ozzie and Harriet* survived (for 14 years) until it became an anachronism well into the 1960s,[48] *The Simpsons* (at the time of writing) is still going after 24 years.

Longevity is not the province of situation comedy. In the USA, *Washington Week*, *60 Minutes* (current affairs), *Saturday Night Live* (comedy), and *Masterpiece Theatre* (classic drama) are all still going after more than 40 years. In the UK, the children's programme *Blue Peter*, the soap opera *Coronation Street*, current affairs programme *Panorama*, the football highlights show *Match of the Day*, the quiz show *University Challenge*, the drama *Dr Who*, and the science programme *The Sky at Night* have an even longer history, beginning in a period between 1953 and 1964. The BBC radio soap opera, *The Archers*, celebrated its sixtieth year by recording its highest recorded listening figures in 2011.[49]

If many of these programmes have been restyled or reinvigorated, the pace of change seems glacial alongside today's permanent revolution in electronic information and entertainment devices. This is, perhaps, because the quality of a cultural experience – or of cultural innovation – is more of a feature of its content than its form. While the size and definition of the image may improve its aesthetics, this is not what moves, inspires, informs or amuses us. If the nature of cultural content moves more slowly than the rapid pace of technological upgrades, it reflects the more gradual nature of shifting social mores and the limited stock of stories available. The pace of change in consumer electronics, by contrast, is often disconnected from day-to-day social life, driven more by the demand for profit in an era of over-production than fulfilment of individual or social needs.

One of the clichés of the media and communications business is to assert that 'content is king': the stories you tell matter more than the equipment you use. This remains true of the quality of our experience: most of us, for example, would rather watch something we like on an old analogue television than something we feel indifferent towards on a state of the art, high definition screen. But it is no longer true of the business model dominating the industry.

Even on a purely technical level questions of quality are often secondary. So, for example, the poor quality speakers on most components – from digital radios and TVs to DVD players, phones and iPods – produce sounds that are demonstrably cruder than an above average stereo system manufactured 30 years ago. This is, in part, because we are less likely to want to invest in high quality components if we don't hang onto to them long enough to make it worthwhile. There is a *kind* of progress here, but it is often narrowly defined around the aesthetics of the consumer object, without any sense of a more profound social, democratic or cultural potential.

From consumer capitalism's point of view, the beauty of the current model is that it creates a public so accustomed to the constant production, reproduction and renewal of media technologies, that we see this – *in itself* – as a mark of progress. This is not to say that the industry's innovations have been pointless – there are plenty of jewels amid the junk, and some of the breakthroughs in digital technology have profound possibilities. But the imperatives of consumer capitalism have pushed us away from exploring (and developing) the social value of these technologies and towards the accumulation – and replacement – of objects. The communication and entertainment businesses are, in this sense, at the cutting edge of consumerism. Their role is both material – they maximize the amount we consume – and ideological – in the sense that they define human development in terms of the sheer volume of choice and the speed with which we buy and replace things.

So, for example, the enthusiasm for digital television often highlighted its potential for interactivity. Television would no longer be a top-down technology, proclaimed enthusiasts, but one where interactivity would lessen the gap between producers and audiences.[50] Here was technology bringing power to the people at the press of a red button. And yet the democratic potential of interactive digital television remains largely ignored, especially by commercial media. Programme makers quickly discovered that – beyond charging people for votes in reality television shows – there was no money in it.[51]

What is both remarkable and disquieting is the ease with which we have accepted – even embraced – this level of built-in obsolescence, while being relaxed about its environmental consequences. A UK government report analysing the costs and benefits of enforcing a switchover to digital TV acknowledged some of the environmental costs of changing technologies, concluding that 'digital switchover will increase energy use and will therefore contribute to climate change'.[52] But the rather questionable mathematics of its cost–benefit analysis – based substantially on the assumption that access to more channels is, by definition, a good thing – trumped these concerns.

The UK's proposed digital radio switchover[53] encapsulates the philosophy that 'more is better'. The move from analogue (FM) to digital (DAB) involves, in many cases, a loss of sound quality, while the environmental costs of such a switch are considerable. Around 100 million appliances would be rendered obsolete at the push of a button, simultaneously *increasing* the energy required to power a radio set (thereby decreasing their portability, and endangering the recent development of wind-up/solar powered radios).[54]

The only significant advantage of digital radio is that it allows more stations onto the spectrum. This assumes, of course, that meaningful choice is purely quantitative. The UK's radio system – with a range of popular, complementary, well-funded public service (BBC) stations – gives listeners a far greater choice of radio programming than a proliferation of commercial channels would allow. Commercial radio stations compete to capture the same lucrative markets at the lowest cost, so we see a proliferation of cheap formats (such as call-ins, sports commentary and pre-recorded music) and very little in the way of drama, situation comedy, documentary, features or live music. Not surprisingly, the most popular radio stations in the UK are run by the BBC,[55] while countries who rely on advertising funded models for radio compare unfavourably with the UK system by almost every measure – not least, by listener satisfaction.[56] The issue, in other words, is less 'spectrum scarcity' than the resources invested in producing high quality radio services designed to offer a range of music and speech programmes.

We see a similar logic in the development of television, where the proliferation of channels has been driven largely by commerce, so that the proportion of publicly funded spaces has shrunk.[57] The UK, for example, has moved from a carefully constructed ecology based on principles of public service broadcasting – with a small

number of well-funded and carefully regulated channels producing a wide range of high quality programming – to a commercial
system with a politically fragile public service component (the
BBC and a small and increasingly reluctant group of commercial
networks).[58] The move to commercial multi-channel broadcasting,
like so many developments in a consumerist culture, is premised
on the idea that choice and proliferation are, in and of themselves,
a celebration of consumer sovereignty and a step forward in the
history of the medium.

A few years ago I attended a visit of a high-level Chinese
delegation to Cardiff University to discuss television policy. The
delegates rebuffed questions about the quality and content of
Chinese media by pointing to the sheer number of channels available to Chinese viewers. 'We have more channels than you do,'
they pointed out with more than a hint of hubris. In short, they
played the classic consumerist card – where freedom is conflated
with freedom of choice, which is, in turn, measured by quantity
rather than quality. There are, of course, good arguments against
this position. Quality, freedom of expression and diversity are not
a consequence of nor guaranteed by quantity. But in making these
arguments we are required to go against the policy assumptions
of our own government, whose policies promoting commercial,
multi-channel television defined choice exactly as our Chinese
guests chose to.

The promotion of choice in television's development is a good
example of how proliferation, on its own, has little to do with
enhancing quality or, in some cases, decreasing price. Proliferation
abounds in a world populated by what Staffan Linder famously
called 'the harried leisure class', where free time becomes increasingly pressed by consumer choice.[59] The rapid expansion of TV
channels – from a few to a multitude – took place in an already
saturated market. In most developed countries TV viewing had
already become near universal before the multi-channel age, with
no increase in the time available to watch it, and more competition from other media (from computer games to social networking
systems). The economic logic of this saturation was generally
ignored in media policy circles by those seduced by a bundle of
associations between choice, freedom and progress.

To increase the number of TV channels – often by a factor of five to twenty times – without increasing the size of the audience – leaves only a limited number of possibilities. Either people would be required or persuaded to pay more for television, or the amount spent on programming would have to decrease. Or, as it turned out, both. Most multi-channel systems are padded out with channels based on cheap programme formats – notably repeats of network programmes, imports, music video,[60] advocacy or propaganda channels (usually religious). While most of these survive on fairly low ratings, they still drain advertising revenue away from the main networks, whose ability to fund original programming is thereby diminished.

In the 1980s the UK provided four well-funded networks, all producing a diverse range of well-resourced genres, for the cost of the licence fee. The advent of multi-channel broadcasting was, initially, a flop. Viewers were – for good reason – unconvinced that the additional channels were worth the cost. The only way to entice viewers to buy the hardware required to view new channels was to create monopoly provision of something many viewers cared about – in this case sport – and charge a premium for it. The franchising of key sporting events to private subscription channels increased viewing costs dramatically – by around 500% for the full package of films and sport – without significantly adding to the range of most television genres. Even after cuts in 2011, the BBC remains by far the main provider of new television and radio programming in the UK on a smaller budget than the main commercial programme provider, BSkyB.[61]

The move towards an emphasis on the quantity rather than the quality of entertainment, information and communication has undoubtedly created a world in which a number of activities have become both faster and easier. The online world is a fantastic repository, with telecommunications increasingly wired to receive its bounty. We have access to a wider range of information and culture than at any time in our history. There is, in theory, a democratic aspect to this digital revolution that is both egalitarian and invigorating.

The problem is not with the technology, but with a model in which the 'upgrade' – whether it be a new version of a software package or a type of TV screen – becomes an end in itself. What we have ignored, in the drive for ever more convenience and capability, is how this potential might best be realized. The burgeoning of content has outstripped our capacity to deal with it. 'When content proliferates,' writes Ioannis Maghiros, 'information consumption can be compared to "trying to drink water out of a fire hose".'[62]

An article in *The Economist* – entitled 'The tyranny of choice' – illustrated this point by drawing attention to the way we disregard plentitude and continue to seek shared cultural experiences (a point made some time ago by scholars trying to understand the pleasures of mass communication).[63] In 2009 the US film industry released 558 movies, with many gigabytes uploaded or shared online. Yet amid this abundance of choice just one of them – James Cameron's *Avatar* – broke all box-office records to become the highest-grossing film in the history of US cinema.

> However many niches there are, in other words, film-goers or TV viewers still want to watch what everybody else is watching, and musicians still manage to release mega-hits. Indeed, in a world that celebrates individualism and freedom, many people decide to watch, wear or listen to exactly the same things as everybody else.[64]

In theory, a world where we have an extraordinary array of easy choices about where we get our information, what programmes we watch, what music we listen to and how we can communicate is a kind of democratic and cultural nirvana. But as Alvin Offer points out, the superfluity of easy choices can quickly become dysfunctional.[65] We have reached a point where our ability to understand the world, to find diversity and meaning, is curtailed by our need to cope with the clutter.

The ease of global communication means we spend an increasing amount of time wading through a digital deluge: unwanted emails; thousands of search engine hits on any given topic; junk mail; unsolicited sales calls; or simply deciding which television programme to watch. Even for those well trained to be discriminating, this can be daunting. Faced with this breathtaking cultural array, most people most of the time will opt for what is familiar and safe. The volume of choice, in other words, exceeds our capacity to deal with it, obliging us to take shelter in familiar genres and brands.

So while digital technology has made many things a great deal easier, it has simultaneously complicated our lives and pushed many people to embrace what they already know rather than seek out more challenging possibilities. It is the irony of the information age: faced with plentiful possibilities we seek ways to narrow our horizons, swept along by an industry that prizes volume and convenience above quality or profundity.

In this context the evidence on quality of life provides a sobering commentary. The revolution in digital technology, with all its possibilities for culture and communication, has not made us happier or our lives more meaningful.[66] The reason for this failure is simple. Most of it is *not designed* to provide richness of experience, happiness or fulfilment. The potential of the technology has been constrained by a consumerist philosophy, geared to the constant reinvention of hardware and software. Its principal modus operandi is to tempt or cajole us into a cycle of replacement.

Steve Jobs, the man behind many of the sleek designs of Apple's digital devices, was hailed by many as a visionary for anticipating consumer taste. 'A lot of times,' he declared, 'people don't know what they want until you show it to them.'[67] Such a statement might once have been associated with a certain kind of Reithian elitism, in which public service media would spread culture to the populace.[68] Today, his statement captures the paternalistic essence of our insatiable age, one in which – as Paul Weller once sang – the public wants what the public gets.[69] This is not to say that Apple's products did not provide a degree of aesthetic pleasure or offer (ever so slightly) distinct utilitarian features, but their business model eventually forced them into the same system of planned obsolescence as their competitors – a 12–18-month production cycle that creates problems just as it solves them.

This cycle of replacements creates its own strains. The costs of constant upgrades places a burden on households, businesses or the public sector, who are forced to invest time and money simply to keep up. At a recent seminar, someone responsible for digital technology in the public sector in the UK recalled a meeting with telecommunications companies, in which he was asked what he wanted from them. His reply was a simple three-word request: 'please slow down'.[70] This was not the response of a technophobe – on the contrary, the speaker was an enthusiastic proponent of the use of digital technology to deliver better public services. But his approach to technology began from a very different premise which, if we put it at its most altruistic, was concerned with the ways in which media and communications might improve people's lives.

Wired but mired

So, how might we assess the contribution that the media and communication industries have made to social or cultural progress? The most obvious technological leaps forward – in the processing and distribution of words, images and numbers (using the internet and convergent digital technology) – have facilitated breakthroughs in research, especially in the social sciences, the natural sciences and medicine. Communication and creativity is now a great deal easier, creating large, living archives of culture and information. From this point of view, the failure to find evidence that these technologies have improved the quality of life is a puzzle.

Back in the analogue age of the 1970s – before personal computing and digital audio-visual reproduction – we were reportedly just as happy and our lives were as meaningful or profound as they are now.[71] And it was not as if we were living in a state of blissful ignorance: people in developed countries had near universal access to a wide range of cultural forms, with an abundance of offerings from film, television, radio, publishing, music and other creative industries. Education, library and news systems provided people with access to large stores of information, while telephone and mail networks enabled communication on a global scale.

For most people at the time, this did not feel like an era of scarcity – in information and cultural terms – but of plenty. The main differences between now and then are twofold: first, abundance is now rife; second, we can move information around much more quickly. There are, of course, some people for whom this speed and abundance has enabled new possibilities – in many fields of medical research, for example. For most of us, though, life is different rather than better.

My contention, in this chapter, is that our ability to take advantage of the information age has been hampered by the way in which we have allowed consumer capitalism to develop the tools of media and communication. This has occurred in three related ways. First, in the drive to sell more – aided and abetted by governments with a crude numerical model of consumer choice – consumer capitalism tends to favour quantity over quality. As Richard Maxwell and Toby Miller put it, this involves embracing a logic that 'more is better' and the consequent idea that 'to advance democracy, media channels must proliferate; to prosper, ICT/CE must be ubiquitous; to enhance pleasure, media technology must spread far and wide; there must be more outlets, more proprietors, more publics, more social networking, more use, more discourse'.[72] It is proving to be an empty philosophy.

Second, to maximize profitability these industries have perfected the planned obsolescence of the objects they produce, forcing our domestic and workplace arrangements into an endless cycle of upgrade and replacement. The pleasures and efficiencies of each step forwards are counterbalanced by the burden of endlessly keeping up.

Third – and perhaps most importantly – they have thereby reinforced the notion that progress is, in Victor Liebow's words, a matter of seeing things 'consumed, burned up, worn out, replaced, and discarded at an ever increasing rate'.[73] It is in this sense that the business model pursued with such skill and occasional flair by the information and entertainment industries has become more than a way of selling things. It imposes upon us an understanding of human development based on the proliferation of objects. This is progress writ small.

9

Imagining a different world

The first part of this final chapter sums up the central arguments made thus far. Consumer capitalism has become increasingly incapable of driving human progress, forcing us into cycles of growth and consumption which, at best, simply keep us where we are. The system is incapable of dealing with the negative psychological and environmental aspects of the over-production on which it depends. Yet our ability to conceive of different forms of progress is limited by the commercial arrangement of our creative industries. We have allowed the most single-minded of those industries – advertising – to adopt a position at the centre of our culture, an ever-present engagement with the story of consumerism. Journalism, by contrast, has the potential to question orthodoxies and explore new ways of thinking, but it remains constrained by the need to manufacture news as a commodity. And the business model of the communication and creative industries as a whole reinforces the idea that progress depends upon the rapid production and consumption of objects rather than the quality of experience.

The second half of this chapter begins a discussion of what we might do to stretch our imaginations. To do so, we must start by addressing the cultural pressures – the dominance of advertising, the move towards disposable news, the primacy of planned obsolescence in the communication and creative industries – that constrain our ability to think critically about consumer capitalism. Only then may we open up spaces that allow and encourage new ways of thinking about human progress.

The (same old) story so far

A few years ago I attended a government seminar whose purpose was to promote public engagement with science. Most of those attending saw scientific and human progress as inextricably linked and during proceedings it was suggested that our starting point should be the notion that science improved the human condition. There is, of course, some truth to this proposition, but whether it is an absolute truth is more questionable. When challenged about the evidence used to support such a wide-reaching claim, the scientists in the room could only offer anecdotes and vague appeals to common sense. Their basic premise, in other words, was not based on scientific evidence but a decidedly unscientific set of assumptions.

They were, in so doing, clutching at a partial truth that conceals as much as it reveals. It is not unreasonable for any natural scientists to measure milestones in human progress by counting the breakthroughs in medicine, engineering, technology and our understanding of the natural world. The two are undoubtedly linked. But there are also ways in which they are *not* linked. New technologies can do harm as well as good – breakthroughs in a manufacturing process, for example, may improve efficiency but they may also increase unemployment, pollution and industrial waste. Or they may simply feed a business model rather than our bodies or souls. The latest clever gadget may provide us with mild amusement, but it may distract us from our more meaningful goals.

Many philosophers, psychologists and social scientists have shown how developments in science and technology occur in a social, political and cultural context that defines their value. To put it another way, not all technology is good technology. So,

for example, how might we compare the contribution of technologies designed to relieve pain and suffering with those (notably
development in weaponry) designed to cause it? Both may involve
scientific breakthroughs of similar complexity, but it would be
crass to see them as making an equal contribution to human
progress. Science may be needed to tackle problems like climate
change, but it is scientific breakthroughs that have helped create
the problem in the first place. And while a great deal of science is
publicly funded for altruistic ends, it is primarily tied to a dominant
business model whose ends are purely commercial.

In much the same way, one of the reasons the relationship
between consumer capitalism and human progress avoids scrutiny
is the assumption that one leads straightforwardly to the other. The
last chapter reviewed some of the technological developments in
the media and communication industries and charted the way in
which these developments have been driven by consumer capitalism, inspired less by an understanding of human progress than by a
profitable way to sustain high levels of production.

How might we assess capitalism as a model for human development? The question is complicated by capitalism's dependence
upon a public sector to regulate it, rescue it in difficult times and
fund those areas (such as health, education and environmental protection) in which a capitalist ethos is widely regarded as capricious
and inadequate. Capitalism's main selling point is that – for all its
inequities, its cyclical crashes, its externalities and its market failures
– it has played a central role in generating wealth. This is a significant claim, since improvement in the wealth of nations has, over
the last few centuries, generally been equated with improvements
in the quality of life.

The link between wealth creation and progress may gloss over a
host of moral inconsistencies, but even critics of consumer capitalism will concede that its productive capacity has aided many forms
of social and cultural development.[1] It has given us the resources
to lead healthier, more comfortable and more interesting lives –
especially when the system is moderated and complemented by a
public sector to create desirable social outcomes.

But how far does this messy, complex truth still hold? For
developed nations in the twenty-first-century world, the evidence

linking capitalism to various measures of human development is looking increasingly threadbare. Which brings us to the point with which this book began: the proposition that consumer capitalism has outgrown itself. A system that was once (depending on your perspective) nimble and dynamic or red in tooth and claw lumbered into the twenty-first century offering superfluity rather than sustenance, excess rather than excellence.

The proliferation of consumer goods in time-strapped societies has become dysfunctional. The optimism that accompanied peace-time growth in the post-war twentieth century was frittered away in a spending spree, replaced by a sense of striving to keep up in an insatiable age. There is an opportunity here: the recent decline of economic growth rates in the developed world coincides with the burgeoning evidence questioning the merits of growth. Yet all we seem capable of doing is reverting to calls for more of the same, desperately clinging to a tired old formula.

We risk failing – as a society – to take stock of where we are and how we might move forward. This is, in part, because consumer capitalism embraces new ideas only within its own constraints. It thereby saps our creative energy away from more profound, original ideas about the human condition. Its undoubted vitality masks a stubborn refusal to think beyond its own limits.

I have, throughout this book, left moral and political critiques of consumer capitalism to one side, not because they are unimportant but to draw attention to the ways in which the system is no longer capable of delivering on its own terms. Worse, without significant adaptation, consumer capitalism threatens to push us towards a world in which we are demonstrably worse off than we are now. Each of the three problems outlined in Part I are sufficient to encourage us to rethink the way we do business. Taken together, they oblige us to.

The most obvious of these (though not so obvious that we are prepared to address it) is the problem of climate change. Governments are able to deal with more immediate environmental problems – such as air pollution or poor public health – if solving them gratifies both political and consumer demands. The problem with climate change (as well as other forms of waste disposal) is that it operates on a time scale that may be alarmingly brief in terms of human history, but where the time-lag between cause and effect exceeds the modus operandi of both government and business.

The volume of greenhouse gases we are currently pumping into the atmosphere – at a rate that, despite more than two decades of well-documented warnings, continues to grow – will have an impact on global temperatures in the years to come. Assessments from the world of climate science become gloomier by the year, with mounting evidence that we are causing irrevocable damage to the planet's eco-systems and a sense of despair that we are doing so little to prevent it. As the certainty of the science linking human activity to global warming has increased, so has the activity (greenhouse gas emissions) that causes the problem. There is almost unanimous agreement among climate scientists that we need radically to reduce emissions as a matter of urgency. The debate is between those who hope this will be enough to ameliorate the worst effects and those who calculate we will be forced to reduce emissions *and* pursue some colossal form of geo-engineering to prevent feedback effects from spinning out of control.[2]

Consumer capitalism, meanwhile, trundles on regardless. Most businesses – including newspapers – issue no clarion calls for action. On the contrary, they complain loudly about the cost of even weak and inadequate environmental regulations in a period of low growth. Modest proposals to use tax revenue to fund clean energy projects are more likely to be greeted with jeers than applause.[3] Politicians – who fear the former and crave the latter – have to submit themselves to elections at regular intervals, creating a reluctance to risk short-term unpopularity for the long-term health of humankind.

The famous phrase adopted by Bill Clinton's first successful presidential campaign – 'it's the economy, stupid' – continues to define political priorities, especially when economic growth slows down. Yet the phrase itself is indicative of an almost wilful ignorance. Franny Armstrong's film *The Age of Stupid*[4] captures this sense of dislocation, of a world moving inexorably towards climatic conditions that will create misery on a global scale, unable to act not through lack of knowledge but lack of will.[5]

We might imagine that the short-term benefits of consumerism must be deeply felt to be so irresistible. Consumer culture is remorselessly upbeat about the life-enhancing capacity of consumer goods, an enthusiasm that underpins the assumptions of most politics and mainstream economics. This brings us to the second major problem with the current model: a growing body of evidence which suggests that we have reached a point where growth in gross domestic product no longer brings improvements in people's quality of life. In the twenty-first century, the unlimited promises of our insatiable age collide with the finite nature of human experience. Our relative affluence, it seems, makes the accumulation of commodities an increasingly empty spectacle.

There is a complication here – one that constrains us as individuals. The data show that *within* a society an individual's quality of life *is* related to his or her social and economic position. But it also shows that, overall, improvements in quality of life in wealthy societies have come to a grinding halt.[6] We have now passed the point where an increase in the volume of consumer goods makes us happier of more fulfilled – indeed, if given a choice, people tend to choose status over money.[7] But because wealth is so strongly associated with purchasing power, the link between consumer goods and quality of life seems more tangible than the data suggest it is.

As individuals it is easy to see how seductive consumer culture becomes as a way of measuring our own value: status, respect, and the sense that we are doing well have become symbolically linked to our purchasing power. If we desire the first, it follows that we seek more of the second. And yet when all of us do this at the same time, our collective income increases but we feel no better off than we were. This may seem to be a paradoxical state of affairs, but only if we think like individuals and not as communities or societies. Collective wisdom, in this sense, is more than a sum of its parts.

Consumer capitalism's waning ability to increase our quality of life is a product of a clash between a system committed to proliferation and a finite world. This is often understood in environmental terms, as capitalism's growth comes up against the limits of the earth's natural resources. There is, however, an even more intractable set of limits on the proliferation of goods: the finite nature of the time we have available to us to buy, use or enjoy them.

Many economists will argue that limits in natural resources can be overcome by human ingenuity. While this is debatable, the resolutely finite nature of human life is not. So while the market provides more goods and more choices, the time we have to exploit (or merely cope with) those choices remains the same. We have now reached a stage where product proliferation has become, even in economic terms, surplus to value.

The more we accumulate, the more the value of each new object diminishes. In a world in which goods increase in volume and decline in (relative) value, and where the time we have to make rational consumer choice remains the same, something has to give. In short, it no longer makes sense to devote the time and energy required to accomplish the increasingly difficult task of choosing the best – or indeed, most ethically produced – product at the best price. As Alvin Offer suggests, on this scale choice becomes less of an opportunity and more of a burden, a way of relinquishing rather than enhancing our independence and self-control. The notion of rationality is intrinsic to an understanding of market economics: if we made purchasing decisions regardless of quality, price, need, self-interest (let alone more altruistic motives) the market becomes chaotic and incoherent. The rational consumer – figuratively and, perhaps, at times, literally – collapses under the weight of the contradiction between time and volume.

Indeed, we have reached a stage where a rational response to the declining benefits of product accumulation is to turn away from the marketplace altogether, to lessen our involvement with consumer culture and focus on those things – relationships, fitness and health, social and civic participation – that provide meaning and contentment. Consumerism undoubtedly has its pleasures and its benefits, but we have a created a society in which too much emphasis has been put on the dead world of objects, and too little on social and cultural forms that generate both pleasure and purpose but that are independent of the marketplace. The truly rational consumer will, reviewing the evidence, draw back from consumerism.

It is, in this sense, not quite so astonishing that within the developed world the health, happiness and energy of nations has little to do with their per capita GDP. The clamour for economic growth – and the increases in consumerism associated with it – is

understandable because growth provides an easy solution to immediate problems, such as creating jobs and funding public services.
But in the long term it distracts us from comprehending the failure
of growth to improve quality of life and imagining how we might
have – in Tim Jackson's words – prosperity without growth.[8]

The evidentiary basis for imagining a world less dominated by
consumer capitalism is already emerging. Richard Wilkinson and
Kate Picket's review of the data in *The Spirit Level*, for example,
suggest that a key variable in the (non-material) prosperity of
nations is equality, with less equal societies – like Portugal or the
United States – experiencing more crime, poorer physical and
mental health and lower levels of well-being. The principle here –
that once we reach a certain level of wealth, we should focus more
on distribution than growth – would seem particularly apposite
at a time when many governments are finding economic growth
difficult to deliver.

Despite this, there has been a striking failure of political parties
to advance the case made by *The Spirit Level*. For parties on the
right, who are philosophically wedded to individualism and the
primacy of the market, this is less surprising. Indeed, there has
been a predictable backlash against their analysis, much of which
seems motivated by a matter of ideological principle than a serious
attempt to deal with the evidence they present.[9] What is more
striking is the failure of left-leaning political parties – for whom
equality is an abiding principle – to embrace these ideas.

If twenty-first-century consumer capitalism has become economically, socially and environmentally dysfunctional, politics
in most developed countries remains deeply committed to the
primacy of consumerism fuelled by economic growth. This is true
on both the left and the right. It is a conservatism sustained by
a culture that makes it difficult to pursue other possibilities, and
which keeps us tied to the status quo. The political left is so caught
up with the breathless pursuit of growth that it has not, thus far,
stepped back to consider the wider aspects of quality of life.

I have, in this book, focused on three aspects of this cultural
quagmire. First, there is the role of the increasingly ubiquitous
advertising industry, outlined in Part II. At a time when the public
funding of the creative industries has come under increasing attack

(not least from the commercial sector), and where the abundance of goods makes stimulating demand more difficult, the advertising industry now occupies pride of place in our culture. It not only underwrites most forms of entertainment and communication, it clutters up those forms. Our cultural environment has thus become a cacophony of commercial come-ons.

Each advertisement is, on its own terms, fairly innocent. And since so much of our creative energy and talent goes into making them, ads can be witty, engaging, ingenious and spectacular. But once we see them as a cumulative presence, they become implicitly political. The stories they present us with may be many and varied, but they are all, in one form or another, versions of one dominant narrative. Happiness, fulfilment, health, status, popularity and every other measure of well-being, they tell us, comes from only one place, the world of consumption. The negative consequences of that consumption, meanwhile (from the miserable working conditions in which goods may be produced to the environmental consequences of current consumption levels) are entirely absent.

The scale of the advertising industry – its presence is almost everywhere we look – means that we are told this limited story countless times a day. Individually, ads are easy to ignore or dismiss, but their cumulative message – in all its subtle, beguiling forms – is unrelenting. It is a cultural environment skewed towards a particular – and highly contestable – world view. It is hardly surprising if we continue to think in these terms, or that we find it difficult to conceive of alternatives to this particular model of consumer capitalism.

Imagine, for a moment, if we freed the creative talent in the advertising industry from commercial constraints. If advertisers were told, instead, to tell any story they wished. The world would immediately become a very different place, one in which our creative resources were limited only by our imaginations. It is possible that in such a world our society would continue to be just as focused on the acquisition of consumer goods is it is now. But it is, at the very least, more likely to embrace a wider range of ideas about progress and the human condition.

Part III considers a second constraint on our collective imagination: a news and information system built, in part, around the idea of built-in obsolescence. There is a strong democratic impulse behind the production of news, and journalists are part of a long-standing ethos whereby 'democracy and journalistic excellence rise or fall together'.[10] This democratic instinct retains a deep cultural resonance, but it is undermined by the development of news as a commodity. The conflict between commercial pressures to titil-late and entertain and a commitment to reporting public affairs is well known, but there is a more profound sense in which a profit motive has defined part of the essence of news as we now understand it.

As a resource, the public value of news depends upon its sub-stance, the degree to which information extends our understanding of the world at home and abroad. As a commodity, the commer-cial value of news depends upon its transience. The more closely news can be tied to the here and now, the more often it can be sold. The 'newness' of news evolved from being a commercial to a cultural imperative. The role of the journalist as a story-teller was thus constrained by an unrelenting obligation to deliver something new.

Journalism is thereby caught between two conflicting instincts. There is, on the one hand, a democratic desire to provide people with useful information, and on the other, to make information a disposable commodity that is, by definition, as transient (and thus in constant need of updating) as possible. The first of these instincts sees the 'newness' of news as a matter of substance, and is intrinsically open to new ideas and new ways of thinking. The second is only interested in 'newness' as a form, a way of packaging or privileging information that makes it quickly dispensable and which offers us a more banal kind of novelty.

The democratic model of news makes journalism, potentially, a scourge of conventional wisdom. The disposable form of news is focused on simply reproducing itself, on questions that create more stories rather than new ideas. Indeed, this embrace of built-in obsolescence makes it conducive to a consumerist ethic, and poorly placed to challenge the dominant conventional wisdom of our age. It is a form that replicates rather than questions consumerism.

While some news outlets have offered glimpses of new ideas,

it is the second instinct that currently holds sway. The idea that growth is automatically good, for example, is represented as an objective truth rather than an increasingly contested idea. Research on quality of life is given an airing, but is invariably sidelined in discussions about the economy, where growth remains the focus and where increases in consumption are always seen as positive. The challenge posed by climate change is generally sidestepped: solutions to climate change focus on technological fixes – replacing one form of energy with another – rather than the problems caused by over-production and a consumerist economy.

If news were a pioneer in the use of planned obsolescence, the media and communications industries as a whole now epitomize a disposable culture. The previous chapter described how a consumerist ethos has pushed those industries towards an emphasis on product proliferation rather than quality, pushing us, in turn, onto a cycle of replacement for its own sake. We acquire more, but it is not clear that we learn or enjoy more. We are led to the edge of a vast cultural world, and in our confusion most of us retreat to what is familiar.

The considerable environmental costs of this vast turnover of production and disposal are largely hidden from most of us. But just as important is the ideological power of this modus operandi. These industries have championed the idea that this is what progress looks like, that moving forward means reducing the lifespan of objects (which nonetheless linger on, unused, in various stages of toxic decay), and that what matters is less what is delivered than how it is delivered.

Technological innovation can, of course, bring all kinds of benefits, and some of the developments in digital technology have been remarkable. Unfortunately, the current consumerist model of development prioritizes change over benefit: it pushes the notion that what matters above all is investing time and money to keep up. This could result in our being better informed, being exposed to more diverse and fulfilling forms of creativity and culture, and improving our quality of life. Under consumerism, to our collective cost, this idea of progress is not what drives technological change. Change is driven by the profits that come from change.

Creating a new economy

Clearly, any swift abandonment of consumer capitalism is both unrealistic and, because of the disruption it would cause, undesirable. For developed countries to shift their energies away from consumer driven GDP growth (as the principal driver of political and social policy) towards a focus on sustainability and quality of life will require gradual reforms alongside a profound shift in cultural values.

So, for example, without economic growth, efficiency gains in productivity will create unemployment,[11] which will, for many of those out of work, lead to a range of negative outcomes. This is a problem that derives, in part, from a cultural shift which values money over time. Despite the increasing demands upon it, the value of time in our culture has diminished, and in recent decades the length of the working week has become static and inflexible, ending the gradual increase in leisure time that occurred during the greater part of the twentieth century. When we become more efficient, the only way in which we (or our employers) reap the benefits is by increasing our purchasing power.

If we regained our appreciation of the value of free time, we might begin to absorb efficiency gains by decreasing the hours we work – maintaining our incomes but increasing our free time – thereby lowering the risks of creating unemployment. Such an exchange would have the added benefit of being more closely aligned to what we now know about well-being: once we reach a certain level of material comfort, we gain more from increasing our free time than we do by increasing our consumption of consumer goods.

These ideas prompted a report by the New Economics Foundation, which called for a move towards a 21-hour working week.[12] Fifty years ago, the idea of a 21-hour week in the twenty-first century seemed entirely plausible.[13] The fact that it now seems almost unimaginable shows how narrow our thinking has become. The case I have tried to make in this book is that this is partly a response to a culture – where advertising is our dominant creative industry, where obsolescence is built in to every purchase – that repeatedly stresses the value of money and ignores the value of time.

How do we get from here to there? From an economy – and way of life – based on a stagnating consumerism, towards one which sustains genuine social progress? This is no leap in the dark: we have a mounting body of evidence about the conditions that promote quality of life and a sustainable life on earth. Andrew Simms has compiled a body of successful policy initiatives from around the globe – some of it coming from unlikely quarters – that prioritize sustainability and quality of life over economic growth.[14] What is lacking is the political will to understand and act upon this evidence – to think outside the confines of consumer capitalism.

This failure is partly a question of power: consumer capitalism is deeply embedded in our dominant institutions. Our economic, social and environmental structures have been crafted, in part, by demands for profit from global businesses. Changing these conditions does not mean being hostile to business or enterprise, but creating a framework in which this energy is more clearly directed towards desirable social and environmental ends.

Telling different stories

I remember, as a child, many comic book visions of what life would look like in the twenty-first century. Some futuristic landscapes were clean and metallic, others were drawn in vivid technicolor. Most of them anticipated advances in the way we moved people and objects around – with flying cars, rocket-powered speed and all manner of robot-assisted conveniences.[15] But if there has been a revolution in the alacrity and agility of movement, it has been in shifting information and images rather than people.

The fastest plane on the planet was developed in the 1960s and has since been decommissioned. Cars remain steadfastly constrained and we are beginning to see a growth in the use of old-fashioned technologies like the bicycle. The speed and breadth of communication have, by contrast, been transformed. This has taken place in a commercial age, so that the expansion of media and communications has precipitated a growth in the role of advertising in every aspect of our cultural life.

This growth – in both the volume and reach of commercial messages – has been gradual enough for each new incursion to pass without notice. The limits governments impose on the spread of advertising grow weaker by the year. They have been seduced by the quest for growth in the creative and information industries, welcoming new advertising opportunities simply as new sources of revenue. The internet age has exacerbated this trend, as virtual content is more difficult to sell in its own right, making it dependent on advertising to generate income. This dependence has become a feature of our contemporary way of life. In a moment of self-reflection, the journalist George Monbiot put it rather dramatically: 'As with all addictions, the first step is to admit to it.'[16]

This has not been the reaction of most policy makers. There has been a general refusal to deal with advertising as our dominant creative industry in its own right. They have tended to disregard its content (unless it offends notions of public taste and decency or peddles flagrant falsehoods) and allowed it to spread like cultural knotweed across the media and cultural industries.

This reached tragi-comic proportions when BMW's sponsorship of a weather system in Germany – 'the Mini Cooper cold front' – came unstuck. The branded cold weather system went on to claim hundreds of lives across Europe in early 2012.[17] For some, the link between weather systems and the automobile industry might conjure up darker and more plausible associations between some of the world's largest corporations promoting the burning of fossil fuels and the looming catastrophe of climate change ('this drought brought to you by Texaco'). For the advertising industry, this was just another attempt to link every facet of life with the selling of goods.

It is an understatement to say that this is not an environment that encourages us to consider consumer capitalism's limits or imagine alternatives. If we are to create a more inspiring cultural environment, one that stimulates new ideas about progress and the human condition, we need to acknowledge that we devote too much of our creative energy to a limited, repetitive set of stories designed to persuade us that the only way to solve problems and engender happiness and fulfilment is through consumption.

According to Richard Layard, the evidence suggests that we would be better off without advertising, and that governments would do more to improve a nation's well-being by banning it than by spreading it.[18] This is not to deny that some advertising, some of the time, provides useful information (especially at the very local level). But we cannot be serious about promoting sustainability without tackling what amounts to an uncoordinated propaganda campaign for an unsustainable lifestyle wedded to relentless consumerism.

While there have been skirmishes around particular forms of advertising – notably for unhealthy food and drink, especially when targeted at children – the critical response to the way in which advertising has colonized our cultural environment has, thus far, been confined to a few voices well outside the mainstream of public debate. Oddly, this is probably more the case today than it was 30 or even 60 years ago. The growth of advertising has, in this sense, been a triumph for consumerism, making it seem an unavoidable, natural part of life.

There are, however, a few signs that this may be beginning to change. Some NGOs – notably those concerned about the environment – have begun to appreciate the political importance of consumer culture. A World Wildlife Fund report in 2011 called for a systematic debate about the social and environmental impact of advertising.[19] In their Foreword, David Norman and Guy Shrubsole argued that 'the potential impacts of advertising should be of pressing concern to a wide range of third sector organizations – irrespective of whether they are working on poverty, climate change, child deprivation and neglect, abuse of human rights, ecological degradation, physical and mental ill health, or failure to place proper value on non-human life'.[20]

The initiative was welcomed in other parts of civil society who have become increasingly exasperated by our collective failure to address looming environmental crises. Oxfam's Martin Kirk, for example, responded thus:

It is hard to overstate the incredible reach of commercial advertising into our lives today – we are wrapped in it from cradle to grave – and yet we have traditionally paid precious little heed to its influence when looking at how to bring about positive social change.[21]

The report ended with some modest suggestions for reversing the tide and creating more commercial-free space. Most of these suggestions – apart from calling for tighter restrictions on advertising to children (and it is hard to think of a serious argument against such a proposal) tended to shy away from regulatory action. This is understandable: indeed, it is testimony to the power of consumerism that we are so tentative in any attempt to constrain it. But we could be bolder than this.

We might begin by introducing – and in many cases, reintroducing – limits on the volume of advertising on television and radio. Oddly – for such a controversial proposal – there would be few losers in a broadcast system with less advertising. Broadcasters could charge more as scarcity drove up the cost of ad-space, viewers would welcome fewer interruptions, and the ads themselves would be less caught up in the clutter of a superabundance of commercial messages.

Second, we could require products to specify the percentage of product cost that has gone on advertising. This may sound radical, but it makes perfect sense within the logic of market economics, allowing people to make rational decisions about the value of what they are buying. This would, at a stroke, make visible the hidden cost of advertising on the price of goods, while encouraging producers to focus on the quality of the commodity rather than its promotion.

Third, we need to put a value on the cost of producing ad-free entertainment and information, and then find ways to fund it. Even in market terms, advertising has distorted the relationship between the media industries and their audiences. The 'market' for most commercial television, web-based media or 'free' newspapers, for example, is not the people who consume it, since they don't pay for it. The market is the advertisers, the audience is merely the product being bought and sold, and the content primarily a way of bringing the two together. If audiences paid for information and entertainment directly, the focus would be on the quality of the content. It is no coincidence, in this sense, that much of the most acclaimed television produced in the USA comes from pay-per-view channels like HBO.

This will inevitably require extending subsidies for ad-free entertainment and news production. There are ways to do this without the risk of direct governmental interference. We could do worse than rekindling an idea proposed by David Sarnoff, the head of the Radio Corporation of America in the 1920s – a period when, even in the USA, the idea of public service media was seen as both necessary and desirable.[22] This would involve taxing the profits from the commercial media and telecommunications sector to divert to an independently administered – perhaps even democratically elected – public media fund.

The cost of such proposal would not be onerous. The world's largest public service broadcaster, the BBC, has a smaller annual turnover than the UK's largest commercial provider, BSkyB, but provides far more content.[23] It is free from commercial pressure and, with no shareholders, is able to plough most of its revenue back into programming. The cost of not doing so, on the other hand, is to bow down to the idea that creativity must always depend on the promotion of consumerism.

Enduring journalism

One beneficiary of a public media fund would be to sustain independent news production. This is not a new idea: news has long been a staple of public service media, while various forms of indirect subsidy have supported – and continue to support – the newspaper industry.[24] Bob McChesney and John Nichols make the case for extending this subsidy – especially in the face of cutbacks and decline in the commercial sector – arguing that journalism is a public good, a necessary basis for a democratic society.[25] If the market cannot support a high quality, diverse information system, providing news at international, national and local levels, then we need to find another way to do it.

But a precondition of such a subsidy should be to re-examine the purpose of news, and to refocus on its core purpose in a democratic society. In the UK, the Leveson Inquiry into the legality and ethics of tabloid journalism became an unedifying spectacle.[26] Evidence to the Inquiry revealed a gaping divide between idealistic rhetoric about the democratic value of a free press and the practices of a small group of powerful news conglomerates. Some contributors made a strong case that, for some newspapers, a mix of ideologically inflected campaigns and the relentless pursuit of gossip and scandal has a negative democratic value, promoting ill-informed opinions and disengaging people from matters of public policy and debate. So, for example, evidence to the Inquiry showed that British newspaper coverage of Muslims and Islam has been shown to be not only tendentious but misleading.[27]

Julian Petley, in his submission to the Inquiry, argued that: 'we need to consider not only the right of the press to publish but the right of readers to receive the information which they need in order to function effectively as citizens of a democratic society'.[28] It is difficult to disagree with this proposition, but to advance it we need a clear understanding of the confluences and conflicts between a commercial and a democratic definition of news.

Laura Stein lists some of the ways in which a market system fails its audience:

> media markets cannot guarantee the production of diverse and high-quality goods and services aimed at meeting the communication needs of all citizens. In fact, efficient market behaviour systematically favours the interests of advertisers, shareholders, and more valued audience segments over those of the broader populace, including the poor, the very young and old, and racial and ethnic minorities.[29]

To which we might add that commercial media markets also favour the views of proprietors, who tend to be right-leaning and sympathetic to the interest of business owners rather than employees. Witness, for example, two of the best news websites in the world – the *BBC* and the *Guardian*. Both were built on financial systems – public funding or a trust – that gave the news providers freedom from the requirement that the enterprise should make a profit. Similarly, the most successful Arab news service, Al-Jazeera, was made possible by government subsidy.[30] This is not to say that these news agencies are all perfect, simply that their success is testimony to the inadequacy of leaving news to the mercy of a consumer economy.

But more fundamental than this is the extent to which commercial journalism has promoted the idea of news as a disposable commodity. Even in public service institutions, unravelling this is difficult: so many ideas that have become intrinsic to the way modern journalism is practised derive from a consumerist ethos. So, for example, the BBC will report the latest salacious crime story – a classic example of disposable news – as enthusiastically as their commercial counterparts, without any serious thought given to the value of such information. Unless we accept that our a 'disposable news' culture often interferes with or contradicts the aim to inform people, we are bound to an information system that owes more to the culture of commerce than to its democratic mission.

Since the internet has left a gaping hole in the finances of an industry (largely) dependent on advertising,[31] we have two choices. We can give up on good, well-funded journalism that informs the way we understand the world, leaving the job to a few news agencies, all of whom will cut their costs and rely on the rising tidal wave of public relations to provide lots of 'new' stories which provide a positive environment for the selling of goods. The 'free press' will be 'free' to consumers but inextricably tied to the business of consumerism. This is our current direction of travel.

Alternatively, we can appreciate that in a world where anyone can be a journalist, good journalism requires a professionalism and a commitment to *provide information that helps us to understand the world*. This requires journalistic investigation, expertise and research. It also requires more critical self-reflection about how we define news, an appreciation that the production of news as a disposable commodity often works against the core democratic values of journalism.

There is a possible role for universities here.[32] These are institutions that are, after all, fairly independent information producers, many of whom teach journalism. They are well placed to create a new model of local news, and, with support, might begin to fill the gap left by the commercial sector. There is also the potential for new technology to lower capital costs and allow new models of local journalism to develop – models less dependent on a disposable news culture.[33] These alternatives do not negate the case for forms of public subsidy: on the contrary, they suggest mechanisms for channelling it.

Whatever the means, for journalism to fulfil its democratic and investigative purpose – to be able to challenge conventional wisdom and find the space to air new ideas – it must be freed from the need to commodify itself. It must sell itself by being relevant and compelling, and it should measured not by the quantity of stories but by the quality of public debate it engenders. We might then be able to debate the way we live now, and how we might do better.

If it's broke, fix it: Tying innovation to sustainability

In their manifesto for more sustainable creative and communication industries, Richard Maxwell and Toby Miller suggest that the figure at the heart of changing the way we do business is the accountant. In a reflection of consumer capitalism's priorities, the corporate world have, thus far, been successful in ensuring that:

> bureaucratic arrangement limits the scope of environmentally sound production practices in the culture industries, because whatever can't be counted also can't be included in the accountant's impact assessment; for example, material or labor costs outside the production sites overseen by accounting or supply chains that are upstream or downstream of creative productions. Accountants know the price of electricity and phone calls but cannot include an audit of carbon emissions generated by their suppliers in the energy and telecommunications sectors.[34]

We have, in this sense, made accountancy a blinkered enterprise, geared towards maximizing profits for companies and spreading the mounting social and environmental costs to the public sector, charities and voluntary groups. We are, in effect, subsidizing the costs of consumerism. The rising public cost of waste disposal alone constrains the capacity of local government to promote better education or healthcare.[35]

If we asked accountants to take a broader view, they could calculate the full cost of production and consumption. So, for example, the cost involved in the manufacture of a television would include:

- offsetting the environmental damage, sickness and injury caused by the mining and processing of minerals;
- the safe disposal of chemicals involved in its manufacture;
- offsetting the greenhouse gas emissions involved in the sourcing of raw material, manufacturing, advertising and distribution;
- the cost of recycling and disposal of the packaging and other publicity material;
- and, when the TV set is discarded, the cost of the safe recycling and disposal of its many toxic and non-biodegradable components.

Most of these activities, at present, are either temporarily ignored (for future generations to clean up) or subsidized by governments and NGOs. If these costs were taken into account – as they should be – a number of consequences might follow.

The first and most conspicuous of these is, on the surface, a negative one: the cost of consumer goods like TV sets would rise. This, of course, is the main argument for adopting a much narrower form of accountancy. However, an accountant taking a broader view would point out that subsidizing production and consumption simply shifts the costs somewhere else: we may have a cheaper TV set, but we have to pay tax to public agencies to cover the environmental costs. The money saved by ending such subsidies might then be used to make sure that the social consequences of the higher costs of goods are borne equitably. So, for example, we might provide tax relief for those on lower incomes to offset the regressive impact of increasing the cost of goods.

Such a change would also create a series of socially desirable incentives. We would see an emphasis on product durability rather than novelty.[36] Companies would shift towards more sustainable forms of production because it would lower their costs, while consumers would save money by buying goods that were longer lasting, easier to fix and less damaging to produce or dispense with. In sum, environmental responsibility – using less packaging or reducing air or road miles – would be rewarded while profligacy would become costly.

As Elizabeth Grossmann points out, this turns our current model on its head:

> Computers, particularly the increasingly popular mobile notebook computers, are not designed to facilitate upgrades in computing capacity. While some manufacturers will, if pressed, explain how memory can be expanded and hard drive capacity increased with an existing computer, most of these changes require using third-party parts that are not covered by the existing computer's warranties. The cost of these upgrades (including labor) often approaches 50 percent of the cost of a new computer, and if there is no warranty to cover repairs on the upgraded machine, extending the life of an existing computer is further deterred.[37]

One of the businesses made almost obsolete by the subsidy of the production, distribution and consumption cycle is that of replacement and repair. It is, these days, invariably cheaper to dump an electronic device than to fix, modify or upgrade it. In 1992, there were over 20,000 electronic repair shops in the USA. Ten years later, there were less than 9,000, a precipitous decline that continues.[38] If waste management and environmental repair were factored into the true cost of production, fixing and adapting technologies would become viable enterprises again.

Indeed, the new accountants might argue that it would make sense to go further, to shift subsidies away from the manufacture of new goods towards businesses devoted to the maintenance and improvement of goods in use. Such investment would be offset not only by savings in the cost of recycling and waste disposal, but also in making job creation less dependent upon environmentally damaging production processes.

This new form of accountancy would tie ingenuity to

sustainability. Built-in obsolescence would become a more expensive option for both producers and consumers. Innovation and skill would, instead, be directed towards longevity. There would, of course, be moments when technological innovation required the dumping and replacement of electronic hardware, but the cost–benefit analysis that accompanies such transitions would be far more discriminating. At its most sophisticated, this means we would have to be persuaded that improvements to technology would *really* mean improvements in our quality of life.

Thinking beyond consumer capitalism

At the heart of these proposals is a recognition that if we are to imagine other forms of human progress, we must create a more open culture, one that does not continually return us to a tired model of consumer capitalism. As long as we cling to a culture where the dominant forms of cultural production and story-telling are defined by a consumerist ethic, we will find it difficult to think beyond its confines.

Expanding our cultural horizons might be worth doing for its own sake. In this book I have tried to make the case that it is also a precondition for human progress. This means reclaiming freedoms that we risk forgetting about: the freedom to tell stories without the need to promote consumption, the freedom to challenge capitalist orthodoxies and debate new ideas, the freedom to innovate for social rather than commercial gain.

From these freedoms, others may then follow. First among these is to recapture the value of one of the most profound forms of freedom in a wealthy society – the time available to us for the pursuit of happiness and meaning – time that we are increasingly squandering as we surf wave after wave of consumer goods.

Notes

1 Introduction

1 Recalling two very different songs: Lieber and Stoller's 'Is that all there is?', written in the 1960s, and D:Ream's 1994 hit 'Things can only get better' adopted by the British Labour Party in their 1997 campaign after 18 years of Conservative rule. If the second is more optimistic, both songs convey a sense of dissatisfaction, but it is Lieber and Stoller's song – written during a period of unparalleled economic growth – that best captures the contemporary zeitgeist.

2 Most famously within Marxist theory, which sees capitalism travers-ing through various phases with an implicit or explicit end point when it reaches a crisis or becomes unsustainable. The idea of 'late capitalism' – characterized by the move towards globalization since 1945 (see, for example, Ernest Mandel's 1975 book *Late Capitalism*) – expresses this idea of a system in its final throws, although in its more sophisticated forms, such as Frederic Jameson's 1991 book, *Postmodernism, or, The Cultural Logic of Late Capitalism*, the moment of decline or crisis becomes more difficult to define.

3 Aided and abetted by the state and public sector, agencies who have softened or averted moments of systemic collapse – most famously in the 1930s and in the late 2000s.

4 Seabrook (1978).
5 Quoted in Durning (1992).
6 While there has been some discussion of this idea – see, for example, Peter Drucker's 1994 book *Post-Capitalist Society*, which anticipates the move from a material to an information age – they have less currency than other forms of 'post' (such as post-feminism or post-modernism). Many would argue that terms like post-feminism are premature, and that the feminist project has some way to go before achieving equality. The idea that capitalism has little more to achieve in developed countries and we should move beyond it is, I would argue, far more credible yet more obscure.
7 Jackson (2010), p. 22.
8 This is not say that this threat has diminished – on the contrary, the trend towards monopoly or oligopoly continues, a systemic issue examined in detail by John Foster and Robert McChesney in their (2012) book *The Endless Crisis: How Monopoly-Finance Capital Produces Stagnation and Upheaval from the USA to China*, New York: Monthly Review Press.
9 These are Universal, Sony and Warner. All three are globally integrated with a wide range of other media industries.
10 As global corporations grow more powerful, of course, the ability of governments to legislate against them is compromised. It is generally easier for governments to ease the path towards oligopoly, even in an area like media and communications, where this drift has implications for democracy and cultural diversity – see, for example, Ben Bagdikian (2004) and Robert McChesney (1999).
11 Fine (1995), p. 129.
12 This is not to say that rational consumers create rational outcomes. Individual rationality can lead to social irrationality (e.g. over fishing) – see Hirsch (1977).
13 Notably impulse buying, advertising or copying other people.
14 So, for example, research on quality of life does suggest a link between well-being and the affluence of societies – *up to a certain point.*
15 Consumer goods can have what Grant McCracken calls 'evocative power', allowing us to express ideas and ourselves in a complex symbolic world (McCracken, 1990).
16 http://www.hm-treasury.gov.uk/d/CLOSED_SHORT_executive _summary.pdf, p. 3. The phrase 'market failure' is, perhaps,

inappropriate, since the problem of climate change is made more critical by consumer capitalism's success. If there is 'market failure' here, it is systemic.

17 http://webarchive.nationalarchives.gov.uk/+/http:/www.hm-treas ury.gov.uk/sternreview_index.htm

18 There are, of course, poorer people in affluent societies who may be said to have these problems, but this is a function of the way we distribute wealth rather than a lack of resources within a society – see, for example, Wilkinson and Pickett (2010).

19 This is not to say that poverty no longer exists in the developed world. Poverty is, however, not a matter of scarcity of wealth or resources *within* these societies. Put simply, there is enough money to go around: developed countries have a choice about whether to redistribute income to minimize poverty or to maintain inequalities.

20 See, for example, Hilton (2013) and Littler (2009).

21 Humphery (2010). Humphery's book criticizes many anti-consumerism movements for their 'overriding tendency to individuate responsibility' (p. 131).

22 Littler (2009).

23 At the time of writing, the *Guardian* reported 750 Occupy protests around the world: http://www.guardian.co.uk/world/occu py-movement

24 The rather more sinister side of this idea – that of shaping people's imaginations in particular ways – has been explored by Henry Geroux and Grace Pollock in their (2010) book, *The Mouse that Roared: Disney and the End of Innocence.*

25 Jhally (2006).

26 Bagdikian (2004) and McChesney (1999).

27 Lovering (1998).

28 Leyshon (2001).

2 Consumer capitalism as a cul-de-sac

1 Or, to borrow from one of Marx's best-known aphorisms, people make history, but not in conditions of their own making. Marx's understanding of the power of economic systems has been a preoccupation of social theorists ever since, while the relationship between economy and culture (in its broadest sense) continues to be a subject

of interrogation and debate. Indeed, this question defines much of the work of some of the central figures in cultural studies – such as Raymond Williams and Stuart Hall – who have grappled with various theoretical traditions in order to understand the nature of the relationship between economic systems, culture and understanding.

2 The relationship between structures (such as economic systems) and agency (individual or group volition) has been widely debated throughout the social sciences and the humanities. While there has been a degree of parodying on both sides (in which structural analyses, such as those developed by the Frankfurt School, are accused of casting us all as witless dupes), I share with many others the view that we have agency within structural constraints.

3 A point well made by Colin Campbell (1989) in *The Romantic Ethic and the Spirit of Modern Consumerism*.

4 A Google search for the phrases 'capitalist societies' and 'capitalist economies' turns up roughly the same number of hits for each, while the singular 'capitalist society' is twice as popular as the phrase 'capitalist economy'.

5 There is a sprawling literature on the relationship between economics and culture, addressed by literary critics, historians, and by social and political scientists. The trajectory of different disciplinary traditions may differ, but they tend to coalesce around the idea that the relationship works in both directions, can be weak at some moments and strong at others. The social theorist Louis Althusser described this relationship as one of 'relative autonomy' (most famously in the essay 'Ideology and ideological state apparatuses' in his 1971 book *Lenin and Philosophy*), and while there have been many critiques of Althusser's position, the idea of 'relative autonomy' has, albeit in various reworked, redefined forms – such as Stuart Hall, Ernesto Laclau and Chantal Mouffe's reworking of Gramsci's notion of 'articulation' (both a link and a speaking through) – charted ways in which cultural and economic practices influence one another.

6 This debate was reduced still further by the assumption – pushed hard by the pro-capitalist side – that communism or socialism was defined by the totalitarian Soviet system, a notion which many Marxists and democratic socialists worked hard to try to dispel. Yet despite their efforts, the dominant strain of Western thought has

assumed that the collapse of the Soviet empire means that socialism is out-dated, irrelevant and discredited.

7 Fukuyama (1992).

8 Packard (1960), p. 33.

9 To use the utilitarian phrase made famous by writers like Jeremy Bentham – see for example, Troyer (2003).

10 The BBC has its commercial wing, of course, and is not immune to commercial pressures, but it is a good example of an instance where the public can outperform the private sector – see, for example, Cushion (2012), for a wealth of evidence to this effect. It is able to offer far more for the cost than Sky, its main commercial rival in the UK – see Lewis (2010b).

11 Although this is a rather misleading phrase, implying as it does that the 'market failures' are kinks in the system rather than aspects of it.

12 Speaking in May, 1973 in the British House of Commons about the activities of Roland 'Tiny' Rowland, a businessman with an African mining empire, Prime Minister Edward Heath referred to 'the unpleasant and unacceptable face of capitalism'.

13 Developed countries have generally been more sympathetic towards cruder, less regulated forms of capitalism in the developing world, where externalities – such as poverty, poor public health and pollution – are well outside their political constituencies.

14 So, for example, Toby Miller shows how even industries we think of as epitomising a commercial market – like Hollywood – are sustained by various forms of public subsidy – see, for example, Miller (2008).

15 See, for example, Wilkinson and Pickett (2010) and Ruut Veenhoven's 'World happiness database', available at: www2. eur. nl/fsw/research/happiness.

16 A shift charted by cultural historians like Stuart Ewen – see, for example, Ewen (2001). Research suggests that the news media in the USA and the UK tend to portray citizens and citizenship in limited, consumerist terms; see Lewis, Inthorn and Wahl-Jorgensen (2005).

17 As Matthew Hilton has shown, consumer movements have been both progressive as well as reactionary – Hilton (2013), p. 339. He distinguishes between those groups seeking 'value for money at the point of sale' (consumer guides) and those seeking 'an active

relationship with the wider concerns of citizenship' (such as the campaigns for fair trade).

18 The interview appeared in *Woman's Own*, 31 October 1987, pp. 8–10.

19 A point developed in Ernst Schumacher's famous collection of essays: *Small is Beautiful: A Study of Economics as if People Mattered* (1977).

20 In December 2000, data compiled by Sarah Anderson and John Cavanagh for the *Institute for Policy Studies* showed that of the world's 100 largest economic institutions, 51 were businesses.

21 Jackson (2010).

22 A number of economists had pointed out the fragility of the lightly regulated banking system. See, for example, Bezemer (2009) and Berry (2013).

23 Soros (2008).

24 Fukuyama (1992).

25 Lury (2011), pp. 1–3.

26 See also Schor (1999).

27 Edwards (2000).

28 See also Sharon Zukin's 2004 book: *Point of Purchase: How Shopping Changed American Culture.*

29 Alan Durning's (1992) book *How Much is Enough?* was a notable and influential broadside against the emptiness and excess of consumer culture, while Barry Smart's (2010) book *Consumer Society: Critical Issues and Environmental Consequences* provides a more recent critique. See also Shove, Trentmann and Wilk (2009) for a collection of essays on consumerism.

30 Sassatelli (2007).

31 Miller, D. (2001).

32 Perhaps best exemplified by the idea of the 'American Dream', whereby the poorest immigrant can go on to become president or a captain of industry – see, for example, Jhally and Lewis (1992).

3 Environmental, economic and social constraints

1 See, for example, McKibben (2006).

2 Wright (2004). Wright argues that the rapid growth in population, technology and consumption places a huge environmental burden

on contemporary societies that a market-based economic system is poorly equipped to address.

3 Jackson (2010); McKibben (2006).

4 Based on the World Bank Development Indicators at http://www.globalissues.org/issue/235/consumption-and-consumerism

5 Jared Diamond, in his book (2005) *Collapse: How Societies Choose or Fail to Succeed* lists 12 environmental problems facing societies today. Historically, he suggests, environmental problems – such as deforestation, overfishing and the burden of population growth on resources – have played a key role in the social and economic collapse of societies throughout the ages. We now face more environmental problems in the twenty-first century than hitherto, increasing the possibility of collapse. Wright (2004), quoted above, makes a similar argument.

6 So, for example, even optimistic estimates see the planet's accessible oil reserves declining in the next few decades, while some analysts argue we are already past the point of 'peak oil' – see, for example, Owen, Inderwildi and King (2010).

7 Jackson (2010).

8 See, for example, Basel Action Network and Silicon Valley Toxics Coalition (2002); Brugge (2008); Crosby (2007); Gabrys (2007); Kuehr and Williams (2003); Maxwell and Miller (2009); and Williams, E. (2004).

9 Figures from the United Nations Environment Programme at http://www.grida.no/publications/vg/waste/page/2861.aspx

10 World Bank (2012).

11 Maxwell and Miller (2012a).

12 http://www.bbc.co.uk/news/science-environment-1799/1993

13 Figures from the United Nations Environment Programme at http://www.grida.no/publications/vg/waste/page/2865.aspx. See also Maxwell and Miller (2012b) for an account of nature of this toxic trade.

14 Figures from the United Nations Environment Programme at http://www.grida.no/publications/vg/waste/page/2860.aspx

15 Houghton, Jenkins and Ephraums (1990).

16 IPCC (2007), p. 44.

17 According to *Forbes* these are: Exxon Mobil, Shell, Petro-China, Petrobras-Petroleo, BP and Chevron. Two other companies on the

list – GE and Berkshire–Hathaway – have direct interests in these sectors. http://www.forbes.com/global2000/list/

18 See, for example, Holmes (2009).

19 Oreskes and Conway (2010).

20 Jackson (2010), p. 6.

21 Druckman and Jackson (2009).

22 Hansen and Sato (2011).

23 IPCC (2007).

24 Tim Jackson lays out the problems created by economic growth in meeting GHG targets clearly in Jackson (2010).

25 Maxwell and Miller (2012a).

26 As Tim Jackson suggests: 'it is entirely fanciful to suppose that "deep" emission and resource cuts can be achieved without confronting the structure of market economies' (Jackson, 2010, p. 57). See also Fournier (2008).

27 IPCC (2007), p. 44.

28 Ibid., p. 69.

29 Hansen et al. (2008).

30 Harvey (2011).

31 A content analysis by Media Tenor in 2012 suggested that coverage peaked with the publication of the 2007 IPCC report, but has generally declined since then. http://www.mediatenor.com/newsletters.php?id_news=384

32 http://people-press.org/report/584/policy-priorities-2010,   June 2010.

33 http://www.bbc.co.uk/insideout/east/docs/OmClimateChange.pdf, June 2010.

34 Beck (1995, 1999).

35 Lewis and Boyce (2009).

36 See Boyce (2007), on the MMR vaccine scare in the UK, where media scare stories significantly reduced the take-up of the vaccine and reduced immunity levels.

37 McGaurr and Lester (2009) argue that Beck's conception of the media's role in a risk society does not take account of the ways in which some risks are stressed while others are not.

38 IPCC (2007), p. 69.

39 Butler and Pidgeon (2009).

40 *Daily Express*, 6 January 2010.

41 http://www.noaanews.noaa.gov/stories2010/20100715_globalstats. html

42 So, for example, a woman taking part in one audience study suggested that a TV character was probably more typical of female lawyers than those she knew – in part because she saw the television character (Claire Huxtable from the *Cosby Show*) as closer to dominant media representations of women in law. See Press (1991); Jhally and Lewis (1992).

43 Lewis (2001).

44 Anderson (1983).

45 One of the breakthroughs of the digital revolution has been the compression of objects into virtual spaces, giving us the capacity to extend radically the spaces available for cultural objects.

46 Cross (1993), p. 3.

47 A paradox charted by Juliet Schor in her book *The Overworked American: The Unexpected Decline of Leisure*, which argues that unlike most European countries the proportion of leisure time available to people in the USA began to decline towards the end of the twentieth century, as capitalism pushed people towards maximizing their ability to buy consumer goods rather than enjoy their free time.

48 'The Tyranny of Choice' *The Economist*, 16 December 2010 http:// www.economist.com/node/17723028

49 In *The Challenge of Affluence* (2006) Avner Offer discusses the idea of rational consumer choice in some detail, and suggests that, despite attempts to rescue the idea, the sheer volume of choice has made this idea a fiction.

50 Giles (1993).

51 Stephen and Gina Antzcak's book *Cosmetics Unmasked* (2001) provides a useful analysis of the content of cosmetic products and what these ingredients do.

52 This survey was conducted by researcher Louise Sutton at Tescos in Cardiff under my supervision.

53 Linder (1970).

54 Iyengar and Lepper (2000).

55 Schwartz (2004).

56 Princen (2002) distinguishes between over-consumption and mis-consumption. The former on an individual level, or even a short-term collective level, may reflect self-interest. The latter occurs

when consumption is not in our self-interest (such as eating too much junk food).

57 Offer (2006).

58 Iyengar and Lepper (2000).

59 BBC Radio 5 Live Breakfast, 16 April 2010.

60 Franco et al. (2007).

61 Political scientists have for some time charted the extent to which citizens remain uninformed about politics and public affairs: see for example, Lewis (2001).

62 Quoted from a report by BBC's *Watchdog* consumer affairs programme on 20 October 2011 at: http://www.bbc.co.uk/blogs/watchdog/2011/10/energy_switching.html

63 See, for example, http://www.fairtrade.org.uk/what_is_fairtrade/facts_and_figures.aspx

64 Klein, N. (2000) *No Logo*, New York: Picador

65 http://fairtradeusa.org/sites/default/files/Almanac%202011.pdf

66 Mohan (2010).

67 Jackson (2010), p. 10.

68 Victor (2008).

69 An example of the crudity of assuming GDP is positive would be a case of two commuters: the first walks or cycles to work; the second drives. The first person arrives at work without incident, refreshed and invigorated by modest exercise. The second gets stuck in traffic and then has an accident on the way, involving a minor collision with another motorist. Both cars require minor repairs. While this clearly adds little to the quality of the journey, it creates a flurry of economic activity. The first journey is much more efficient and enjoyable, but it is the second that has a positive impact on GDP.

70 See, for example, Anderson (1991).

71 Notwithstanding the symbolic value we attach to goods, which is partly a product of the work of advertising, explored in the next section. The key point here is that there are other ways of extending our social and symbolic experiences that do not depend on the acquisition of commodities.

72 Paul Wachtel's (1983) book *The Poverty of Affluence – A Psychological Portrait of the American Way of Life* is one the earlier critiques of the ecological and well-being consequences of consumerism, while Alan Durning (1992) points out that although the world has consumed

as many goods and service since 1950 as all the previous generation put together, Americans are no happier now than they were in the 1950s.

73 James (2007).

74 Humphery (2010).

75 Available at: http://worlddatabaseofhappiness.eur.nl/

76 Inglehart, Ronald and Klingemann (2000); Layard (2003, 2011); Bok (2010); Wilkinson and Pickett (2010).

77 Wilkinson and Pickett (2010).

78 Bok (2010).

79 Layard (2003, 2011). We should be careful about the word 'happiness' here: happiness is an important aspect of human experience, but it is only part of what constitutes quality of life. Fulfilment is not the same as happiness, but is a highly valued part of human experience. Since the data refers to a much broader set of human emotions and experience, we can substitute Layard's use of the word 'happiness' with 'quality of life'.

80 Jackson (2006), p. 9.

81 Oswald (2003).

82 Layard (2003, 2011).

83 James (2007).

84 Argyle (1987) provides evidence that points to the importance of social relations over material wealth.

85 Kahnerman et al. (2004), p. 429.

86 Coote, Simms and Franklin (2010).

87 Linder (1970).

88 Bok (2010).

89 Frey and Stutzer (2001).

90 Kasser (2002).

91 Schor (2004), p. 167.

92 Wilkinson and Pickett (2010).

4 The insatiable age

1 So, for example, a well researched documentary series for PBS in the USA described the early years of the twentieth century the 'Age of Hope'. It featured remarkable interviews with people alive during this period who conveyed a deep sense of optimism and possibility.

http://www.pbs.org/wgbh/peoplescentury/episodes/ageofhope/description.html.

2 Budd, Craig and Steinman (2004), p. 7.

3 Campbell (1989), p. 37.

4 Ibid.

5 Bradshaw (1927), p. 492.

6 Ewen (2001), pp. 178–9.

7 Ibid., p. 179.

8 Strasser (2009), pp. 32–3.

9 Phelps (1929), p. 251.

10 Morgan (2002). Gerbner was writing not just about advertising but about commercial media in general.

11 A process vividly documented by Stuart Ewen (2001).

12 Veblen (1994).

13 Brierley (2002), p. 7.

14 Marcuse (1964).

15 Galbraith (1958), p. 153.

16 Goldthorpe (1963). Even though access to consumer goods has increased since then, it is hard to imagine the term 'affluent' being used in these contexts today.

17 Packard (1960), p. 21. This sentiment contradicted a position he adopted in his 1957 book, *The Hidden Persuaders*, which suggested that (honest, overt) advertising played a vital role in the creation of economic growth.

18 Strasser (2009), p. 35.

19 Cross (1993).

20 Hunnicutt (1984).

21 By the Independent Commission on International Development Issues, chaired by former Chancellor of West Germany, Willy Brandt.

22 See, for example, Quilligan (2002).

23 Brierley (2002), p. 7.

24 Budd, Craig and Steinman (2004). There are other figures for advertising spend during this period which vary a little, but which nonetheless show a similar rate of increase – see Smart (2010).

25 Ewen (2001), pp. 40–1.

26 Ibid., pp. 22–3.

27 Galbraith (1958), p. 153.

28 Ibid., p. 24.

29 Packard (1957).
30 As Colin Campbell points out, traditional economics lacks any psychological or anthropological depth, and is thus ill-equipped to investigate why people buy things or to what end – see Campbell (1989).
31 Goldthorpe (1963).
32 Alexander, Crompton and Shrubsole (2011).
33 Berger (2004), p. 1.
34 Jung and Seldon (1995).
35 Molinari and Turino (2009).
36 Law (1994), p. 28.
37 In 2010 over 70% of global spending on advertising was in Western Europe and North America; see 'Mobile Shines Amid Rising Digital Ad Spending' *eMarketer Digital Intelligence*, 13 October 2011. http://www.emarketer.com/Article.aspx?R=1008639
38 A figure of $32.6 billion – Verrier (2012).
39 Smart (2010), p. 74.
40 Ewen (2001), p. 1.
41 Although the dynamism of the industry during that period was pioneered by smaller, independent record labels whose motivations were often cultural (the love of certain kinds of music) rather than commercial (making money was not their primary goal).
42 Curran and Seaton (1997); Williams, K. (1998).
43 Fabos (2004).
44 R. L. Rutsky describes the counter culture around the early days of the digital age, whose technologies were seen as 'inherently liberating . . . because of their ability to decentralize or disperse information' (Rutsky, 2005), p. 63.
45 See, for example, Tracey (1998); Rowland and Tracey (1990).
46 Lewis (2010a).
47 *UK Marketing News*, http://www.ukmarketingnews.com/uk-consumers-watch-48-ads-and-four-hours-of-tv-a-day/ viewed December 2010.
48 According to TNS Media Intelligence, http://www.marketingcharts.com/television/average-hour-long-show-is-36-commercials-9002/
49 The *Sunday Herald Sun*, http://www.news.com.au/national/tv-stations-exceeded-prescribed-limits-with-ads/story-e6frfkx0-122579 5498281

50 Credos, Credos Forum: Monitoring Public Opinion of Advertising, May 2011, pp. 16–19.

51 Smythe (1980). This idea has been developed by Leiss, Kilne and Jhally (1986) and Jhally (1990).

52 See Miller and Kim (2008).

53 Wernick (1991).

54 See blogs.guardian.co.uk/organgrinder/2006/07/itvs_summer_of_doom_1.html – 56k (26 April 2007).

55 Gilens and Hertzman (2000).

56 A survey for the Press Complaints Commission found that 54% knew little about or had never heard of the PCC, and 58% knew little about or had never heard of Ofcom. Less than one in five knew more than 'just a little' about either (www.pcc.org.uk/news, May 2007).

57 Miller, T. (2009).

58 See Galician (2004); Jacobson and Mazur (1995); Kretchmer (2004); Wasko, Phillips and Purdie (1993).

59 http://www.mediaawareness.ca/english/resources/educational/teachable_moments/word_from_our_sponsor.cfm, December 2010.

60 *Behind the Screens: Hollywood goes* Hypercommercia, Media Education Foundation, Northampton Massachusetts, 2000.

61 *Money for Nothing: Behind the Business of Pop Music*, Media Education Foundation, Northampton Massachusetts, 2001.

62 Klein (2009).

63 In their (2012) book *Misunderstanding the Internet*, James Curran, Natalie Fenton and Des Freedman provide a much needed corrective to the common tendency to assume that all that matters about the internet is the possibility of the technology. The internet, they argue, is a product of the commercial conditions that have shaped it.

64 Rutsky (2005), p. 67.

65 There are some exceptions here. Niche products (like the *Financial Times*) that appeal to wealthy consumers are able to charge online subscriptions. But it is not at all clear that, with so much available for nothing, people will be willing to pay as much for information or culture as they were before the online age.

66 Moreover, as Robert McChesney points out, the online world has drifted toward monopoly provision with remarkable speed, with over 90% of the operating systems (Microsoft) and 97% of the mobile

search market (Google) owned by single companies (McChesney, 2013).

67 Monbiot (2011).

68 This emerged as a key point of contention at the Community Journalism conference in at Cardiff University (15 January 2013).

5 Tales of sales

1 See Lewis (2010a).

2 By contrast Gwyneth Lewis's poetic lines carved through solid slate on the side of the Wales Millennium Centre – 'In these stones horizons sing' – challenge us to imagine creativity without such constraint.

3 Brennan (2001).

4 Budd, Craig and Steinman (2004), p. 6.

5 Offer (2006), pp. 122–5.

6 McAllister (2003).

7 McChesney (1989).

8 According to a study by the *Wall Street Journal*, the average broadcast time for an American football game is three hours, while the ball is in open play for an average of just 11 minutes. Biderman (2010).

9 Football has, of course, thrived in countries with commercial television. What makes the USA an especially difficult climate for football – or soccer – is that advertising has dominated US broadcasting since the 1920s, allowing American football to be transformed from an elite college game (like Rugby in England) to a mass sport tailored to broadcasters' requirements – see McChesney (1989).

10 Williamson (1995); Kilbourne (2000).

11 Raymond Williams' idea that the central experience of watching television is one of programmes and commercials *flowing* into one another is still germane (Williams, R., 1974). Audience research now incorporates people's viewing of programmes they record (described as consolidated viewing figures by the BARB in the UK and as Time Shift Viewing by Nielsen in the USA). This suggests that despite the widespread availability of technology which makes it easier to construct ones own menu, the great majority of people still watch television in real time (http://www.tamireland.ie/time-shifted-viewing-tsv-effect-on-viewing.html)

12 See Humphery (2010) for a detailed analysis of the contemporary politics of anti-consumerism.

13 Azcuenaga (1997).

14 Ibid.

15 Ibid.

16 See, for example, US Department of Health and Human Services, National Cancer Institute, 'The role of the media in promoting and reducing tobacco use', NCI Tobacco Control Monograph Series No. 19, 2008, Available at: http://cancercontrol.cancer.gov/tcrb/monographs/19/m19_complete.pdf.

17 An Australian study, for example, found that 66% of commercial during popular children's programmes were for high-fat, high-sugar foods – see Kelly et al. (2007).

18 Packard (1957).

19 A point made by critics for some time – see, for example, Mander (1977), pp. 126–7.

20 Berger (2004), p. 32.

21 Schudson (1986), p. 210, critiqued in Ewen (2001).

22 Nava (1997), p. 40.

23 Postman (1985). Part of the problem with Postman's critique is that much of it applies to American-style *commercial* television rather than television per se.

24 See for example, Ellis (1992).

25 O'Donohoe (1997).

26 Much of the research on media influence has become bogged down in a debate between those who stress an individual's capacity for making meanings and those who focus on media's power to influence. The great weight of research suggests that while we may be active consumers of media, capable of creative or critical responses, media does provide us with an informational climate which influences our understanding. See Lewis (2001, 2008).

27 Livingstone (2006); Story, Neumark-Sztainer and French (2002).

28 Magnus et al. (2009).

29 Hawkes (2007).

30 Livingstone and Helsper (2006). Their review of 60 studies found that 41 indicated clear effects, 13 mixed effects and 6 no impact. Interestingly, 5 of the 6 studies that found no impact were for children in the 2-6 age bracket. As the authors suggest, this does not

necessarily mean that young children are (counter-intuitively) less susceptible to the influence of advertising, since this is an age group where measuring impact is methodologically challenging.

31 Lewis and Jhally (1998).

32 See, for example, http://stakeholders.ofcom.org.uk/binaries/resear ch/media-literacy/media-literacy-bulletin/mlb-issue-41.pdf

33 In the UK, broadcast advertising is regulated by the Television and Radio Advertising Standards Code, which prohibits advertising on behalf of political bodies for political ends (unless it is part of an agreed quota for political parties).

34 Tim Edwards observes that 'consumerism as an ethos and a practice is expanding in importance at a near exponential rate to incorporate everything from health and insurance to education and recreation' – Edwards (2000), p. 188.

35 Williamson (1995).

36 Edwards (2000), p. 189.

37 Ibid., p.191.

38 Layard (2011).

39 Jhally (2006).

40 Berger (1972), p. 132.

41 Jhally (1990).

42 Frey and Stutzer (2001).

43 http://www.youtube.com/watch?v=FuBPw5lvnM8

44 http://www.youtube.com/watch?v=o72M-Z6qhJg

45 http://www.youtube.com/watch?v=NyH2eW9SfmU

46 http://www.youtube.com/watch?v=zO9GUdpRodQ

47 http://www.youtube.com/watch?v=MzveOdha0zk&feature=related

48 http://www.youtube.com/watch?v=Oom7ZAHpFXY

49 Chaney (1983).

50 Hastings et al. (2010).

51 Colin Campbell, for example, argues that the emotions people attach to objects are just as real as the objects themselves; Campbell (1989), p. 48.

52 Offer (2006), p. 104.

53 Iyengar and Lepper (2000).

54 Mander (1977), p. 128.

55 Wernick (1991), p. 192.

56 Leiss, Kline and Jhally (1986), p. 16.

57 Kasser (2002), p. 167.
58 Linder (1970).
59 Economic History Association: http://eh.net/encyclopedia/article/whaples.work.hours.us
60 Fogel (2000).
61 Schor (1991).
62 The Directive was eventually introduced in the UK on 1 August 2009.
63 Coote, Simms and Franklin (2010).
64 Wilkinson and Pickett (2010).
65 Bok (2010), p. 29.
66 Kahnerman et al. (2004) p. 429.
67 Bok (2010), p. 30.
68 Cowling and Poolsombat (2007).
69 Schor (1991).
70 Fraser and Paton (2003).
71 Jackson (2010).
72 Wilkinson and Pickett (2010).
73 Williams, R. (1993), p. 421.
74 Layard (2003).

6 Disposable news and democracy

1 Although research suggests that people are more likely to be represented as passive consumers than as active citizens – see Lewis, Inthorn and Wahl-Jorgensen (2005).
2 See, for example, Soley and Craig (1992), p. 1.
3 See Lewis, Williams and Franklin (2008).
4 See Hardy (2010), pp. 104–5.
5 See, for example, Herman and Chomsky (1988); Franklin (1997); Kellner (1990); Bagdikian (2004); Entman (2004).
6 Research suggests that in the UK, there are roughly the same number of print journalists as there were 20 years ago, but they produce three time as much copy. See Lewis, Williams and Franklin (2008); Davies (2008).
7 They note the ways in which this has been acknowledged by various forms of public subsidy, and suggest extending these to promote public interest journalism – McChesney and Nichols (2010).

8 Daniel Hallin discusses these conflicting pressures in Hallin (2000).

9 http://www.ipsos-mori.com/Assets/Docs/Polls/Veracity2011.pdf
This is far lower than most other professions: teachers, doctors, professors, judges and clergymen all tend to be trusted by 70% to 90% of the those surveyed.

10 http://www.gallup.com/poll/145043/nurses-top-honesty-ethics-list-11-year.aspx

11 http://www.levesoninquiry.org.uk/

12 Jackson (2010), p. 22.

13 Research into news production and news routines has long established the way in which news routines are linked to elite agendas, beginning with classic newsroom studies such as Tuchman (1978); Schlesinger (1978); Gans (1979); and Born (2005).

14 First released in 1987, the song's first verse runs:

> The higher you build your barriers
> The taller I become
> The farther you take my rights away
> The faster I will run
> You can deny me
> You can decide to turn your face away
> No matter, cos there's . . .
> Something inside so strong.

15 *The War on Democracy* in 2007, about US foreign policy in Latin America.

16 Franklin (1997)

17 McManus (2009), p. 218.

18 Hutchins, R. and the Commission on Freedom of the Press (1947), p. 57.

19 McManus (2009) p. 219.

20 There is a sociological literature on the nature of news – beginning with Galtung and Ruge (1973), and developed by Harcup and O'Neill (2001) and Brighton and Foy (2007). These accounts – indirectly – show how news values encompass both civic and commercial imperatives.

21 See, for example, Charity (1995).

22 As Colin Sparks points out: Newspapers in Britain are first and foremost businesses. 'They do not exist . . . to act as watchdogs for the public, to be a check on the doings of government, to defend the

ordinary citizen against abuses of power, to unearth scandals or to do any of the other fine and noble things that are sometimes claimed for the press. They exist to make money, just as any other business does. To the extent that they discharge any of their public functions, they do so in order to succeed as businesses.' Sparks (1999), p. 46.

23 Rantanen (2009).

24 Lewis (2010c).

25 *Chicago Tribune*, 1916.

26 McNair (2000).

27 Thompson (1968).

28 *Poor Man's Guardian*, 19 October 1833.

29 Allan (2000).

30 Allan (2000), p. 13.

31 Stamp duty was repealed two years later, and paper duty in 1861.

32 Curran and Seaton (1997), p. 20.

33 Curran and Seaton (1997).

34 Ibid., p. 9.

35 Tom Streeter (1996) discusses the complex relationship between ideas of public and private ownership in the history of broadcasting in *Selling the Air: A Critique of the Policy of Commercial Broadcasting in the United States*.

36 Kaplan (2010).

37 Cushion and Lewis (2009).

38 Barnhurst and Nerone (2001).

39 Rantanen (2009).

40 Victor Liebow quoted in Packard (1960), p. 33.

41 Perhaps most famously, John Birt and Peter Jay (1975) wrote a series of articles in *The Times* in the 1970s about journalism's mission to explain.

42 Lewis, Cushion and Thomas (2005).

43 Cushion (2010).

44 Lewis and Cushion (2009).

45 Lambert (2002), p. 14

46 Lewis and Cushion (2009).

47 Ibid.

48 We were commissioned by the BBC to conduct a series of reports into the twenty-four news service offered by the BBC and its rivals. Our reports repeatedly demonstrated the limits of 'breaking news',

and yet reporters at the channels found it difficult to avoid embracing it. When forced to announce cutbacks in 2011, the BBC's mission for the channel was to 'focus on core and breaking news, with less money spent elsewhere. More repeats, less spent on reporting areas such as arts, culture and science.' http://www.bbc.co.uk/news/entertainment-arts-15186116.

49 Reardon (2013).
50 Boorstin (1977).
51 Livingston and Bennett (2003).
52 Lewis, Cushion and Thomas (2005).
53 Lewis and Cushion (2009).

7 *Disposable news, consumerism and growth*

1   Iyengar (1991).
2   Harrison (2006).
3   Williams, K. (1998).
4   Franklin (1997).
5   Allan (2000), p. 13.
6   Barnhurst and Nerone (2001) .
7   Lewis and Cushion (2009).
8   Reiner, Livingstone and Allen (2003).
9   Apart from very local news in areas where crime is low, and where the dramatic threshold is considerably lower.
10 *Independent*, 9 May 2007.
11 Jewell (2008).
12 Lewis (2008).
13 Because it not subject to changes in police operations, the British Crime Survey is widely regarded as the most reliable indicator of crime trends.
14 Rajan (2009).
15 Lewis and Cushion (2009).
16 Davies (2008).
17 Packard (1960), p. 20.
18 Galbraith (1958), p. 127.
19 BBC News 25 November 2010 at http://www.bbc.co.uk/news/uk-11833241
20 Wilkinson and Pickett (2010) and Ruut Veenhoven's 'World

happiness database', available at: www2. eur.nl/fsw/research/happiness.

21 Research by Maxwell Boykoff and Maria Mansfield suggests that global media coverage of climate changed peaked in late 2009/10, and has since declined. Indeed, by late early 2012 coverage had declined to 2005 levels. http://sciencepolicy.colorado.edu/media_coverage/ It is also worth noting that much recent coverage about climate change has focused on 'controversies' casting doubt on the scientific consensus.

22 *Washington Post*, 29 May 1999.

23 As Soroka and Wlezien (2002) point out, 'as a public priority, defense spending is pervasively unpopular. Indeed, with the exception of the first 2 years of the Reagan administration, we know of no surveys in Europe or the United States in which defense spending is not substantially less popular than spending on health, education, and social security', p. 401.

24 Lewis and Hunt (2011).

25 The Stockholm International Peace Research Institute (one of the most authoritative sources on global military expenditure, used by the UK Ministry of Defence to provide comparative figures) calculated in its *2009 Yearbook* that the UK now spends more than Russia, being third equal (with France) on the list of military spenders, behind only the United States and China, with the UK the second highest per capita spender of the major military powers (www.sipri.org). According to SIPRI's figures, the USA spend around as much as the next twenty largest military powers (most of them allies) combined, while UK military budget rose by 75% between 1997 and 2009. Most other European countries saw much smaller increases – Germany's military budget, for example, rose by 12% over the same period.

26 Glasgow Media Group (1976, 1980, 1982).

27 So, for example, research by Cardiff University for the BBC Trust found that between 2007 and 2012 the voice of trade unions on a number of key issues in BBC news outlets had gone from minimal to non-existent.

28 Roush (2006).

29 See Merrill (2013).

30 Svennevig (2007).

31 Anderson and Cavanagh (2000).

32 Svennevig (2007), p. 5.

33 BBC Trust (2007), pp. 15–16.

34 Ibid., p. 19.

35 Brecher and Costello (1994).

36 Merrill (2013), p. 70.

37 Berry (2013). See also Schechter (2009).

38 Svennevig (2007).

39 Doyle (2006).

40 Tambini (2010).

41 Doyle (2006), p. 447. See also Fahy, O'Brien and Poti (2010).

42 For a fuller account of this study see Lewis and Thomas (2013).

43 From 29 September 2010 to 20 July 2011.

44 These were the *Chicago Tribune*, the *LA Times*, the *New York Times* and the *Washington Post* in the USA and the *Guardian*, *Independent*, *Telegraph* and *The Times* in the UK.

45 *Guardian*, 29 June 2011.

46 *New York Times*, 20 May 2011.

47 *Daily Telegraph*, 24 November 2010.

48 *Washington Post*, 29 April 2011.

49 *The Times*, 24 March 2011.

50 Lewis and Hunt (2011).

51 *The Times*, 21 June 2011.

52 *The Times*, 17 May 2011.

53 Lewis and Boyce (2009).

54 Jackson (2010).

55 On 9 February 2011.

56 We did find a series of three article in the *Independent* that featured NEF sources just outside our sample period (in September 2010), but no other newspapers picked up the story.

57 *New York Times*, 31 July 2011.

58 See, for example, McChesney and Nichols (2010).

59 Wright (2004), p. 131.

8 *Obsessed with obsolescence*

1 Maghiros (2009).

2 VSS Historical Database, available at www.vss.com/historical09

3   'Global consumer tech device spending to surpass $1 trillion in 2012', *Business Wire*. www.businesswire.com/news/home/201201080050 73/en/Global-Consumer-Tech-Device-Spending-Surpass-1.

4   VSS Historical Database, available at www.vss.com/historical09.

5   Doyle (2009).

6   http://www.gartner.com/it/page.jsp?id=503867

7   Maxwell and Miller (2012b), ch. 1.

8   Lipovetsky (1994), p. 134.

9   Wark (1991).

10   Grossman (2010), p. 7.

11   Schor (2010).

12   Taussig (1993), p. 232.

13   Maxwell and Miller (2009).

14   Crosby (2007); Mooallem (2008). Mooallem makes the point that most phones are retired because of psychological, not technological, obsolescence, highlighting the importance of promotional and advertising strategies in the process.

15   Sterne (2007), p. 7.

16   See, for example, http://electronics.howstuffworks.com/question 487.htm

17   See, for example, http://downlode.org/Etext/negativland_shiny. html

18   Reported by the *Guardian* at http://www.guardian.co.uk/music/ musicblog/2009/dec/02/vinyl-frontier-record-sales

19   Greenburg (2011).

20   Wasko and Sirois (2011).

21   Although the poor sound quality of downloads leaves a great of room for future upgrades.

22   See Hargreaves (2011).

23   As Kembrew McLeod has documented, the question of property ownership is often morally questionable, as large corporations police the use of music whose origins and derivation is quite independent of them, while limiting new forms of creativity – see McLeod (2001, 2005).

24   Walker (2009).

25   Maxwell and Miller (2009).

26   Brugge (2008).

27   Maxwell and Miller (2012), ch. 1.

28 Ibid.
29 Thompson (1979).
30 Hawkins (2003).
31 Strasser (1999).
32 http://www.dosomething.org/tipsandtools/11-facts-about-e-waste,
     June 2010.
33 Sterne (2007), p. 10.
34 Maxwell and Miller (2009).
35 Grossman (2010), p. 2.
36 Grossman (2010), p. 8.
37 Grossman (2010).
38 Gabrys (2007).
39 Basel Action Network and Silicon Valley Toxics Coalition (2002).
40 Maxwell and Miller (2012), ch. 5.
41 Grossman (2010), p. 17.
42 Williams, E. (2004).
43 Kuehr and Williams (2003).
44 Gabrys (2007), p. 1.
45 Quoted in Packard (1960), p. 33.
46 Straw (2000).
47 Carey (2005), p. 445.
48 From 1952 to 1966.
49 http://www.bbc.co.uk/blogs/thearchers/2011/05/record_listening_
     figures_for_t.html
50 Walker (2009).
51 Curran (2010).
52 Department for Culture, Media and Sport Department for Trade and
     Industry (2005) *Regulatory and Environmental Impact Assessment: the
     timing of digital switchover*, p. 28. Available at http://www.digitaltel-
     evision.gov.uk/pdf_documents/consultations/ria_timingof_ds2.pdf.
     Their calculations were based on very limited and optimistic assump-
     tions about the use of new technology the switch would generate,
     focusing only on the take-up on set-top boxes, and underestimating
     the stimulus it would give to the consumption of less energy efficient
     TV screens.
53 Initially proposed for 2015, but put on the back-burner mainly due
     to the lack of consumer demand.
54 Vallely (2010).

55 The three most popular stations in the UK are BBC Radio 1, Radio 2 and Radio 4.

56 Ofcom's Communication Market Report found 94% satisfaction among radio listeners with the radio content they receive. Ofcom's Digital Radio Report found that a total of 93% of respondents said that they would not acquire a digital radio because there was 'no need' – see http://www.which.co.uk/documents/pdf/digital-radio-switch-over-which-briefing-252743.pdf

57 Pauwels (1999); Tracey (1998).

58 For whom public service requirements put them at a competitive disadvantage.

59 Linder (1970).

60 The success of music video as a TV format relies upon its commercial function – since the videos are, in effect, advertisements for the music, they are supplied to channels at little or no cost.

61 Lewis (2010b).

62 Maghiros (2009), p. 47.

63 See, for example, Scannell (1996).

64 http://www.economist.com/node/17723028

65 Offer (2006).

66 As detailed in Chapter 3, most studies show that the period encompassed by the digital revolution in developed countries over the last two decades has not been accompanied by an increase in well-being or quality of life.

67 Quoted in *BusinessWeek*, 12 May 1998 at http://www.businessweek.com/bwdaily/dnflash/may1998/nf80512d.htm

68 Ouellette and Lewis (2000).

69   People might say that I should strive for more,
      But I'm so happy I can't see the point . . .
      And the public wants what the public gets
      But I don't get what this society wants.

                  From 'Going Underground' by the Jam

70 This was one of series of seminars bringing together senior staff at the Welsh government and Cardiff University, held on 19 October 2011.

71 See, for example, Helliwell, Layard and Sachs (2012).

72 Maxwell and Miller (2012).

73 Quoted in Packard (1960), p. 33.

9 Imagining a different world

1 So, for example, while both Wilkinson and Pickett and Tim Jackson focus on the flaws in consumer capitalism, they acknowledge that there is, up to a certain point, a correlation between economic growth and well-being.

2 See, for example, the report by The Royal Society (2009).

3 So, for example, a *Daily Mail* front-page headline on 24 November 2011, blared out: GREEN 'TAX' TO RISE EVERY YEAR, displaying a vigilance about the threat of tax increases alongside a disregard for the problem of climate change.

4 Released in 2009 by Banner Films.

5 This issue – the urgency of tackling climate change and our relaxed attitude towards it – is dealt with more directly by the Irish documentary, *A Burning Question* (distributed by the Media Education Foundation).

6 According to Wilkinson and Pickett, an average medium income of about $20,000 a year.

7 Assuming the value of money is constant, when asked to choose between a world in which we earn $40,000 where average incomes are $50,000, or one where we earn $30,000 and average incomes are $20,000, most of us opt for the latter.

8 Jackson (2010).

9 Wilkinson and Pickett discuss this point in the 2010 edition of the book, in which they address the issues raised by their critics, and point out the keen ideological inflections behind much of the criticism.

10 Scheuer (2008), p. xii.

11 Discussed in detail by Jackson (2010).

12 Coote, Simms and Franklin (2010).

13 Indeed, as discussed in Part II, economists imagined an even greater reduction, in line with trends established in the first half of the twentieth century.

14 Simms (2013).

15 This began to change in the 1980s, when more dystopian visions began to appear. Channel Four's *Max Headroom* depicted a world in which a TV company, desperate for an edge in the competition for ad revenue, creates 'blipverts' which condense 30-second spots

into three seconds. The blipverts had the unfortunate side effect of causing certain more obese viewers to spontaneously combust.

16 Monbiot (2011).
17 Reported in the *Independent*, 2 February 2012 thus: 'It's a Mini disaster! BMW sponsors deadly cold front: Car firm pays to name weather system after new model – then sees it kill scores across Europe'. http://www.independent.co.uk/news/world/europe/its-a-mini-dis aster-bmw-sponsors-deadly-cold-front-6298210.html
18 Layard (2003, 2011).
19 Alexander, Crompton and Shrubsole (2011).
20 Ibid., p. 7.
21 Ibid., p. 4.
22 Douglas (1987).
23 Lewis (2010b).
24 McChesney and Nichols (2010).
25 Ibid.
26 http://www.levesoninquiry.org.uk/
27 Lewis, Mason and Moore (2009).
28 http://www.levesoninquiry.org.uk/wp-content/uploads/2011/12/ Witness-Statement-of-Professor-Julian-Petley1.pdf
29 Stein (2006).
30 Sakr (2005).
31 Franklin (2011).
32 See, for example, New York University's collaboration with the *New York Times* at http://nyulocal.com/on-campus/2010/09/13/ nyu-nytimes-launch-hyper-local-news-blog-for-east-village/. In the UK, the Centre for Community Journalism at Cardiff University is different type of initiative to develop a new hyper-local news sector.
33 Mair, Fowler and Reeves (2012).
34 Maxwell and Miller (2012).
35 As outlined in Chapter 3 – figures from the United Nations Environment Programme at http://www.grida.no/publications/vg/ waste/page/2861.aspx and World Bank (2012).
36 Schor (1998).
37 Grossmann (2010) p. 13.
38 *USA Today*, 14 January 2004. http://www.usatoday.com/tech/ news/2004-01-14-electronic-repairs_x.htm

References

Azcuenaga, M. (1997) *The Role of Advertising and Advertising Regulation In the Free Market*, Federal Trade Commission, at http://www.ftc.gov/speeches/azcuenaga/turkey97.shtm

Alexander, J., Crompton, T. and Shrubsole, G. (2011) *Think Of Me As Evil? Opening The Ethical Debates In Advertising*, Public Interest Research Centre and WWF-UK at http://valuesandframes.org/download/reports/Think%20Of%20Me%20As%20Evil%20-%20PIRC-WWF%20Oct%202011.pdf

Allan, S. (2000) *News Culture*, Milton Keynes: Open University Press

Althusser, L. (1971) 'Ideology and ideological state apparatuses' in *Lenin and Philosophy*, New York: Monthly Review Press

Anderson, B. (1983) *Imagined Communities: Reflections on the Origin and Spread of Nationalism*, London: Verso

Anderson, S. and Cavanagh, J. (2000) *Top 200: The Rise of Global Corporate Power*, Washington, Institute for Policy Studies.

Anderson, V. (1991) *Alternative Economic Indicators*, London: Routledge

Antzcak, S. and Antzcak, G. (2001) *Cosmetics Unmasked*, London: Harper Collins

Argyle, M. (1987) *The Psychology of Happiness*, New York, Methuen

Bagdikian, B. (2004) *The New Media Monopoly*, Boston: Beacon Press

Barnhurst, K. and Nerone, J. (2001) *The Form of News: A History*, New York: Guilford.

Basel Action Network and Silicon Valley Toxics Coalition (25 February 2002). *Exporting Harm: The High-Tech Trashing of Asia*, at www.ban.org/E-waste/technotrashfinalcomp.pdf

BBC Trust (2007) *Report of the Independent Panel for the BBC Trust on Impartiality of BBC Business Coverage*, London: BBC Trust; April 2007, pp. 15–16, at http://www.bbc.co.uk/bbctrust/assets/files/pdf/review_report_research/impartiality_business/business_impartiality_report.pdf

Beck, U. (1995) *Ecological Politics in an Age of Risk*, Cambridge: Polity

Beck, U. (1999) *World Risk Society*, Cambridge: Polity

Berger, A. A. (2004) *Ads, Fads and Consumer Culture* (2nd edn), Maryland: Rowman and Littlefield

Berger, J. (1972) *Ways of Seeing*, London: Penguin

Berry, M. (2013) 'The Today programme and the banking crisis', *Journalism, Theory and Practice*, forthcoming

Bezemer, D. J. (2009) 'No one saw this coming: Understanding financial crisis through accounting models', MPRA Paper no. 1582, at http://mpra.ub.uni-muenchen.de/15892/1/MPRA_paper_15892.pdf>

Biderman, D. (2010) '11 minutes of action', *Wall Street Journal*, 15 January 2010, at http://online.wsj.com/article_email/SB10001424052748704281204575002852055561406-lMyQjAxMTAwMDEwNTExNDUyWj.html

Birt, J. and Jay, P. (1975) 'The radical changes needed to remedy TV's bias against understanding', *The Times*, 1 October 1975, p.14.

Bok, D. (2010) *The Politics of Happiness: What Government Can Learn from the New Research on Well-Being*, Princeton: Princeton University Press

Boorstin, D. (1977) *The Image: A Guide to Pseudo-Events in America*, New York: Atheneum

Born, G. (2005) *Uncertain Vision: Birt, Dyke and the Reinvention of the BBC*, London: Vintage

Boyce, T. (2007) *Health, Risk and News*, New York: Peter Lang

Bradshaw, P. V. (1927) *Art in Advertising*, London: The Press Art School

Brecher, J. and Costello, T. (1994) *Global Village or Global Pillage: Economic Reconstruction From the Bottom Up*, Cambridge MA: South End Press

Brennan, L. (2001) *Writing the TV Spec Script*, Writing-World.Com at http://www.writing-world.com/screen/TV.shtml

Brierley, S. (2002) *The Advertising Handbook* (2nd edn), London: Routledge

Brighton, P. and Foy, D. (2007) *News Values*, London: Sage

Brugge, P. (2008) Consumer Electronics Association, Presentation to E-Scrap Conference, September 17

Budd, M., Craig, S. and Steinman, C. (2004) *Consuming Environments: Television and Commercial Culture* (2nd edn), New Jersey: Rutgers University Press

Butler, C. and Pidgeon, N. (2009) 'Media communications and public understanding of climate change: Reporting scientific consensus of anthropogenic warming' in Boyce, T. and Lewis, J., *Climate Change and the Media*, New York: Peter Lang

Campbell, C. (1989) in *The Romantic Ethic and the Spirit of Modern Consumerism*, Oxford: Blackwell

Carey, J. (2005) Historical pragmatism and the Internet', *New Media and Society*, 7(4): 443–55

Chaney, D. (1983) `The department store as a cultural form', *Theory, Culture and Society*, 1(3): 22–31

Charity, A. (1995) *Doing Public Journalism*, New York: Guilford

Coote, A. Simms, A. and Franklin, J. (2010) *21 Hours: Why a Shorter Working Week Can Help Us All to Flourish in The 21st Century.* http://www.neweconomics.org/publications/21-hours

Cowling, K. and Poolsombat, R. (2007) *Advertising and Labour Supply: Why do Americans Work Such Long Hours?* Warwick Economic Research Papers no. 789

Crosby, J. (2007, 29 June) 'The mania over Apple's latest product could translate into an avalanche of electronic waste', *Star Tribune* p. 1D

Cross, G. (1993) *Time and Money: The Making of Consumer Culture*, London: Routledge

Curran, J. (2010) 'Technology foretold' in Fenton, N. (ed.), *New Media, Old News*, London: Sage

Curran, J. and Seaton, J. (1997) *Power without Responsibility*, London: Routledge

Curran, J., Fenton, N. and Freedman, D. (2012) *Misunderstanding the Internet*, London: Routledge

Cushion, S. (2012) *The Democratic Value of News: Why Public Service Media Matters*, Basingstoke: Palgrave

Cushion, S. (2010) 'Rolling service, market logic: The race to be Britain's most watched news channel' in Cushion, S. and Lewis, J. (eds). (2010) *The Rise of 24-Hour News Television*, New York: Peter Lang

Cushion, S. and Lewis, J. (2009) 'Towards a "foxification" of 24-hour news channels in Britain? An analysis of market driven and publicly funded news coverage' in *Journalism: Theory, Practice and Criticism*, 10 (2): 131–53

Davies, N. (2008) *Flat Earth News*, London: Chatto and Windus

Diamond, J. (2005) *Collapse: How Societies Choose or Fail to Succeed*, New York: Viking Press

Douglas, S. J. (1987) *Inventing American Broadcasting, 1899–1922*, Baltimore: Johns Hopkins University Press

Doyle, G. (2006) 'Financial news journalism: A post-Enron analysis of approaches towards economic and financial news production in the UK', *Journalism*, 7 (4): 433–52.

Doyle, J. (2009) 'Climate action and environmental activism' in Boyce, T. and Lewis, J., *Climate Change and the Media*, New York: Peter Lang

Drucker, P. (1994) *Post-Capitalist Society*, New York: Harper Collins

Druckman, A. and Jackson, T. (2009) 'The carbon footprint of UK households 1990–2004: A socioeconomically disaggregated, quasi-multi-regional input-output model', *Ecological Economics*, 68 (7): 2066–77

Durning, A. (1992) *How Much is Enough: The Consumer Society and the Future of the Earth*, Boston: Worldwatch Institute

Edwards, T. (2000) *Contradictions of Consumption*, Buckingham: Open University Press, 2000

Elliott, L. and Atkinson, D. (2008) *The Gods that Failed: How Blind Faith in Markets has Cost us our Future*, London: Bodley Head

Ellis, J. (1992) *Visible Fictions*, London: Routledge

Entman, R. (2004) *Projections of Power: Framing News, Public Opinion, and U.S. Foreign Policy*, Chicago: University of Chicago Press

Ewen, S. (2001) *Captains of Consciousness: Advertising and the Social Roots of Consumer Culture*, 25th anniversary edn, New York: Basic Books

Fabos, B. (2004) *Wrong Turn on the Information Superhighway: Education and the Commercialization of the Internet*, New York: Teachers College Press

Fahy, D., O'Brien, M. and Poti, V. (2010) 'From boom to bust: A post-Celtic tiger analysis of the norms, values and roles of Irish financial journalists, *Irish Communications Review*, 12: 5-20

Fine, B. (1995) 'From political economy to consumption' in Miller, D. *Acknowledging Consumption*, London: Routledge

Fogel, R. (2000) *The Fourth Great Awakening and the Future of Egalitarianism*, Chicago: University of Chicago Press

Foster, J. and McChesney, R. (2012) *The Endless Crisis: How Monopoly-Finance Capital Produces Stagnation and Upheaval from the USA to China*, New York: Monthly Review Press

Fournier, V. (2008) 'Escaping from the economy: The politics of degrowth', *International Journal of Sociology and Social Policy*, 28 (11/12): 528–45

Franco, M., Orduñez, P., Caballero, B., Granados, J. A., Lazo, M., Bernal, J. L., Guallar, E. and Cooper, R. S. (2007) 'Impact of energy intake, physical activity, and population-wide weight loss on cardiovascular disease and diabetes mortality in Cuba, 1980–2005', *Journal of Epidemiology*, 166: 1374–80

Franklin, B. (1997) *Newszak and News Media*, London: Arnold

Franklin, B. (2011) 'Sources, credibility and the continuing crisis of UK journalism' in B. Franklin and M. Carlson (eds.), *Journalists, Sources and Credibility*, New York: Routledge

Fraser, S. and Paton, D. (2003) 'Does advertising increase labour supply? Time series evidence from the UK', *Applied Economics*, 35: 1357–68

Frey, B. and Stutzer, A. (2001) *Happiness and Economics: How the Economy and Institutions Affect Human Well-Being*, New Jersey: Princeton University Press

Fukuyama, F. (1992) *The End of History and the Last Man*, Free Press

Gabrys, J. (2007) ' Media in the dump' in *Alphabet City: Trash*, ed. John Knechtel, Cambridge: MIT Press, pp. 156–65

Galbraith, J. K. (1958) *The Affluent Society*, Harmondsworth: Penguin

Galtung, J. and Ruge, M. (1973) 'Structuring and selecting news' in S. Cohen and J. Young (eds.), *The Manufacture of News: Deviance, Social Problems and the Mass Media*, London: Constable, pp. 52–64

Galician, M. (ed.) (2004) *Handbook of Product Placement in the Mass Media*, New York: Haworth

Gans, H. (1979) *Deciding What's News*, New York: Random House

Geroux, H. and Pollock, G. (2010) *The Mouse that Roared: Disney and the End of Innocence*, 2nd edn, Rowman and Littlefield

Giles, M. (1993) 'Indigestion: A survey of the food industry', *The Economist* (4 December): 1–18

Gilens, M. and Hertzman, C. (2000) 'Corporate ownership and news bias: Newspaper coverage of the 1996 Telecommunications Bill', *Journal of Politics*, 62(2): 369–86

Glasgow Media Group (1976) *Bad News*, London: Routledge

Glasgow Media Group (1980) *More Bad News*, London: Routledge

Glasgow Media Group (1982) *Really Bad News*, London: Routledge

Goldthorpe, J. (1963) *The Affluent Worker: Political Attitudes and Behaviour.* Cambridge: Cambridge University Press

Greenburg, Z. (2011) 'Vinyl vs. CDs: The tables are turning' *Forbes Magazine*, 18 July, http://www.forbes.com/sites/zackomalleygreenburg/2011/07/13/vinyl-vs-cd-the-tables-are-turning-rolling-stones-dom-lyor-cohen/

Grossman, E. (2010) *Tackling High-Tech Trash: The E-Waste Explosion and What We Can Do About It*, New York at Demos.http://www.demos.org/sites/default/files/publications/High_Tech_Trash-Demos.pdf

Hallin, D. C. (2000) 'Commercialism and professionalism in the American news media' in J. Curran and M. Gurevitch (eds.), *Mass Media and Society* (3rd edn), London: Arnold

Hansen, J. et al. (2008) 'Target atmospheric CO2: Where should humanity aim?' p.17 at http://arxiv.org/ftp/arxiv/papers/0804/0804.1126.pdf

Hansen, J. and Sato, M. (2011) *Paleoclimate Implications for Human-Made Climate Change*, New York: NASA Goddard Institute for Space Studies and Columbia University Earth Institute at http://www.columbia.edu/%7Ejeh1/mailings/2011/20110118_MilankovicPaper.pdf

Harcup, T. and O'Neill, D. (2001) 'What is news? Galtung and Ruge revisited', *Journalism Studies*, 2 (2): 261–80

Hardy, J. (2010) *Cross-Media Promotion*, New York: Peter Lang

Hargreaves, I. (2011) *Digital Opportunity: A Review of Intellectual Opportunity and Growth*, London: UK Government, at http://www.ipo.gov.uk/ipreview-finalreport.pdf

Harrison, J. (2006) *News*, London: Routledge

Harvey, F. (2011)'World headed for irreversible climate change in five years, IEA warns', *Guardian*, 9 November 2011, at http://www.guardian.co.uk/environment/2011/nov/09/fossil-fuel-infrastructure-climate-change

Hastings, G., Brooks, O., Stead, M., Angus, K., Anker, T. and Farrell T. (2010) 'Alcohol advertising: The last chance saloon: Failure of self regulation of UK alcohol advertising', *British Medical Journal* (international edn), 340: 184–6

Hawkes, C. (2007) 'Regulating and litigating in the public interest: Regulating food marketing to young people worldwide: Trends and policy drivers', *American Journal of Public Health*, 97(11): 1962–73.

Hawkins, G. (2003) 'Down the drain: Shit and the politics of disturbance' in G. Hawkins and S. Muecke (eds.), *Culture and Waste: The Creation and Destruction of Value*, Lanham, MD: Rowman and Littlefield, pp. 39–52

Helliwell, J., Layard, R. and Sachs, J. (2012) *World Happiness Report*, Columbia University Earth Institute

Herman, E. and Chomsky, N. (1988) *The Manufacture of Consent*, New York: Pantheon

Hilton, M. (2013) *Consumerism in Twentieth-Century Britain*, Cambridge: Cambridge University Press

Hirsch, F. (1977) *Social Limits to Growth*, London: Routledge

Holmes, T. (2009) 'Balancing acts: PR, 'impartiality,' and power in mass media coverage of climate change' in Boyce, T. and Lewis, J. (eds.), *Climate Change and the Media*, New York: Peter Lang

Houghton, J. T., Jenkins, G. J. and Ephraums, J. J. (eds.) (1990) *Report prepared for Intergovernmental Panel on Climate Change by Working Group 1*, Cambridge: Cambridge University Press

Humphery, K. (2010*) Excess: Anti-Consumerism in the West*, Cambridge: Polity

Hunnicutt, B. K. (1984) 'The end of shorter hours', *Labor History*, 25 (Summer): 373–404

Hutchins, R. and the Commission on Freedom of the Press (1947) *A Free and Responsible Press: A General Report on Mass Communication*, Chicago: University of Chicago Press

Inglehart, R. and Klingemann, H. D. (2000) *Genes, Culture and Happiness.* Boston: MIT Press

Intergovernmental Panel on Climate Change (1990)

Intergovernmental Panel on Climate Change (2007) *Climate Change 2007 – Synthesis Report*, Cambridge: Cambridge University Press

Intergovernmental Panel on Climate Change (2007) *Climate Change 2007: Mitigation. Contribution of Working Group III to the Fourth Assessment Report of the Intergovernmental Panel on Climate Change*, Cambridge: Cambridge University Press

Iyengar, S. (1991) *Is Anyone Responsible?* Chicago: University of Chicago Press

Iyengar, S. and Lepper, M. (2000) 'When choice is demotivating: Can one desire too much of a good thing?' *Journal of Personality and Social Psychology*, 79 (6): 995–1006

Jackson, T. (ed.) (2006) *Reader in Sustainable Consumption*, London: Earthscan

Jackson, T. (2010) *Prosperity Without Growth? The Transition to a Sustainable Economy*, London: Sustainable Development Commission

Jacobson, M. and Mazur A. (1995) 'Product placement' in *Marketing Madness: A Survival Guide for a Consumer Society*, Denver: Westview Press

James, O. (2007) *Affluenza*, London: Vermilion

Jameson, F. (1991) *Postmodernism, or, The Cultural Logic of Late Capitalism*, London: Verso

Jewell, J. (2008) *The Media Coverage of the Disappearance of Madeleine McCann*. In MeCCSA Conference 2008 , 9–11 January 2008, School of Journalism Media and Cultural Studies, Cardiff University

Jhally, S. (1990) *The Codes of Advertising*, New York: Routledge

Jhally, S. (2006) 'Advertising at the edge of the apocalypse' in Jhally, S. *The Spectacle of Accumulation*, New York: Peter Lang

Jhally, S. and Lewis, J. (1992) *Enlightened Racism: The Cosby Show and the Myth of the American Dream*, New York: Westview

Jung, C. and Seldon, B. J. (1995) 'The macroeconomic relationship between advertising and consumption', *Southern Economic Journal*, 61: 577–87

Kahnerman, D., Krueger, A., Schkade, D., Schwartz, N. and Stone, A. (2004) 'Toward national well-being accounts', *American Economic Review*, 94: 429

Kaplan, R. (2010) 'The origins of objectivity in American journalism' in Allan, S. (ed.), *The Routledge Companion to News and Journalism*, New York: Routledge

Kasser, T. (2002) *The High Price of Materialism*, Cambridge MA: MIT Press

Kelly, B., Smith, B., King, L., Flood, V. and Bauman, A. (2007) 'Television food advertising to children: The extent and nature of exposure', *Public Health Nutrition*, 5: 1–7

Kellner, D. (1990) *Television and the Crisis of Democracy*, Boulder: Westview

Kilbourne, J. (2000) *Killing Us Softly 3: Advertising's Image of Women*, Northampton, MA: Media Education Foundation

Klein, B. (2009) *As Heard on TV: Popular Music in Advertising*, Surrey: Ashgate

Klein, N. (2000) *No Logo*, New York: Picador

Kretchmer, S. B. (2004) 'Advertainment: The evolution of product placement as a mass media marketing strategy', *Journal of Promotion Management*, 10 (1/2): 37–55

Kuehr, R. and Williams, E. (eds.) (2003) *Computers and the Environment: Understanding and Managing their Impacts*, Dordrecht: Kluwer Academic Publishers

Lambert, R. (2002) 'Independent Review of News 24', London: Department of Culture, Media and Sport, Broadcasting Policy

Law, A. (1994) 'How to ride the wave of change', *Admap*, 26 (1)

Layard, R. (2003) *Lionel Robbins Memorial Lectures* 2002/3, delivered on 3, 4, 5 March 2003 at the London School of Economics

Layard, R. (2011) *Happiness, Lessons from a New Science*, London: Penguin

Leiss, W., Kilne, S. and Jhally, S. (1986) *Social Communication in Advertising*, New York: Methuen

Lewis, J. (2001) *Constructing Public Opinion*, New York: Columbia University Press

Lewis, J. (2008) 'Thinking by numbers: Cultural analysis and the use of data' in Bennett, T. and Frow, J. (eds.), *Handbook of Cultural Analysis*, London: Sage

Lewis, J. (2010a) 'The myth of commercialism: Why a market approach to broadcasting doesn't work' in Klaehn, J. (ed.), *Media and Power*, New York: Peter Lang

Lewis, J. (2010b) *A Monster Threatens UK Broadcasting? It's Sky, not the BBC* at http://www.opendemocracy.net/ourkingdom/justin-lewis/monster-threatens-uk-broadcasting-its-sky-not-bbc

Lewis, J. (2010c) 'Democratic or disposable? 24-hour news, consumer culture and built-in obsolescence' in Cushion, S. and Lewis, J. (eds.), *The Rise of 24-Hour News Television*, New York: Peter Lang

Lewis, J. and Boyce, T. (2009) 'Climate change and the media: The scale of the challenge' in Boyce, T. and Lewis, J., *Climate Change and the Media*, New York: Peter Lang

Lewis, J. and Cushion, S. (2009) 'The thirst to be first: An analysis of breaking news stories and their impact on the quality of 24-hour news coverage in the UK', *Journalism Practice*, 3 (3): 304–18

Lewis, J., Cushion, S. and Thomas, J. (2005) 'Immediacy, convenience or engagement? An analysis of 24-hour news channels in the UK', *Journalism Studies*, 6 (4): 461–78.

Lewis, J. and Hunt, J. (2011) 'Press coverage of the UK military budget: 1987 to 2009', *Media, War and Conflict*, 4 (2): 162–84

Lewis, J., Inthorn, S. and Wahl-Jorgensen, K. (2005) *Citizens or Consumers: The Media and the Decline of Political Participation*, Maidenhead: Open University Press

Lewis, J. and Jhally, S. (1998) 'The struggle over media literacy', *Journal of Communication*, 48 (1): 109–20

Lewis, J., Mason, P. and Moore, K. (2009) 'Islamic terrorism – the repression of the political' in Marsden, L. and Savigny, H. (eds.), *Media, Religion and Conflict*, Ashgate

Lewis, J. and Thomas, R. (2013) 'More of the same: News, economic growth and the recycling of conventional wisdom' in Murdock, G. (ed.), *Money Matters* (forthcoming)

Lewis, J., Williams, A. and Franklin, B. (2008) 'A compromised fourth estate? UK news journalism, public relations and news sources', *Journalism Studies*, 9 (1): 1–20

Lewis, J., Williams, A. and Franklin, B. (2008) 'Four rumours and an explanation: A political economic account of journalists' changing newsgathering and reporting practices', *Journalism Practice*, 2 (1): 27–45

Leyshon, A. (2001) 'Time – space (and digital) compression: Software formats, musical networks, and the reorganisation of the music industry', *Environment and Planning*, 33: 49–77

Linder, S. (1970) *The Harried Leisure Class*, New York: Columbia University Press

Lipovetsky, G. (1994) *The Empire of Fashion: Dressing Modern Democracy* (Porter, C. trans.), Princeton: Princeton University Press

Littler, J. (2009) *Radical Consumption: Shopping For Change In Contemporary Culture*, Maidenhead: Open University Press

Livingston, S. and Bennett, W. L. (2003) 'Gatekeeping, indexing and live-event news: Is technology altering the construction of news?' *Political Communication* 20 (4): 363–80

Livingstone, S. (2006) 'Does TV advertising make children fat? What the evidence tells us', *Public Policy Research*, 13 (1): 54–61.

Livingstone, S. and Helsper, E. (2006) 'Does advertising literacy mediate the effects of advertising on children? A critical examination of two linked research literatures in relation to obesity and food choice', *Journal of Communication*, 56 (3): 560–84

Lovering, J. (1998) 'The global music industry: Contradictions in the commodification of the sublime' in A. Leyshon, D. Matless and G. Revill (eds.), *The Place of Music*, New York: The Guilford Press

Lury, C. (2011) *Consumer Culture* (2nd edn), Cambridge: Polity

McAllister, M. P. (2003) 'Is commercial culture popular culture?: A question for popular communication scholars' , *Popular Communication*, 1(1): 41–9

McChesney, R. (1989) 'Media made sport: A history of sports coverage in the United States' in Wenner, L. (1989) *Media, Sports and Society*, California: Sage, pp. 49–69.

McChesney, R. (1999) *Rich Media, Poor Democracy*, University of Illinois Press

McChesney, R. (2013) *Digital Disconnect: How Capitalism is Turning the Internet Against Democracy*, New York: New Press

McChesney, R. and Nichols, J (2010) *The Death and Life of American Journalism: The Media Revolution that Will Begin the World Again*, Nation Books

McCracken, G. (1990) *Culture and Consumption.* Bloomington: Indiana University Press

McGaurr, L. and Lester, L. (2009) 'Complementary problems, competing risks: Climate change, nuclear energy and the *Australian*' in Boyce, T. and Lewis, J., *Climate Change and the Media*, New York: Peter Lang

McKibben, W. (2006) *The End of Nature*, New York: Random House

McLeod, K. (2001) *Owning Culture: Authorship, Ownership and Intellectual Property Law*, New York: Peter Lang Publishers

McLeod, K. (2005) *Freedom of Expression: Overzealous Copyright Bozos and Other Enemies of Creativity*, New York: Random House/Doubleday

McManus, J. (2009) 'The commercialization of news' in Wahl-Jorgensen, K. and Hanitzsch, T. (eds.), *The Handbook of Journalism Studies*, New York: Routledge

McNair, B. (2000) *Journalism and Democracy: A Qualitative Evaluation of the Political Public Sphere*, London: Routledge

Maghiros, I. (2009) 'Information, telecommunications technologies and media convergence challenges' in Pauwels, C., Kalimo, H., Donders. K. and Van Rompuy, B. (eds.), *Rethinking European Media and Communications Policy*, Brussels: Brussels University Press

Mair, J., Fowler, J. and Reeves, I. (2012) *What Do We Mean By Local?* Bury St Edmunds: Abramis

Magnus, A., Haby, M., Carter, R. and Swinburn, B. (2009) 'The cost-effectiveness of removing television advertising of high-fat and/or high-sugar food and beverages to Australian children', *International Journal of Obesity*, 33: 1094–102

Mandel, E. (1975) *Late Capitalism*, London: Humanities Press

Mander, J. (1977) *Four Arguments for the Elimination of Television*, New York: William Murrow

Marcuse, H. (1964) *One-Dimensional Man: Studies in the Ideology of Advanced Industrial Society*, Boston: Beacon

Maxwell, R. and Miller, T. (2009) 'Talking rubbish: Green citizenship, media and the environment' in Boyce, T. and Lewis, J., *Climate Change and the Media*, New York: Peter Lang

Maxwell, R. and Miller, T. (2012a) 'The great illusion of media and communications', *European Financial Review*, 19 June http://www.euro peanfinancialreview.com/?p=5283

Maxwell, R. and Miller, T. (2012b) *Greening The Media*, Oxford: Oxford University Press

Merrill, G. (2013) 'Profits or prophets: economics and business journalism in Britain from 1999 to 2008.' Ph.D thesis, Goldsmiths College, University of London.

Miller, D. (2001) 'The poverty of morality', *Journal of Consumer Culture* 1 (2): 225–43

Miller, T. (2008) 'The vernacular economist's guide to media and culture' in Ruccio, F. (ed.), *Economic Representations: Academic and Everyday*, London: Routledge, 200–10

Miller, T. (2009) *Television Studies: The Basics*, New York: Routledge

Miller, T. and Kim, L. (2008) 'Overview: It isn't TV, it's the "Real King of the Ring"' in Edgerton, G. and Jones, J. P.(eds.), *The Essential HBO Reader*, University of Kentucky Press, 2007, pp. 217–38

Mohan, S. (2010) *Fair Trade Without the Froth: A Dispassionate Economic Analysis of Fair Trade* London: Institute of Economic Affairs

Molinari, B. and Turino, F. (2009) 'Advertising and business cycle fluctuations', Working Papers, Series AD 2009-09, S.A. (Ivie): Instituto

Valenciano de Investigaciones Económicas, at: http://www.ivie.es/downloads/docs/wpasad/wpasad-2009-09.pdf

Monbiot, G. (2011) 'Sucking out our brains through our eyes', *Guardian*, 24 October 2011. Also available at http://www.monbiot.com/2011/10/24/sucking-out-our-brains-through-our-eyes/

Mooallem, J. (2008) 'The afterlife of cellphones', *New York Times*, 13 January. http://www.nytimes.com/2008/01/13/magazine/13Cellphone-t.html?pagewanted=all

Morgan, M .(ed.) (2002) *Against the Mainstream: The Selection Works of George Gerbner*, New York: Peters Lang

Mueller, B. (2006) *Dynamics of International Advertising*, New York: Peter Lang

Nava, M. (1997) 'Framing advertising: Cultural analysis and the incrimination of visual texts' in Nava, M., Blake, A., MacRury, I. and Richards, B. (eds.), *Buy this Book: Studies in Advertising and Consumption*, London: Routledge

O'Donohoe, S. (1997) 'Leaky boundaries: Intertextuality and young adult experiences of advertising' in Nava, M., Blake, A., MacRury, I. and Richards, B. (eds.), *Buy this Book: Studies in Advertising and Consumption*, London: Routledge

Offer, A. (2006) *The Challenge of Affluence: Self-Control and Well-Being in the United States and Britain since 1950*, Oxford: Oxford University Press

Oreskes, N. and Conway, E. (2010) *Merchants of Doubt: How a Handful of Scientists Obscured the Truth on Issues from Tobacco Smoke to Global Warming*, New York: Bloomsbury

Oswald, A. (2003) 'How much do external factors affect wellbeing? A way to use "happiness economics" to decide', *The Psychologist*, 16: 140–1

Ouellette, L. and Lewis, J. (2000) 'Moving beyond the "vast wasteland": cultural policy and television in the United States', *Television and New Media*, 2(1): 93–113.

Owen, N., Inderwildi, O. and King, D. (2010) 'The status of conventional world oil reserves: Hype or cause for concern?' *Energy Policy*, 38: 4743

Packard, V. (1957) *The Hidden Persuaders*, London: Longman

Packard, V. (1960) *The Waste Makers*, Harmondsworth: Penguin

Pauwels, C. (1999) 'From citizenship to consumer sovereignty: The paradigm shift in European audiovisual policy' in Calabrese, A. and Burgelman, J-C. (eds.), *Communication, Citizenship, and Social Policy: Rethinking the Limits of the Welfare State*, Lanham: Rowman and Littlefield

Pauwels, C., Kalimo, H., Donders. K. and Van Rompuy, B. (eds.) (2009) *Rethinking European Media and Communications Policy*, Brussels: Brussels University Press

Phelps, G. H. (1929) *Tomorrow's Advertisers and their Advertising Agencies*, New York: Harper

Postman, N. (1985) *Amusing Ourselves to Death: Public Discourse in the Age of Show Business*, New York: Penguin

Press, A. (1991) *Women Watching Television*, Philadelphia, University of Pennsylvania Press

Princen, Thomas (2002) 'Consumption and its externalities: Where economy meets ecology' in Princen, T., Maniates, M. and Concha, K. (eds.), *Confronting Consumption*, Cambridge: MIT Press

Quilligan, J. (2002) *The Brandt Equation: 21st Century Blueprint for the New Global Economy*, at http://www.brandt21forum.info/BrandtEquation-19Sept04.pdf

Rajan, A.(2009) 'The big question: Why are public perceptions of crime so at odds with the official statistics? *Independent*, 17 July

Rantanen, T. (2009) *When News Was New*, New York: Wiley-Blackwell

Reardon, S. (2013) Ph.D thesis, School of Journalism, Media and Cultural Studies, Cardiff University

Reiner, R., Livingstone, S., and Allen, J (2003) 'From law and order to lynch mobs: Crime news since the Second World War' in Mason, P. *Criminal Visions: Media Representations of Crime and Justice*, Cullompton: Willan

Roush, C. (2006) 'The need for more business education in mass communication schools', *Journalism and Mass Communication Educator*, 61 (2): 196–204

Rowland, W. D. and Tracey, M. (1990) 'Worldwide challenges to public service broadcasting', *Journal of Communication*, 40 (2): 8–27

Royal Society (2009) *Geoengineering the Climate: Science, Governance and Uncertainty*, London at http://royalsociety.org/uploadedFiles/Royal_Society_Content/policy/publications/2009/8693.pdf

Rutsky, R.L. (2005) 'Information wants to be consumed' in Rutsky,

R. L. and Cohen, S. (eds.), *Consumption in an Age of Information*, Oxford/New York: Berg, pp. 61–78

Sakr, N. (2005) 'Maverick or model: Al Jazeera's impact on Arab satellite television' in Chalaby, J. (ed.), *Transnational Television Worldwide: Towards a New Media Order*, London: I. B. Tauris, pp. 66–95

Sassatelli, R. (2007) *Consumer Culture: History, Theory, Politics*, London, Sage

Scannell, P. (1996) *Radio, Television, and Modern Life: A Phenomenological Approach*, Oxford: Blackwell Publishers

Schechter, D. (2009) Credit crisis: How did we miss it? *British Journalism Review*, 20 (1): 19–26.

Scheuer, J. (2008) *The Big Picture: Why Democracies Need Journalistic Excellence*, New York: Routledge

Schlesinger, P. (1978) *Putting Reality Together*, London: Methuen

Schor, J. (1991)*The Overworked American: The Unexpected Decline of Leisure*, New York: Basic Books

Schor, J. (1998) *The Overspent American: Upscaling, Downshifting and the New Consumer*, New York: Basic Books

Schor, J. (1999) *The Overspent American: Why We Want What We Don't Need*, New York: HarperCollins

Schor, J. (2004) *Born to Buy*, New York: Scribner

Schor, J. (2010) *Plenitude: The New Economics of True Wealth*, New York: Penguin

Schudson, M. (1986) *Advertising: The Uneasy Persuasion. Its Dubious Impact on American Society*, New York: Basic Books

Schumacher, E. (1977) *Small is Beautiful: A Study of Economics as if People Mattered*, London: Abacus

Shove, E., Trentmann, F. and Wilk, R. (eds.) (2009) *Time, Consumption and Everyday Life: Practice, Materiality and Culture*, Oxford: Berg

Schwartz, B (2004) *The Paradox of Choice: Why More is Less*, New York: HarperCollins

Smart, B. (2010) *Consumer Society: Critical Issues and Environmental Consequences*, London: Sage

Smythe, D. (1980) *Dependency Road*, Norwood, NJ: Ablex

Seabrook, J. (1978) *What Went Wrong?* New York: Pantheon

Simms, A. (2013) *Cancel the Apocalypse*, London: Little Brown Books

Soley, L. C. and Craig, R. L. (1992) 'Advertising pressures on newspapers: A survey', *Journal of Advertising*, 21(4): 1–9.

Soroka, S. and Wlezien, C. (2002) 'Opinion-policy dynamics: Public preferences and public expenditure in the United Kingdom'. Paper delivered to the Elections, Public Opinion and Parties Annual Conference, September, Salford, UK, p. 401

Soros, G. (2008) *The New Paradigm for Financial Markets. The Credit Crisis of 2008 and What it Means*, London: Public Affairs

Sparks, C. (1999) 'The press', in Jane Stokes and Anna Reading (eds), *The Media in Britain: Current Debates and Developments*, Basingstoke: Macmillan Press Ltd

Stein, L. (2006) *Speech Rights in America*, Urbana and Chicago: University of Illinois Press

Stern, N. (2006) *Stern Review on the Economics of Climate Change*, HM Treasury, UK government, http://www.hm-treasury.gov.uk/d/CLOSED_SHORT_executive_summary.pdf

Sterne, J. (2007) 'Out with the trash: On the future of new media' in C. R. Acland (ed.), *Residual Media*, Minneapolis, MN: University of Minnesota Press, pp. 16–31

Story, M., Neumark-Sztainer, D. and French, S. (2002) 'Individual and environmental influences on adolescent eating behaviors', *Journal of the American Dietetic Association*, 102(3): S40–S51.

Strasser, S. (1999) *Waste and Want: A Social History of Trash*, New York: Metropolitan Books

Strasser, S. (2009) 'The alien past: Consumer culture in historical perspective' in Turow, J. and McAllister, M. (eds.), *The Advertising and Consumer Culture Reader*, London: Routledge, pp. 32–3

Straw, W. (2000) 'Exhausted commodities: The material culture of music', *Canadian Journal of Communication*, 25 (1)

Streeter, T. (1996) *Selling the Air: A Critique of the Policy of Commercial Broadcasting in the United States*, Chicago: University of Chicago Press

Svoboda, M. (2011) *Advertising Climate Change: A Study of Green Ads*, Yale Forum on Climate Change and the Media, 6 July 2011 at http://www.yaleclimatemediaforum.org

Svennevig, M (2007) *BBC Coverage of Business in the UK: A Content Analysis of Business News Coverage*, London: BBC Trust.

Tambini, D. (2010) 'What are financial journalists for?' *Journalism Studies*, 11 (2): 158–174.

Taussig, M. (1993) *Mimesis and Alterity: A Particular History of the Senses*, New York and London: Routledge

Thompson, E. P. (1968) *The Making of the English Working Classes*, Harmondsworth: Penguin

Thompson, M. (1979) *Rubbish Theory: The Creation and Destruction of Value*. Oxford: Oxford University Press

Tracey, M. (1998) *The Decline and Fall of Public Service Broadcasting*, London: Oxford University Press

Troyer, J. (2003) *The Classical Utilitarians: Bentham and Mill*, Hackett Publishing

Tuchman, G. (1978) *Making News*, New York: Beverley Press

US Department of Health and Human Services, National Cancer Institute, (2008) 'The role of the media in promoting and reducing tobacco use', *NCI Tobacco Control Monograph* Series No.19 at: http://cancercontrol.cancer.gov/tcrb/monographs/19/m19_complete.pdf.

Vallely, P. (2010) 'The big question: Is the analogue/digital switchover destined to lead to chaos?' *Independent*, 30 March 2010, Available at http://www.independent.co.uk/extras/big-question/the-big-question-is-the-analoguedigital-switchover-destined-to-lead-to-chaos-1930692.html

Veblen, T. (1994) [1899] *The Theory of the Leisure Class*, New York: Penguin

Veenhoven, R. 'World happiness database', available at: www2.eur.nl/fsw/research/happiness.

Verrier, R (2012) 'Global box-office receipts rise 3% in 2011, MPAA reports', *Los Angeles Times*, 23 March at http://articles.latimes.com/2012/mar/23/business/la-fi-ct-mpaa-stats-20120323

Victor, P. (2008) *Managing without Growth – Slower by Design not Disaster*, Cheltenham: Edward Elgar

VSS Historical database, available at www.vss.com/historical09

Wachtel, P. (1983) *The Poverty of Affluence – A Psychological Portrait of the American Way of Life*, New York: Free Press

Walker, K. (2009) 'Reality check: Interactivity, reality TV and empowerment' in Burnett, J., Senker, P. and Walker, K (eds.), *The Myths of Technology: Innovation and Inequality*, New York: Peter Lang, pp. 97–112.

Wark, M. (1991) 'Fashioning the future: Fashion, clothing, and the manufacturing of post-fordist culture', *Cultural Studies*, 5(1): 61–76

Wasko, J., Phillips, M. and Purdie, C. (1993) 'Hollywood meets Madison Avenue: The commercialization of US films', *Media, Culture and Society* 15 (2): 271–93

Wasko, J and Sirois, A. (2011) 'The political economy of the recorded music industry: Redefinitions and new trajectories' in Wasko, J., Murdock, G. and Sousa H., *The Handbook of Political Economy of Communications*, Chichester: Wiley Blackwell, pp. 331–58

Wernick, A. (1991) *Promotional Culture: Advertising, Ideology and Symbolic Expression*, London: Sage

Wilkinson, R. and Pickett, K. (2010) *The Spirit Level: Why Equality is Better for Everyone*, London: Penguin

Williams, E. (2004) Energy intensity of computer manufacturing: Hybrid assessment combining process and economic input–output methods, *Environmental Science and Technology*, 38(22): 6166–74

Williams, K. (1998) *'Get Me a Murder a Day!' A History of Mass Communications in Britain*, London: Arnold

Williams, R. (1974) *Television, Technology and Cultural Form*, London: Fontana

Williams, R. (1993) 'Advertising: The magic system' in During, S. (ed.), *The Cultural Studies Reader*, London: Routledge, pp. 411–23

Williamson, J. (1995) *Decoding Advertisements: Ideology and Meaning in Advertising* (4th impression), London: Marion Boyars

World Bank (2012) *What a Waste: A Global Review of Solid Waste Management*, at http://siteresources.worldbank.org/INTURBANDEVELOPMENT /Resources/336387-1334852610766/What_a_Waste2012_Final.pdf

Wright, R (2004) *A Short History of Progress*, Toronto: House of Anansi Press

Zukin, S. (2004) *Point of Purchase: How Shopping Changed American Culture*, New York: Routledge

Index